The Lord's Song in a Strange Land

THE LORD'S SONG IN A STRANGE LAND

Music and Identity in Contemporary Jewish Worship

Jeffrey A. Summit

OXFORD
UNIVERSITY PRESS

OXFORD

UNIVERSITY PRESS

Oxford   New York

Auckland   Bangkok   Bogotá   Buenos Aires   Cape Town
Chennai   Dar es Salaam   Delhi   Hong Kong   Istanbul   Karachi
Kolkata   Kuala Lumpur   Madrid   Melbourne   Mexico City   Mumbai
Nairobi   São Paulo   Shanghai   Taipei   Tokyo   Toronto

Library of Congress Cataloging-in-Publication Data
Summit, Jeffrey A.
The Lord's song in a strange land : music and identity in
contemporary Jewish worship / Jeffrey A. Summit.
p. cm.—(American musicpheres)
Discography: p
Includes bibliographical references and index.
ISBN 0-19-511677-1; 0-19-516181-5 (pbk.)
1. Jews—Music—History and criticism. 2. Synagogue
music—Massachusetts—Boston—History and criticism.
3. Judaism—Liturgy.   I. Title. II. Series
ML3195 .S96 2000
296.4'62—dc21   99-047436

This book has been printed digitally and produced in a standard
specification to ensure its continuing availability. The audio files on the
referenced companion CD are available online at www.oup.com/us/lordssong.

1 3 5 7 9 8 6 4 2

Printed in the United States of America
on acid-free paper

Series Foreword

Spheres within spheres—this is what American music looks like in the early twenty-first century. Overlapping, intersecting, sharp at the core and fuzzy at the edges: large and small music systems surround Americans and project the region's sound to the world. This is a multidimensional, surprising set of worlds in collision. The machinery of marketing and media struggle to straighten out the shapes, styles, and meanings. Tinges of domination, accommodation, and reciprocity color the picture.

"America" here means the several cultural spaces that center on the United States, both magnet and generator of musical energy. This nation-state once understood its musical map as an overlay of "white" on "black," with "color" added by continuous overlays of absorbed populations, some brought in by aggressive territorial expansion, others by the pull of immigration or the push of disaster. It took the whole twentieth century to shift to a more nuanced sense of internal cultural ferment. Now we can see any musician or audience as an influencer or receptor. Groups actively seek to control their own definition, often consciously crossing cultural and national borders. The media both empower and disempower musical taste and direction through target marketing.

This series will present concise, focused accounts of a sampling of spheres. Some studies will describe a localized group, but show how a micromusic is implicated in broad trends and constantly changing ways of thinking about musical choices. Some books survey "networks," circuits of sensibility that bind people regionally or nationally. Others will introduce an individual as a prism that refracts and breaks down the harsh beam of American life into an intensely hued pattern of musical light. Yet others might seize on a musical moment of particular intensity.

The overall aim: to avoid defining musical "villages," to move away from neat periodization, and to give terms like "folk," "traditional," "ethnic," and "popular" a well-deserved rest. American music studies needs new perspectives; this series hopes to suggest some.

MARK SLOBIN
Series Editor
American Musicspheres

Acknowledgments

The Talmud says that a person who properly acknowledges sources brings redemption to the world (Babylonian Talmud, *Megillah* 15a). While I believe in aiming high, this is at least an opportunity to thank my teachers, friends, and colleagues for their guidance and generous support. A number of scholars helped tremendously when this book was in its earlier form. Throughout my graduate work and this project, Mark Slobin provided invaluable direction and encouragement. His work has been a model for my own work in ethnomusicology. I learned a great amount from the other members of my doctoral committee at Tufts: my advisor David Locke, Mark DeVoto, and Joel Rosenberg. Their insight and careful critique shaped this study in its earlier version. Other enthomusicologists have helped in important ways. Jeff Todd Titon's initial encouragement as director of the Tufts program in ethnomusicology brought me to this field, and I have benefited greatly over the years from his thoughtful critiques. I also wish to thank Philip Bohlman, both for many important conversations about these topics and for inviting me to present a paper at the conference he organized at the University of Chicago, "Music in American Religious Experience." That paper formed the basis for chapter 3 of this book. I deeply appreciate Mark Kligman's insightful comments and suggestions after reading the manuscript. My brother-in-law, Samuel Heilman, has taught me a great deal about participant/observer research and has been generous in his observations and suggestions. Richard Israel, author, rabbi, and astute observer of American Jewish life, has served as editor, friend, and thoughtful critic. My work is better for his sharp pencil and sharper eye. I also want to acknowledge and thank other scholars who have answered my many questions and offered their advice and perspectives on various issues: Joshua Jacobson, Jonathan Sarna, Hankus Netsky, Arthur Green, Ruth Langer, Eliahu Schliefer, Uri Sharvit, Velvel Pasternak, Marc Perlman, Moshe Waldoks, Abraham Shonfeld, and Brian Mayer. I am deeply appreciative of their guidance and insights during the various stages in this work.

My editors at Oxford University Press, Maribeth Payne, Jonathan Wiener, Maureen Buja, and Robert Milks, provided extremely valuable direction throughout this project. I want to thank R. Berred Ouellette for his involvement in the digital recordings and production of the CD master. My good friend and photographer Richard Sobol was sensitive and creative in his approach to the worship communities pictured in this book. Sol Gittleman, senior vice-president and provost at Tufts University, has been a continuing source of support and encouragement. I appreciate the financial support to produce the enclosed CD received from the Lucius N. Littauer Foundation and from the office of the Vice-president of Arts, Sciences and Technology and the office of the Graduate School of Arts and Sciences at Tufts. I also want to express my appreciation to the Hillel Foundation at Tufts University and the Hillel Council of Greater Boston for my sabbatical during the spring of 1998. I am deeply grateful to the National Foundation for Jewish Culture who awarded the book the Sidney and Hadassah Musher Publication Prize in 2000.

Much of this work was written "from the inside out"; that is to say, I was interested primarily in the participants' understanding of music in the liturgy of contemporary American Jewish worship communities. My work rests on the generous insights and gracious help of the worshippers from the five communities I interviewed for this study, as well as from other communities. While I spoke with many more people than are listed below, here I wish to acknowledge and thank those who did formal interviews: Miriam Acevedo-Naters, Ira Axelrod, Larry Brown, Robert Bullock, Lea Campolo, Jonathan Carden, Stuart B. Chizzik, Jeffrey Cohen, Carol Diamond, Shelly Dorf, Marshall Einhorn, Roy Einhorn, Joe Eudivich, Sally Finestone, Lev Friedman, Jenna Gerstel, Samuel Goldberg, Carla Golembi, Melinda Gordon-Tepper, Halona Gropper, Debra Grumet, Seth M. Haaz, Levi Yitzhak Horowitz, Mayer Horowitz, Naftali Horowitz, Joshua Jacobson, Jim Jubelirer, Lauren Jubelirer, Laura Kahn, Naomi Kalish, Aaron Katchen, David Krohn, Shira Levi, Julie Levitt, Benjamin Linden, Aliza Lipschitz, Jennifer Madan, Alex Mandell, Thomas R. McKibbens, Scotty McLennan, Bernard Mehlman, Daniel Michaeli, Richard Moline, Marisa Morgan, Frank Olney, Frances S. Putnoi, Joan Rachlin, Randy Ravitz, Avi Rockoff, Michael Ross, Adam Rothchild, John Stendahl, David Stern, Marylyn Stern, Scott Tepper, Neil Tow, Moshe Waldoks, David Webner, Joshua A. Weingram, Elyse Winick, and Elaine Zecher.

The following people recorded melodies from their respective services for the enclosed CD. From B'nai Or: Matia Rania Angelou, Lev Friedman, Michaela Friedman, Shayndel Kahn, Ruven Washor Liebhaber, Joyce Rosen-Friedman, Laurel Smith, Ron Sweet, Sharon Teitelbaum, Scott A. Tepper. From Temple Israel: Ann Abrams, Ruth Alpers, Roy Einhorn, Bob Feldman, Alan Fisch, Allene Fisch, Priscilla Golding, Ruth Goran, Carol Kur, Sam Lampert, Carol B. Michael, Averi Miles, Manja Miles, Marc Miles, Todd Miles, Edie Mueller, David F. Passer, Frances S. Putnoi, Deborah Rivlin, Michael J. Ross, Ellen Rovner, Michael A. Sandman, Nancy G. Sandman, Jeff Stock, Gary Stone, Rachel Warner, Michael Zimman. From

Tufts Hillel: Stuart B. Chizzik, Marshall Einhorn, Halona Gropper, Debra Grumet, Seth M. Haaz, Aliza Lipschitz, Jennifer Madan, Marisa Morgan, Jeffrey A. Summit, Neil Tow, Joshua A. Weingram. From Shaarei Tefillah: Larry Brown, Yehuda Brown, Gene E. Fax, Samuel Goldberg, Joshua Jacobson, Aaron Katchen, Jeremy Newberger, Avi Rockoff, Jules Rosenberg. From Beth Pinchas: Mayer Horowitz.

I especially want to thank my three children, Aleza, Ariela, and Zachary, who have seen this book take shape over time and who have understood and supported my enthusiasm for this work. My wife, Gail Kaufman, has unequivocally encouraged this project. In the words from the book of Proverbs, "Many women have done extraordinary things. You excel them all" (31:29).

Contents

A Note on Transliteration

Hebrew words are transliterated in a way that best facilitates their pronunciation. For certain words, such as *havurah* (fellowship community), I present the conventional English spelling, even though this leads to orthographic inconsistencies. When a word in Hebrew, Yiddish, or Aramaic is introduced, it is italicized and translated at the first mention; subsequent usage is neither italicized nor translated. Frequently used foreign words are defined in the glossary at the end of the book. The guttural sounds "ch" and "kh" are pronounced like the "ch" in Bach. Hebrew names of synagogues or organizations are spelled as the groups spell them. Quotes from written sources retain the original author's transliterations. Throughout, I italicize the titles of Hebrew prayers and hymns, such as *Lekhah dodi*. Only the first word of a hymn's title is capitalized.

The Lord's Song in a Strange Land

Introduction

After being appointed head of the Talmudic academy in Israel, the great Babylonian teacher Hillel was asked, "Master, we are obligated to bring an animal as a sacrifice for Passover. But what if Passover falls on the eve of the Sabbath? We know it is forbidden to do any work on the Sabbath, even to carry the slaughtering knife. If one forgot to bring the knife beforehand, how does one transport it to the Temple in order to fulfill the obligation to do the sacrifice?" As hard as he tried, Hillel could not remember the answer to their question. He finally said, "Let us see what the people do; if they are not prophets, they surely are the children of prophets!" On the next day, Hillel watched as people brought the animals they were about to sacrifice to the Temple. If it was a sheep, they stuck the knife in the sheep's wool. If it was a goat, they affixed the knife between the goat's horns. Thus the animals did the work of carrying and no prohibition was transgressed. "Ah, yes!" said Hillel, *"That* was the tradition as I learned it from my teachers!" (text after passage in the Babylonian Talmud [central text of rabbinic Judaism, redacted in the sixth century], *Pesachim* 66a)

This is a book about what Jews do, in one metropolitan setting at the end of the twentieth century, as they choose the music for the performance of prayer in communal worship. I begin with the story of Hillel because it lays out many questions that are crucial to my study. How are traditions and laws established: by legal ruling or by the people's practice? What is the relationship between what people do and what leaders, teachers, rabbis, and in the case of liturgical music, cantors, composers, and musicians, think they *should* do? Who leads and who follows in the establishment of traditions? Where is the locus of authority for a community's practices? How does creative expression become tradition? Although Jews have struggled with these questions for thousands of years, the Jewish experience in America, with its exceptional freedom and possibility of diverse practice, presents rich opportunities to examine the dynamics that drive this dialectic between creativity and tradition.

Across America, modern urban Jews come together every week to sing and pray in a wide variety of worship communities. Through this music, made by and for ordinary folk, these Jews define and redefine their relationship to the continuity of Jewish tradition and the realities of American life. Today Jewish ethnicity and identity are increasingly voluntary, a matter of choice. For many Jews, music and the choice of musical settings function as a basic, defining component of identity and affiliation.

This book considers Jews across denominational lines, including Hasidim, Modern Orthodox, Conservative college students in a university setting, Reform, and members of a "new age" *havurah* (fellowship group). It examines how choice of melody helps them present and maintain their religious and cultural identity. There is tremendous diversity within the broader Jewish community, and nowhere are the distinctions among subcommunities as obvious as in the approaches to the performance of liturgical and scriptural text. These Jews "vote with their feet" and with their pocketbooks, as they attend and support different synagogues with particular melodies and styles of liturgical performance. Even while members express strong loyalty to their own group, there is considerable interaction among these subcommunities. The musical choices in one community are often part of an unspoken dialogue with other subcommunities. Through song, members affirm who they are—and who they are not—as Jews.

Through oral histories and an analysis of recordings, this book shows the fluid interaction within this American musicsphere. Melodies are continually shared and borrowed, not only from traditional and contemporary Jewish sources, but from mainstream American culture and alternative sources as diverse as Sufi chant, Christmas carols, rock and roll, and Israeli popular music. While the same melody may be used in different congregations, its meaning and significance can vary dramatically from one community to another, even when these worship groups are located only a few miles apart.

I examine the construction of identity among these Jews in three ways. The focus throughout will be on Friday evening worship, which includes *Kabbalat Shabbat* (Welcoming the Sabbath) and the Sabbath *Maariv* (evening) service.[1] First, I consider a single piece of liturgical repertoire, the popular hymn *Lekhah dodi* (Come, my beloved). An examination of this tune shows the extent to which performance has given way to participation as a value embraced simultaneously by congregants and leaders in all of these worship communities. Members collect, trade, borrow, steal, and compose melodies for this central hymn with an eye toward constructing a worship experience that expresses the values and ideals of their particular community.

Broadening the range of vision, I next look at the term *nusach* (traditional chant), an insider's concept which is used in many different ways by worshippers in the construction of their identity. Contemporary conceptions of nusach are informed by these Jews' struggles with modernity and their search for historical authority and authenticity. For some, nusach serves as a powerful connection to Jewish community, tradition, and traditional texts. Others see it as the key to a more participatory prayer experience. Surprisingly, many Reform Jews, though they are friendly to innovation, hold traditional chant as dear and central as do their Orthodox counterparts, though they define the expression and the meaning of these musical traditions quite differently.

Finally, I examine how Jewish worshippers choose melodies in prayer. There is tremendous experimentation, cross-fertilization, and interaction within and among these subcommunities. Here we see how the choice of melody helps American Jews to negotiate living in two cultures, to create or diffuse boundaries between themselves and other segments of the Jewish community, and to define their relationship with the non-Jewish American superculture.

Through close study of selected Jewish subcommunities in one metropolitan area, we will see issues continually arise that are common to the varieties of middle-class religion in America. Across denominational lines, these Jews exhibit local variations of larger American supercultural themes, attitudes, and folkways. To illustrate, at the end of the book I briefly "walk across the street" and visit some of the Protestant and Catholic churches in the neighborhoods where these Jews live and worship. As much as these Jews are influenced by Jewish history and practice, they also present an American ethos, shaped by American history and culture. While this work explores the networks of musical interaction among Jewish worship circles in Boston, it also contributes to a larger understanding of American religious expression and Americans' accompanying search for cultural authority and spiritual meaning.

"*Nu?* [So?] Are You *Davening* [Praying] or Conducting Research?"

James Clifford, a noted anthropologist, describes modern ethnography as "a pervasive condition of off-centeredness in a world of distinct meaning systems, a state of being in culture while looking at culture" (1988:9). As a committed Jew, I come to this state well equipped by my religious and cultural background. The Jewish tradition has defined this condition for the past two millennia as being in *galut* (exile), a condition that transcends the physical, encompassing psychological, and spiritual disjuncture. When I attended services at each of the five worship communities studied in this book, I felt like both a guest observer and a participant, which in all honesty is how I feel in most of my life.

When I grew up in Connecticut, my family was affiliated first with the Conservative and later, the Reform movement. My parents and grandparents were very active in the Jewish community. My American-born maternal grandfather was among the founders of the Reform temple in Waterbury, my father served as temple president, my mother taught in the Hebrew school. My paternal grandparents were immigrants from Rumania, spoke Yiddish, and kept a kosher home. Although I never considered a career in the rabbinate during high school or most of college, I was president of my temple's high school youth group and a song leader at regional and national youth conferences. While my Jewish identity and commitment were strong, my knowledge of Hebrew, traditional liturgy, and ritual practice were weak, a common situation among liberal Jews. During college I studied English literature and American civilization, planning to attend law school after graduation. However, I was influenced by the social action of religious leaders in the civil rights and antiwar movements of the 1960s and chose to apply to the Hebrew Union College–Jewish Institute of Religion, the rabbinic school of the Reform movement, in 1972. It was only after study in rabbinic school and extended periods living in Israel that I became comfortable with Hebrew. Although I had learned Torah and *Haftarah* (Prophets) cantillation for my bar mitzvah, I had long forgotten them after that singular performance/rite of passage. While it was not required by my rabbinic school, I set about to relearn cantillation and learn traditional davening.

Over the years I have become increasingly more traditional in my ritual observance, and at one point spent several months studying at an Orthodox yeshiva in Jerusalem. I find denominational labels constricting and limiting. This view is reflected by my career choice, working as a rabbi with a diverse Jewish population on a college campus. Officially I belong to the Reform rabbinical association, the Central Conference of American Rabbis. However, my professional organizational affiliation has been primarily in the cross-denominational Association of Hillel and Jewish Campus Professionals, where I served as national president. Our family belongs to the Newton Center Minyan, a worship community in which the service is basically Orthodox except for the full participation of women. Our three children have attended Solomon Schechter, the bilingual day school of the Conservative movement.

My polymorphic relationship to the Jewish community influences my approach to research. Jews often tend to be opinionated and judgmental of Jewish traditions and synagogues not their own. Yet I am hard pressed to find any sincere Jewish spiritual expression that does not feel authentic and genuine. Throughout this research I was encountering people who were simultaneously "me" and "not me." As I studied others' identities, my identity was constantly in flux, a situation common to researchers engaged in fieldwork.[2] The complexity of my participant/observer status was underscored by an exchange at one research venue, the Orthodox synagogue Shaarei Tefillah (Gates of Prayer). When I came to services on Friday evening, one of the members wished me "Good Shabbos," and asked, "Nu?

Are you davening or conducting research?" As I surveyed the room, noted the melody that the leader had chosen, and leafed through my *siddur* (prayer book) as I prepared to begin praying, I answered honestly, "Like *I* should know?" Upon deeper reflection, the answer to his question was clearly "both," a situation that complicated and enriched my role as a participant observer.[3]

I grew up playing and performing music. As with many children in our predominantly Italian neighborhood, my first instrument was the accordion. When I was fourteen, I fell in love with blues and unceremoniously pawned my accordion to buy a guitar. Throughout high school and college I performed both contemporary Jewish music and traditional American folk music, at one point recording an album of original material written about my experiences in Israel during the Yom Kippur War. My introduction to the field of ethnomusicology began at Hebrew Union College in Cincinnati while I was conducting research for my rabbinic thesis analyzing the biblical cantillation of the Yemenite Jews. I struggled to explain atypical cantillation signs in a Yemenite manuscript of the Song of Songs. My teacher, David Weisberg, suggested that I continue my research in Israel, living and studying with Yemenite teachers to see if they could explain the unusual accentuation in the manuscript. In addition to this fieldwork, I did research in the National Sound Archives at Hebrew University and met Israeli ethnomusicologists who graciously encouraged my work. Later, at Tufts, I was drawn to the work of Jeff Todd Titon when he was directing Tufts' program in ethnomusicology. My master's thesis examined the role of the part-time cantor and was done as a member of the research team for Mark Slobin's book *Chosen Voices*, the first study of the American cantorate. My doctoral work at Tufts is the basis for this book.

Long before I chose the five worship communities for this study, they were all important stops along my own religious journey. My experiences with some of them reach back more than thirty years. As a teenager, I would often visit the Reform congregation Temple Israel on youth group retreats for discussion, singing, socializing, social action projects, and prayer. I remember the imposing sanctuary and how we members of the youth group had struggled to write our own informal, creative services in contradistinction to the impressive, formal worship in that temple.

I knew Lev Friedman, the talented musician and founder of the Boston havurah B'nai Or (Children of Light) when he was still Larry Friedman and taught folk guitar at the Music Emporium in Cambridge. I was a regular patron of that store when Lev was becoming increasingly involved in the Jewish community. We discussed the possibility of his going to cantorial or rabbinic school at the time when B'nai Or in Boston was just beginning. My connection with B'nai Or actually began during my freshman year at Brandeis University in the spring of 1969 when I studied the psychology of religion with Rabbi Zalman Schachter (now Schachter-Shalomi), who later founded B'nai Or's national parent organization. Seven years later, while in rabbinic school, I worked with Reb Zalman at the National Hillel Summer Institute, leading prayer and teaching music. It was Zalman who first sent me to the Bostoner *Rebbe*, the spiritual leader of the Bostoner Hasidim, to experience some "real *leibadick* davenen" (lively prayer, Yiddish). I remember as a college student being deeply affected by the singing, dancing, and teaching at the Rebbe's. The music and intensity of the davening made a profound impression on me, whetting my taste for more regular davening with the Bratslav Hasidim in Jerusalem during the three years I lived there. Shaarei Tefillah is one of the three Orthodox synagogues in my neighborhood in Newton. The *shul* (synagogue, Yiddish) is a short walk from our home; the four homes next to ours are all owned by families who belong to that congregation. When I do not have to be at my job as the rabbi at Tufts, I daven at the Newton Center Minyan on Saturday morning, but our group seldom meets on Friday night for Kabbalat Shabbat. Then I enjoy going to Shaarei Tefillah, where a friend recently warned me that if I kept coming there I was going to become "one of them."

I have davened weekly at the Conservative service at Tufts Hillel for the past twenty years. For the first ten years or so I often led this service, then I came to believe that it was more important for college students to learn how to lead prayer themselves and this honor and responsibility moved to community members. Now I regularly give a short informal sermon at this service and in the last two years have split my time between the Conservative and the Reform services on campus.

I realize that my experiences as a traveler among these worship communities are amplified by my personal and professional interest. However, as I discuss below, contact and cross-pollination among these groups is not unusual as these Jews wander and explore the rich resources before them in Boston.

The Participating Observer

Initially I assumed that my research would be easier and better because of my insider status with a number of these worship communities. I am a *shaliach tsibbur* (prayer leader) and have planned and led services in settings similar to all those I was researching, with the exception of the Bostoner Rebbe's. I assumed that as an insider, I would both know the right questions to ask and have a deeper intrinsic understanding of these informants' feelings about music and prayer. My position offered me access to these synagogues and informants, as well as a broad understanding of the ritual and facility in both the Hebrew language and traditional liturgy. Now I see that while these advantages are blessings, they are mixed blessings.

As an insider, I found that I had to pay careful attention to avoid certain pitfalls. I took care not to talk with informants in the "shorthand" that knowledgeable insiders tend to use. I also tried not to be too quick to understand informants' responses: I might cut short valuable observations and explanations. As a rabbi, shaliach tsibbur, and musician, I had to be careful not to show off my knowledge of Jewish liturgy or music for fear that I might intimidate informants and keep them from sharing information.

Is it better for a researcher to be a cultural insider or not? While it is important to be thoughtful about the question, I see no compelling reason why one's personal history should determine, or preclude, an area of research. We are drawn to work with a particular topic for complex reasons: to satisfy our intellectual curiosity, to spend more time studying something that we love, to uncover who we are, and not least, by chance and luck. Every researcher comes with a history, and each personal history will have *some* effect upon one's relationship with informants. I have found that people are too complex to predict neatly what that effect will be. In dealing with informants, who are after all our teachers and occasionally our students and our friends, researchers need to bring to bear all the skills reserved for managing other precious relationships in our lives: honesty, resourcefulness, humor, generosity, responsibility, sensitivity, and humility. Through gestures, large and small, I have tried to build relationships with the people in these five worship communities based on these values. I have found this a challenging course to navigate and, in James Clifford's words, I see participant observation as "tacking between the 'inside' and the 'outside' of events: on the one hand grasping the sense of specific occurrences and gestures empathetically, on the other stepping back to situate these meanings in wider contexts" (1988:34).

There are particular challenges when the researcher is a bona fide member of a community being studied. For example, I was well into writing this book before it struck me that something was missing in my analysis of the Conservative service at Tufts Hillel. *I* was missing! That section lacked the voice of the rabbi who had been a leader of that worship community for almost twenty years. Rather than "interview myself," which felt silly, I worked to reposition myself in order to think about, and then write about, my experiences with that community from the perspective of a founding member, rabbi, teacher, and organizer. I then stepped back once more in order to add that voice to the others from that worship community. If anything, it felt more rather than less natural to be reflective and critical of my role and use of self in that community. As a rabbi, I have thought about this topic regularly over the years with the help of supervisors, friends, and teachers. For that matter, I do not think my experience "tacking between the inside and outside of events" here was radically different from that of other informants I interviewed in these groups. Many were academics, social workers, counselors, and psychologists, people with years of graduate schooling, who brought a well-honed reflexivity to their observations about Jewish worship and music as well as their participation in these worship communities.

Recording Unrecordable Music

Ethnomusicologists value field recordings. We enter our research settings increasingly well equipped to bring back and share music as we heard and experienced it. In many Jewish worship communities, however, the music of the Sabbath service is simply unrecordable. Traditional Jews do not use electricity on the Sabbath. This prohibition includes the use of an audio or video recorder. Thus I was not able to record actual *Shabbat* (Sabbath) evening services at three of these worship communities. The leaders at the two liberal settings said that it was fine to make discreet recordings of the service and I did so at the beginning of my research. However, by the time I was ready to make the recordings for the CD accompanying this book, I had spoken to a number of members in these congregations who were hesitant to have me record actual worship. Thus I gathered members during the week, wherever possible in the same locations where they davened on Shabbat, and recorded key segments of the Friday evening service.

Not being able to record these services live was both a loss and a gain. On one hand, I would have loved to collect and preserve the music of each of these five services, capturing the music *in situ* for the compact disc. However, the Jewish legal restrictions on recording Sabbath music underscore a truth that ethnomusicology has been confronting in its full complexity. A musical event has its own singular nature, not capturable on tape, video, or notational transcription. When the Sabbath is described as *Shabbat Kodesh* (holy Sabbath), the meaning of the Hebrew word *kodesh* indicates that this is a time set apart, unlike any other, nonreproducible. Understanding this point is both good Judaism and good ethnomusicology. There is a tendency to view the representation of an event as if it were the event itself. It was instructive to work within the constraints of Jewish law that underscored the sanctity and singularity of specific ritual performances.

Members assembled during the week to record specific musical selections and, in some cases, full versions of the Friday evening service. All agreed that it felt strange to gather in a group and record this time-bound music out of its liturgical and temporal context. I was surprised to find, again and again, that even knowledgeable informants had difficulty recalling specific tunes out of the context of the service.[4] Still, the request to make a tape of the music was not unusual for these Jews. The technology of the cassette tape has been adopted and used for the transmission of all of these communities' musical traditions.[5] Members often make and share tapes of liturgical music, both for their own pleasure and as teaching tools for their children and new members. Specific worship communities were quick to make use of the copies of these tapes that I returned to them. For example, at Tufts Hillel, student leaders distributed cassettes to both newcomers and students who wanted to learn how to lead a service or improve their davening skills. I stress that the immediacy, intensity, and full sound montage of traditional davening is not adequately reproduced when a group is artificially assembled on a Tuesday night to re-create or record selections from a Shabbat service. We lose the interplay between leader and congregation so integral to the function of the shaliach tsibbur. Of course, one person singing a version of his or her nusach or a particular tune does not reproduce the feeling of a group engaged in communal worship. As Anthony Seeger explained, the sounds of the village and its "entire social orchestra" are an integral part of the ceremonies that he recorded and studied among the Suya in Brazil (1987:65–87). So too, recordings from these re-created services do not provide the full range of ambient sounds of a congregation in prayer.

Finally, I faced issues specific to communities composed of highly literate informants. The anthropologist Jack Kugelmass observes that "one curious feature about research among American Jewry is that the subjects of the studies are likely consumers of the finished products" (1988:20). I found this true in regard to my previous writings, which were avidly read by many of my informants and their friends. They told me of the fine time they had in deciphering the pseudonyms I had assigned the informants. Many people I interviewed expressed interest in reading my finished work. Some of them are colleagues, neighbors, and friends. For better and worse, our lives are connected in complex ways and my role as a dispassionate researcher was at times difficult, if not impossible, to maintain. It was especially hard to decide whether or not I should cite informants, and even communities, anonymously.

The people in these worship communities expressed their support and enthusiasm for my research. Many told me they were pleased that their group was being studied and that their music would be recorded. It felt disrespectful to rename these very real worship communities with pseudonyms. It then followed that if I was to identify the communities I was studying, it made little sense to disguise their leaders, who are well known in Boston. It was more of a problem to determine how to treat the more than fifty men and women with whom I conducted formal interviews. I thought long and hard about folklorist Henry Glassie's words that our informants are "real people" and it would be "unkind and ungrateful . . . to murder them prematurely with anonymity or pseudonyms" (1982:xv). Yet in dealing with five worship communities, I was not fully able to develop the character and complexity of these men and women as individuals. Often I spoke with a person for hours then chose only one quote from the interview for the book. That quote could reveal an important truth about a community but might give a skewed picture of an individual. A person could easily ask, why would you choose *that* quote to represent me from a whole interview? Thus I acknowledge and thank by name all the people with whom I recorded formal interviews, but I quote them anonymously.

People sometimes shared sensitive or potentially embarrassing stories about themselves and other community members. When these stories shed significant light on my research topics, I disguised sources or slightly changed the context of some stories. If in doubt, I asked for permission to relate the story. Even in the interest of scientific truth, I do not believe I serve their interests or mine in revealing anything that should not be revealed. The Jewish tradition teaches that to embarrass a person publicly deprives you of your place in the world to come (Babylonian Talmud, *Baba Metsia* 59a). I tried to be careful and not betray the trust of those who were so gracious in answering my questions and discussing these issues. I hope that I succeeded.

"We Are One"—Are You One Too?
Jewish Community and Subculture

Jews assume community. This is simply how Jews think, an idea born out of need, religious requirement, tradition, and history. Whether it is the quorum of ten Jews required for a full communal prayer service, the organization needed to collect and distribute charity, enough dancers at a wedding, or people to argue with, Jews require other Jews to fully express, celebrate, and realize Jewish culture. When Patrick Henry said, "Give me liberty or give me death," he was stating a particularly American ideal. The Jewish version of this statement was expressed in the Talmud in the story of Honi Hameagel, a Jewish Rip van Winkle, who sleeps for seventy years and is distraught to wake and find he has no friends left alive. His story ends with the observation, "Give me community or give me death!" (Babylonian Talmud, *Taanit* 23a). Generations of forced isolation and separation from Christian society in Europe made it imperative that Jews organize their economic, cultural, and religious lives. In Europe it was the *kehilah,* the organized Jewish community, that administrated every aspect of Jewish life: communal welfare, medical care, education, charity, public works, and religious practice. There were benefits from this cradle-to-grave control, but one had little opportunity to leave or escape it. Until the Enlightenment and Emancipation of the eighteenth century, a Jew who stepped out of the ghetto had no status, opportunity, or freedom in most of Europe. When one left the Jewish community, there was simply no place else to go. Even after the ghetto gates opened and assimilation was common both in Europe and America, this sense of the Jews as one people was underscored by the tragedy of the Holocaust. At that time, Jews were branded as members of one people regardless of their religious affiliation or cultural expression. Even formal conversion to Christianity offered no escape from the fate of the Jews under Nazi control. So today Jews continue to think in terms of "the Jewish community," even knowing that there are deep religious, cultural, and philosophical divisions that separate Jews into smaller groups.

In America, freedom from both government regulation and religious direction from a centralized Jewish authority have allowed Jews to develop many different ways to be Jewish. This autonomy, combined with the Protestant ethos of an America that supported local control and a broad spectrum of individual choice in worship, led to the development of a Jewish community rich in diverse religious and cultural expression. For many years the motto of the national United Jewish Appeal charity campaign was "We are one," a motto more telling in hope than in reality.

American Jewry is often glibly referred to as if it were a uniform subculture. American Jews do share many factors in common. Income levels, education, and professional attainment are remarkably similar among suburban Reform, Conservative, and Orthodox Jews. But even if we exclude such groups as the Hasidic, Sephardic, and recently arrived Russian Jews, the expressive religious culture of the American Jewish community is far from homogeneous. Influenced by an American assumption of unlimited opportunity and practicing a form of spiritual consumerism, Jews exercise tremendous choice as they form themselves into small worship communities in which they can feel at home, comfortable and authentically Jewish. Belonging to different kinds of worship congregations is not a new thing for Jews in America. Early in this century, the lower east side of New York was filled with "landsman shuls," each exhibiting the particular traditions of its hometown synagogue in Europe. The members grouped together to re-create worship with the same music, custom, and style that bound them together in the Old World. What is different about the worship communities examined in this book is the degree of freedom with which these contemporary Jews shape and invent specific traditions, choose and compose melodies, and define a style that best expresses their religious identity.

Religious, ethnic, and cultural divisions tend to be painted with broad strokes in America. Differences among American Jews have historically been described in terms of large national groups such as German vs. Eastern European.[6] This study gives greater attention to finer distinctions within this subculture. In my experience, we tend to define ourselves in relation to people who are similar in basic ways yet different in particularities. For that matter, examining the internecine divisions within particular communities often provides a better understanding of how their members construct and present their identities than does considering the grosser distinctions between a subculture and its superculture.[7]

This book concentrates on five "sub-subcultures" within the subculture of the Boston Jewish community.[8] I also call these groups "worship communities," because it is around worship that their organizational life is structured. The term "community" is used as well, because that is how the members themselves refer to these groups. Furthermore, in every case, members pay dues or contribute financially to the group, engage together in special projects, and together mark major events in their lives and in the Jewish calendar. These groups represent the three major movements—Reform, Conservative, and Orthodox—and include two "edges" of the Jewish community: the Hasidim of the Bostoner Rebbe (on the religious right) and a "New Age" havurah, B'nai Or (on the religious left). While these communities offer a cross-denominational perspective on music and identity in Jewish worship, they are not meant to present a representative picture of American Jewry.

For example, individual congregations exercise so much autonomous control, and local *minhag* (custom) is so strong, that it is difficult to speak of even a "representative" Reform congregation in the Greater Boston area. At one Reform temple the feeling is "neo-Hasidic": they sing *niggunim* (pl., Hasidic tunes, often wordless; sing., *niggun*) to guitar accompaniment. At another Reform temple an organist accompanies a choir led by a non-Jewish cantorial soloist.[9] So too, while I include an important perspective on the Conservative movement by considering Conservative students in a university setting, I do not examine a Conservative synagogue.

I focus on Ashkenazi Jews and thus omit the three Sephardic congregations in Boston. I do not address the recent immigration of Russian Jews to Boston, the two Reconstructionist congregations, or the *havurot* (pl.) made up of post-college age Jews in Brookline, Cambridge, and Somerville. Very little work in ethnomusicology has been done on the music of middle-class religion in America, let alone on the music of the Jewish community (Reck, Slobin, Titon 1996:498). I hope others will document these important traditions.

Jewish Boston

Greater Boston is a large metropolitan area (pop. 2,852,000), currently home to a population of 233,000 Jews (Israel 1997:14).[10] Solomon Franco, possibly the first Jew in America, arrived in Boston in 1649. His arrival was inauspicious; following a financial dispute with the colony's governor, he was asked to leave shortly after his arrival (Smith 1995:23). Indeed, early Jewish settlement was slow. While Sephardic Jews in the shipping trade established small communities in other ports along the eastern seaboard, Boston was less welcoming than other port cities. The Puritans were not eager to receive either members of other religious groups or competing merchants. Trade opportunities were better in New York and in the West Indies (ibid.:24, 25). Until the 1890s the Jewish population in Boston numbered less than 5,000. The first significant Jewish settlement dates back to the mid-nineteenth century, when German and Polish Jews settled and established the oldest three synagogues in Boston: Ohabei Shalom (1842), Adath Israel (1854), and Mishkan Tefila (1858). Boston's experience was atypical in that Polish Jews outnumbered German Jews throughout the nineteenth century. Then the Eastern European Jewish immigration at the end of the century greatly increased Boston's Jewish population, which rose from 3,000 in 1875 to 40,000 at the beginning of the twentieth century. Boston is known for its "pioneering role in the development of communal structures" (Elazar 1967:240) and was the first Jewish community in America to establish a Jewish federation (1895) to aid in the settlement, welfare, and acculturation of these new Jewish immigrants. The religious and communal institutions established by this wave of Eastern European immigration served as the models for the present organizational structure of the Boston Jewish community.

Greater Boston has approximately 114 congregations, served by 160 religious professionals, 107 rabbis and 53 cantors.[11] The population is heterogeneous: a full range of denominational affiliation is represented. Approximately 47 percent of Boston's Jews are affiliated, that is, dues-paying members of a congregation (Israel 1997:40).[12] Boston also hosts more than 200 other Jewish organizations serving the intellectual, educational, cultural, and social needs of the community (Rosenzweig 1995). Combined Jewish Philanthropies, Boston's Jewish federation, is a professionally staffed umbrella organization with active lay leadership that both raises and allocates funds for these groups. A distinguishing mark of the community is the high percentage of young Jewish adults, students, and young professionals who remain in the area after completing university (Israel 1997:16). The academic Jewish community in Boston supports many active Hillel Foundations and has contributed to the growth of local havurot and other alternative Jewish worshipping communities, adding to the diversity of the Boston Jewish community.

The Roots of Jewish Denominations

The diversity found in the Jewish community in Boston is common to many metropolitan areas in America (Sarna and Smith 1995:3). How did these religious variations develop? While the Jewish denominations examined in this study evolved in a particular American context, their roots go back to Europe and grow out of Judaism's responses to modernity in the eighteenth century. The emancipation of the Jews from the ghettos of Europe in the late eighteenth and nineteenth centuries gave birth to a variety of attempts to reconcile traditional Jewish belief and practice with the modern world. Throughout the Middle Ages, Jews were isolated within ghettos, segregated from gentile society. New approaches in science, the humanistic movement, and the economic, social, and religious revolutions all combined to create a mood of liberal opinion and religious tolerance (Rudavsky 1967:17). Christian advocates of religious freedom, such as Count Mirabeau and Montesquieu, paved the way for France to grant the Jews full citizenship and equality in 1791.

As the gates of the ghetto started to open to the outside world, Judaism began to change from within. In the spirit of the *Haskalah* (Jewish Enlightenment), philosophers redefined and reinterpreted traditional Judaism. As Napoleon swept across Europe, he carried with him the principles of political and social emancipation championed by the French Revolution. A century before, the Jews were ill prepared for life outside the confines of the ghetto. By the early nineteenth century, many were ready and eager to enter the outside world as citizens.

The Enlightenment and the Emancipation opened a range of economic, philosophical, and religious options for Europe's Jews. When free to choose, many Jews left the Jewish community, preferring the baptismal font to the difficult struggle to reconcile traditional Jewish practice and contemporary values. Conversion was often the key to economic and social advancement. Movements arose to stem the tide of assimilation and place Jewish views in accord with rationalism. Doing so necessitated a break from traditional Orthodoxy and led to the rise of a variety of religious movements: Reform Judaism; the Historical School, which was the precursor of the Conservative movement; and neo-Orthodoxy. By the early 1800s, Reform Jewish leadership in Germany implemented many changes in Jewish worship, shortening the service and allowing both mixed seating and mixed choirs in the synagogue.[13] Traditionally, instrumental music was forbidden on the Sabbath, both as a sign of mourning for the destruction of the First and Second Temples in Jerusalem and as a precaution against doing the forbidden work of repairing an instrument, should it break on the Sabbath. Yet the early reformers introduced instrumental music on the Sabbath; the organ was a defining fixture in the early Reform congregations in Berlin and Hamburg. In reaction, the Historical School rejected Reform's more radical departures and encouraged moderate change, believing that the true spirit of Judaism could be found in the observance of its traditions and practice. They believed that it was essential to preserve the use of Hebrew in worship, adherence to the dietary laws, and Sabbath observance. However, they insisted that change was possible if based upon a careful and critical inquiry of Jewish law. Still, not all leaders accepted even moderate change. Traditional Jewish thinkers such as Samson Raphael Hirsch (1808–1888), a leading figure of German neo-Orthodoxy, rejected the notion that Judaism was a dynamic, changing force. Even while embracing modernism, the Orthodox believed that rabbinic law was decisive and the customs of the past were unalterable. In Rudavsky's terminology, these movements represent the European "roots" or prototypes out of which grew their American "shoots" or counterparts (1967:97).

America offered unparalleled freedom and opportunity to Jewish settlers, beginning with the earliest Jewish immigrants in the mid-seventeenth century.[14] Although the origins of Jewish denominationalism reach back to Western Europe, the Reform, Conservative, Orthodox and, finally, Reconstructionist[15] movements developed as American institutions beginning in the mid-nineteenth century. With a few exceptions,[16] Jews were free to practice their religion from the time of earliest Jewish immigration to America.

Certain factors, such as the publication of prayer books for each movement,[17] professional training in each movement's rabbinic and cantorial schools,[18] and the existence of youth groups[19] and summer programs, contribute to the standardization of worship and practice within denominational movements. Still, none of these movements fully controls religious practice in individual congregations. The influence of America's founding fathers, who were nonconformist Protestants, set the tone for Jewish congregational affiliation and practice. Each individual congregation exercises primary control over its customs, service, and music. For example, on the east coast, Reform Jewish practice is considerably more traditional than in the midwest. Conservative congregations run the gamut from right-wing Reform to left-wing Orthodox. American Judaism is an American institution and has remained highly resistant to centralized control and authority.

Music and Identity

In this study the term "identity" indicates a sense of belonging, of membership, of place, and of connection to a particular community.[20] One belongs to a community by participating in the social and religious activities of that group. Identity is functionally determined by a series of individual and collective choices, made by technical means—about how one dresses, eats, socializes, worships, and sings.[21]

When melodies are selected in Jewish worship, a series of musical decisions are made that are not always apparent to the majority of participants interviewed in this study. What tune is chosen for a particular prayer? How many times is a niggun repeated? How does a prayer leader ornament liturgical chant? What vocal style do congregants see as appropriate for praying? An analysis of these decisions and members' thoughts about the role of music in worship show how these five Jewish congregations define themselves. This study will examine both worshippers' and leaders' conceptions of music and prayer.[22]

While much of the current discussion of identity is relational, that is, how one strategically situates oneself in relation to others who form an ethnic, religious, racial, or social group, we can also think of identity as the expression of a person's core essence.[23] William James spoke of this essence in terms of a person's character: "A man's character is discernible in the mental or moral attitude in which, when it came upon him, he felt himself most deeply and intensely active and alive. At such moments there is a voice inside which speaks and says: *This* is the real me!" (James 1920: 199 in Erikson 1968:19). When conducting ethnographic research, how best can we hear that individual's voice, our living connection to every culture that is in motion? We know from our conversations with our closest friends that those moments of personal revelation are privileged and rare. The truths that we uncover are hard-won and precious. They feel both timeless and as if emanating from a particular moment and place. All at once, realizations about the nature of our core self are concrete, spiritual, personal, and relational.

Music is a deep vessel, a form of expressive culture that can combine and hold many expressions of identity. The nature of music makes it possible to blend and layer such components as language, text, tune, rhythm, vocal timbre, and instrumentation. A thoughtful consideration of the role and function of music in our lives enables us to access the multileveled meanings and associations that constitute our core selves. As a discipline, ethnomusicology is especially suited to untangle and analyze these layers of constructed identity. Mark Slobin borrows terminology from sociolinguistics to describe this process as *code-layering;* it will be explored in greater depth in chapter 4. He explains: "A band playing a song can pull together not just text and tune, but timbre, rhythm, and instrumentation for several performers simultaneously in a stratified system I call code-layering, style upon style upon style—then shift any number of the variables in the next section to produce a new kaleidoscopic code combination. Analysis becomes a process of untying a musical knot and seeing where all the strings come from before proceeding to the next node in the fabric" (1992:63). In this way, music carries a complex, even conflicting set of identity markers and indications, a situation I found repeatedly in my research. For example, a modern Orthodox congregation can sing a Hasidic niggun but be very strict about repeating it only once in the service.

By doing so, they control and moderate the spontaneity and emotional expression originally associated with the tune. Members of a havurah can chant the English translation of a Hebrew prayer to nusach, creating worship that feels both new and old as they negotiate their complex relationship to tradition and modernity by their choice of melody.

I found in my research that one does not have to be a musician, a composer, or a cantor to have strong feelings about music and its function in Jewish worship. Furthermore, one does not have to be a specialist to have a working vocabulary to describe musical complexity. People spoke easily about rhythm, harmony, fancy or simple vocal style, instrumentation, old and new melodies. In each worship community, I was often steered to members who were "really into music." Yet it was just as important to speak to those members who were *not* participating, not singing, because they were as much a part of the musical event as were their more vocal counterparts. Members express who they are as Jews as much when they don't sing as when they do. Through strategic use of silence, congregational members can influence a leader's style of performance and the choice of melodies in worship. To understand the many reasons for and significance of silence in an event in expressive culture takes an understanding of both the *halakhah* (Jewish legal regulations) governing prayer and the dynamics of the social network that control and order this musical performance. In this study I consider all of these variables, realizing that the music of Jewish worship is both "an event and a process" (Behague 1984:4; also cf. Qureshi 1986:xiv) and cannot be productively abstracted from its cultural and religious context.

I found, again and again, when these nonspecialists spoke about music in Jewish worship they were in fact talking about the deepest spiritual questions in their lives. What tunes and chant represented the essence of who they were and what they believed as Jews? What music constituted authentic practice? What was their relationship to their ethnic and religious history? Where and when did they feel truly comfortable and fully at home? In my many conversations and interviews, we spoke about music, but the real conversation was about the locus of core meaning in their lives.[24] Their feelings about music illuminated their experience as bearers of an ancient tradition and as active participants in modern America who were trying many different models to integrate Judaism's lessons into their lives and carry that tradition into the next millennium. So while this book examines Jewish identity through music, it is really a study of the men and women who make that music.[25]

Bruce A. Phillips observes that much study of Jewish identity has been conceptualized and measured by change-orientation models, considering Jewish observance and formal and informal ties to other Jews, such as organizational affiliation, activism on behalf of Israel, and intermarriage.[26] This approach to Jewish identity has tended to plot Jews on a continuum from nonobservant to ritually observant, from assimilated to identified. Yet my experience with these subcommunities of the Jewish community in Boston is that they do not fit easily on a continuum. I repeatedly found that while identity constructs such as denominational labels describe a great deal, we must look beyond them in order to understand the complex religious and cultural identity of these American Jews. For example, Reform Jews spoke passionately about the importance of traditional prayer modes. Feminists embraced traditional worship while challenging and redefining gender roles. Orthodox Jews innovated and introduced new tunes in worship while insisting that nothing had changed. I believe flexible discourse is essential in order to describe and discuss the construction of identity at this time of tremendous personal freedom and choice.[27]

One might assume that worship would be a bastion of tradition, an area where practice is firmly established, where all the choices have already been made. In fact, in every community that I examined, musical aspects of the service underwent constant, strategic negotiation, both by leaders and by worshippers (cf. Royce 1982:184–215). Throughout this study I examine "junctures of choice" within the Friday evening service. These junctures are broad in some worship communities, narrow in others. Yet by examining these choices, and the processes by which they are made, we learn about the locus of authority and power of tradition in each community. We see which community boundaries are permeable and which are inviolable. This process of textual and melodic choice is as old as the history of Jewish worship. The inclusion and exclusion of specific liturgical texts have been debated throughout the development of Jewish liturgy.[28] The existence of variant editions of the siddur attests to the successful efforts of individual communities to define and assert their own identities within the broader Jewish community.[29] Melodic choice and the proper role of music in synagogue worship have been topics of discussion from the talmudic period to the present,[30] but its present realization is in certain ways unique. American Jewish communities now enjoy unprecedented social and religious freedom. They draw from an increasingly larger range of musical resources when "building a service" (Slobin 1989:287–97). Each community works hard to find a *style* of worship that properly expresses who its members are as Jews and as Americans.

Style functions as a symbolic expression of core values and identity. In the field of cultural studies, Dick Hebdige discusses the function of style as an essential differentiator in subculture: "Style in subculture is . . . pregnant with significance. . . . Our task [is] to discern the hidden messages inscribed in code on the glossy surfaces of style, to trace them out as 'maps of meaning'" (1979:18). According to Hebdige, people continually borrow cultural expressions and redefine them, reinterpreting their meaning and significance. As melodies are appropriated, they become infused with meaning that is specific to a particular group. For example, worshippers have strong feelings about the vocal style chosen by a cantor or lay prayer leader and will associate certain values and attitudes with that musical style. Earlier in this century, a leader who sang in a bel canto, operatic vocal style was seen as cultured and artistic—an American. Now this approach can brand a leader as being formal, egotistical, and oriented toward performance. A leader's vocal style, a cantor's use of a guitar, an Israeli folk song in the liturgy all convey symbolic meaning to the listener. Many Jews take the pulse of a congregation very quickly by noting the style of music used in worship.

I spoke with many Jews who had left congregations where they felt the patient was barely breathing. For them, prayer in those communities was simply uninspired, lacking spirit, breath, and life. I know this too from my experience as a Jew who participates in communal worship, both as a worshipper and as a leader of prayer. I often find prayer a meaningful, and occasionally a transformative, experience. Yet in certain settings the style of music makes the worship feel dead to me. I am personally and professionally conscious that Jewish prayer, and the siddur in particular, are not especially user-friendly to the uninitiated. The rich, multileveled Hebrew language of the traditional prayer book is incomprehensible to many worshippers, and even for the dedicated student it takes years to develop linguistic fluency with the *tefillot* (prayers). Thus music becomes increasingly important in worship. Both the prayer leaders and worshippers in this study were extremely conscious of even minor differences in the style of musical performance in worship (cf. Slobin 1992:62). I am convinced that style of worship, even more than the content of the liturgy, plays a major factor in whether or not many Jews find prayer meaningful and fulfilling. Style makes people feel either at home or uncomfortable and alienated from communal prayer. Ultimately, it can affect whether or not they attend and affiliate with synagogues.[31]

While the construction of any religious, cultural, and ethnic identity is complicated, Jewish identity is especially complex. Mordecai Kaplan described Judaism as "something far more comprehensive than Jewish religion. It includes that nexus of a history, literature, language, social organization, folk sanctions, standards of conduct, social and spiritual ideals, esthetic values which in their totality form a civilization" (1981 [1957]:178). The Jews with whom I spoke understood their Judaism in many ways: as a culture, an organized religion, a people, a denominational movement, a homeland, an ethnic or national group, an ongoing spiritual exploration. On one hand, Jewish identity was voluntary, a matter of choice. Which synagogue would you join? How ritually observant would you be? Would you wear a Jewish star pendant inside or outside your shirt, or not at all? Most of these Jews enjoyed tremendous freedom in choosing particular forms of cultural and religious expression. On the other hand, Jewish identity was experienced as involuntary, ascribed by the dominant culture. To what extent would you be stereotyped by non-Jewish classmates? Would you be admitted to certain schools or private clubs? Up until very recently, America always reminded Jews they were different, a religious and ethnic minority. Members of all of these worship communities, or their parents, had experienced anti-Semitism. The specter of the Holocaust hung over the individual and collective history of even the most assimilated of these Jews.

There are other factors that complicate Jewish identity in the United States. Jews are not the only people in America who relate to an ancestral homeland and address the experience of being in diaspora: the terms African American and Asian American suggest similar relationships. Yet the majority of the men and women I interviewed had strong and complex relationships with Israel. Many were swept up in the resurgence of Jewish identity following Israel's victory in the 1967 Six Day War. Most were deeply supportive of Israel; others expressed ambivalence in regard to government policy and frustration with the slow peace process. Many of these Jews were especially aware that Israel and her political fortunes receive an inordinate amount of attention in the American press. All were conscious of the struggle for political and religious power in Israel between the Orthodox rabbinate and Israel's small Reform and Conservative movements. Yet these Jews do not experience much intradenominational conflict in Boston, where their own subcommunities have tremendous local autonomy and little institutional reason to have contact, let alone conflict, with one another. All of these factors combine to create a research field that is complicated and diverse. Even from the inside, American Judaism is confusing. With so many different congregations and organizations, so many ways to "be Jewish," it often feels as if Jews share little common ground.

Music is one of the common reference points, where we find significant overlap among certain groups of Jews in America. Even between services that differ greatly, such as the Hasidic and Reform service, there was common ground created by shared liturgical text, similar visions of the nature, purpose, and sanctity of the Sabbath. Melodies, and the memory of melodies accepted and rejected, were held in common. When the Hasidic Bostoner Rebbe described how he chose a tune for *Lekhah dodi*, he discussed Louis Lewandowski's setting for the hymn. The Rebbe stressed that this tune was boring and repetitious and did not create the proper spiritual mood for welcoming the Sabbath. That same tune was used and held dear by worshippers at Temple Israel, the Reform Temple in this study, yet they had greatly modified its performance and text in response to these same issues. The Reform community has the freedom to make such changes, use instrumental music, and give women the opportunity to lead services. These are not options in Hasidic worship. Still, they share many common reference points: nusach, venerated tunes for hymns, and the interplay of leader and congregation in Jewish prayer.

I also found considerable, and surprisingly fluid, musical contact among these worship communities. Personal friendships, spiritual search, curiosity, and the simple fact of living in relatively close proximity bring Jews from these very different worship communities together. Lay and professional leaders visit different services. Members at the modern Orthodox shul Shaarei Tefillah cut their teeth at the Conservative services at Harvard and Brandeis Hillel. Members of the havurah B'nai Or visit the Bostoner Rebbe's Hasidic community for, in the words of one member, a "spiritual shot in the arm." Conservative university students join their Reform friends to attend a concert by Debbie Friedman, one of the Reform movement's most influential and charismatic liturgical composers. Even at the Rebbe's, two bearded Hasids warmly approached to wish me good Shabbos. They had both been students at Tufts years before they found their place as members of the Rebbe's community. All of these Jews talk to God through prayer. Though they express themselves in different ways, their vocabularies overlap as that conversation is carried out in song.

1

An Introduction to Jewish Worship

The Nature of Jewish Worship

There are Jews in every denomination who venerate worship traditions as if they had been passed down from God to Moses on Mount Sinai. Most communities have congregants who insist that the service always be conducted exactly the same way and who come to synagogue vigilantly to watch that nothing be changed. In fact, the history of Jewish liturgy has been one of continual development and evolution, a balance between tradition and innovation. The very institutionalization of obligatory, communal prayer services as the official means to thank, praise, and petition God was developed by creative rabbis after the destruction of the Second Temple in Jerusalem by the Romans in 70 C.E. The Temple had been the religious, economic, and political center of the Jewish state, and when it was destroyed, so was the institution of the daily and holiday sacrifices and offerings, together with the vocal and instrumental pageantry of the Levites, the Temple musicians. That direct path to God was cut off: no longer would the sweet smell of incense and animal smoke rise to the heavens from the Temple altar in Jerusalem. In a radical leap born of necessity, the rabbis stressed that prayer would be equal to the sacrifices that had been offered in the Temple.[1] So closely were worship services modeled after the daily and holiday sacrifices that some of the services, such as *Minchah* (afternoon) and *Musaf* (additional service on Shabbat and holiday mornings) even took the sacrifices' names.

We do have examples of personal prayer that date back to the Bible, such as when Moses prayed for God to heal his sister Miriam when she was struck with leprosy (Num. 12:13). The Psalms also contained personal prayers of thanksgiving, praise, and petition that were eventually collected into one book. During the period of the Second Temple, these biblical passages and elaborately orchestrated psalms were recited in conjunction with the sacrifices. The Jewish commonwealth was divided into twenty-four districts, or *Maamadot*, which would send representatives to Jerusalem to participate in the Temple service. Those who stayed at home would join together to recite biblical passages. These Maamadot became one of the precursors of the modern synagogue, and the rites conducted there set the stage for the establishment of the decentralized prayer service. In the early rabbinic period the rabbis of the *Mishnah* (rabbinic legal code that forms the basis of the Talmud, second century C.E.) begin to codify these biblical passages, psalms, and prayers into a formal order, or *seder*, from the same Hebrew root as siddur, the name of the book that eventually contained them. Prayer became obligatory at that time, and Jewish men were expected to pray three times a day. While women are allowed, and often encouraged, to pray, they traditionally do not have as many liturgical obligations as men since such "time-bound" *mitzvot* (commandments, pl.) might conflict with their primary responsibilities to home and family.

Every traditional service is composed of a set liturgy that the congregation is required to recite.[2] Certain popular prayers can be recited only in the presence of a *minyan*, a quorum of ten worshippers. The morning and evening worship service is structured around two central prayers: the *Shema* (Listen! [Israel]), the statement of God's unity; and the *Amidah* (standing prayer), a series of nineteen benedictions that thank, praise, and petition God. The *Shema* is a series of three biblical passages beginning with the central creedal statement, "Listen Israel! Adonai is our God, Adonai alone." This last phrase is also translated "the Lord is one." The other paragraphs of the *Shema* stress the obligation to teach and model that unity in daily life and the reward or punishment for observing or transgressing the commandments. The *Shema* is preceded by two blessings; the first emphasizes God's creation of the world, and the second teaches that the Torah was revealed as a sign of God's love for Israel. The *Shema* is followed by a blessing stressing redemption. In the evening, a second blessing follows the *Shema* thanking God for peace and protection. The *Amidah*, or standing prayer, is so central that it is also referred to simply as *Hatefillah, the* prayer. Yet another name for this prayer is the *Shemoneh Esrai* (Eighteen), because it originally contained eighteen rather than nineteen benedictions. It begins by praising God for maintaining connection with the Jews through history, by acknowledging God's power, and by declaring God's holiness. This is followed by a series of petitionary requests, among them health, peace, protection, and ingathering of the dispersed Jewish exiles to Israel. On the Sabbath, the *Amidah* is shortened to seven benedictions, eliminating the prayers of petition. On Friday evening an abbreviated repetition of the Tefillah, *Magen avot* (Protector of the patriarchs), is added.

Services are introduced with a section of psalms. At the service's conclusion the *Alenu* (It is our obligation [to praise God]) recapitulates the main themes of the service. After the *Alenu*, mourners are given the honor of reciting the *Kaddish* (Sanctification); this prayer makes no mention of death but rather affirms God's majesty and holiness.

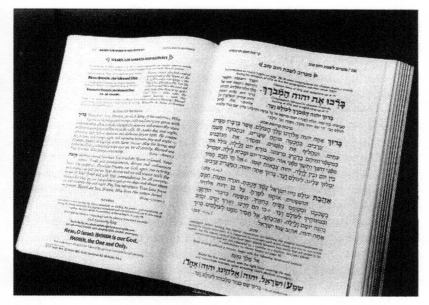

Figure 1.1. A traditional siddur (prayer book), Shaarei Tefillah. Photo: Richard Sobol.

Services vary in length and complexity, according to the time of day (morning, afternoon, and evening) and whether it is a weekday, Sabbath, or holiday. A traditional weekday evening service might take only 20 minutes. A Friday evening service might last 45 minutes. However, a Sabbath morning service will usually run for two and a half hours, a High Holiday service for four hours.

Historically, the siddur is a multilayered text. The oldest prayers are biblical sections, which over time have been supplemented with compositions by the rabbis of the talmudic (third to sixth century c.e.), geonic (sixth to eleventh century c.e.), and later periods. In fact, each generation added its own prayers and meditations to the service; the most popular ones stuck and were integrated into the siddur. Until the early Reform movement began to shorten the service in the mid-1800s, it was more common to add prayers to the service than to take them away. Over time, the siddur grew from a text that could have fit into a small pamphlet to the substantial volume it is today.

Jewish prayer is sacred text performed. Scholars have compared a congregation involved in traditional Jewish prayer to a jazz band (Heilman 1976:212; Hoffman 1997:3). At times the leader solos, at times the congregation sings a melody along with the leader, at times all the participants are "doing their own thing."[3] While the whole congregation is an orchestra, praising and petitioning God, the prayer leader is both soloist and conductor. Traditional prayers are divided into individual units, and the leader chants the beginning lines (*petichah*, literally "opening") and ending lines (*hatimah*, literally "sealing") of certain prayers. In this way, the leader marks the place and sets the pace of the service. Such Jewish prayer often sounds like a cacophony of voices. Individuals proceed at varying speeds; rarely are two people chanting exactly the same words at the same time. Worshippers chant in a undertone, each choosing a comfortable key.

In traditional Jewish worship the leader and congregation do not "pray" or "read prayers"; they *daven*. In Yiddish, *daven* means simply "to pray." Yet davening (in Yiddish, *davenen*), has a much more involved, participatory implication. At least in Eastern European tradition, to daven is to sing, chant, move, and sway. One must bring an emotional intensity and involvement to the recitation of the prayers. To daven, one must have proper *kavanah*, the piety, devotion, concentration, and intention to consider the meaning of the prayers and say them as though one means them.[4] The term "to daven" can mean both "to pray" and "to lead prayer." A worshipper might ask, "Where are you going to daven on Shabbos?" A cantor might say, "The congregation hired me to daven on Rosh Hashanah" (cf. Kon 1971:38, 39).

Certain prayers are chanted in a call-and-response pattern. The leader begins solo and the congregation responds together, answering or in some cases repeating the leader's words. In other places the leader chants certain words out loud to signal that the congregation should have arrived at a certain part of the service. Some congregations join together as the leader sings the opening or closing lines of a particular prayer. Yet the individual worshipper is not obligated to sing with the leader if he has completed the prayer himself. Sometimes the worshipper will just listen to the leader chant the last lines of the prayer, respond "Amen," and proceed to the next prayer. In fact, a worshipper who is unfamiliar with the Hebrew text can technically fulfill the religious obligation to pray by simply listening to the leader's prayer and responding "Amen."[5]

While following the basic structure of the traditional liturgy, the style of worship in a Reform Temple is different. Early Reform Jews in Germany wished to re-create prayer as an aesthetic experience more in keeping with their modern, post-Enlightenment sensibilities. They instituted a number of radical changes to eliminate the noise, repetition and, to their perceptions, "disorderliness" of traditional davening. The service was accordingly shortened, and many prayers were read in unison either in the vernacular or Hebrew. In America it also became common to do responsive readings in English, with the rabbi reading one line of a psalm or creative prayer and the congregation answering by reading the next. Key sections of the liturgy are read in English, or depending on the particular synagogue, chanted in unison in Hebrew. In many settings the choir, together with the cantor or cantorial soloist, sings key sections of the liturgy in Hebrew or English. Because many liberal Jews are not able to read Hebrew, or at least to read well, the role of the professional becomes more important in communal worship.

In traditional terminology, the leader of prayer is called the *shaliach tsibbur*, the community's liturgical agent or representative of the congregation. One can position the musical/liturgical leadership in the synagogue on a continuum of professionalism. At one end is the skilled but unpaid congregational member who will accept the honor of serving as shaliach tsibbur and leading the congregation in prayer, either occasionally or regularly. At the other is the full-time, professional *hazzan* (cantor) who has completed a course of graduate study to become a cantor. The term *baal tefillah* (master of prayer) is also used as an honorific to signify a leader who is especially well versed in liturgical chant and the laws of correct liturgical practice. A shaliach tsibbur may or may not be a baal tefillah, depending on one's level of liturgical expertise. If a congregation needs additional help or cannot support a full-time cantor, it may hire a part-time cantor, either for the Sabbath or, more likely, for the High Holidays (Summit 1988). Some Reform temples employ cantorial soloists, musicians who possess a good voice but may have little or no facility in Hebrew or knowledge of Jewish liturgy. It is not unusual for such a musical soloist to be non-Jewish.

The cantor, part-time or full-time, remains the most active and central liturgical leader in Conservative and Orthodox synagogues and plays an increasingly important role in Reform temples. While the rabbi enjoys a higher professional and economic status, only in Reform congregations does the rabbi have a more active role than the cantor in leading services. In an Orthodox synagogue, any adult male member of the congregation who regularly attends services and possesses the requisite liturgical skills is an acceptable leader. It is an honor to lead the congregation in prayer, and in traditional settings the *gabbai* (a lay leader in charge of assigning ritual tasks), is careful to distribute these honors fairly among congregants and guests.[6]

It is assumed that the prayer leader is familiar with the Hebrew and Aramaic text of the liturgy and will chant the service in the correct *nusach*, the term for Ashkenazi traditional chant. (Nusach is discussed at length in chapter 3.) There is a special nusach for the High Holidays, for Shabbat morning, and for weekday afternoon services. Samuel Heilman defines nusach as a "combination of sprechgesang and aria which concludes, corrects and leads the prayers" (1976:288). Because of its relatively free nature, nusach allows the leader certain opportunities for improvisation (cf. Slobin 1989:256–79).

The choice of the music used in worship is greatly determined by local minhag (custom). This is especially true for the metrical hymns in the services, such as *Lekhah dodi* or *Adon olam* (Master of the universe), which the leader and congregation sing together. In every worship community there are certain points in the service where the leader can—and is expected to—make musical choices. Certain tunes and melodies are also used for other sections of the liturgy. A congregation might know several different tunes that it accepts and uses for a particular prayer. It is the leader's

Figure 1.2. The town and mountains of Safed, Israel. Photo: David Rubinger.

prerogative to choose one of these tunes, within the bounds accepted by the congregation. The leader then controls the key, tempo, dynamics, and how long the congregation sings and repeats the tune.

The Kabbalat Shabbat Service

Kabbalat Shabbat was introduced as a liturgical innovation by the Jewish mystics during the mid-sixteenth century in the town of Safed in northern Israel.[7] Enthralled with the mystical personification of the Sabbath as Israel's bride and inspired by the natural beauty of Safed, high in the mountains, these mystics dressed in fine clothing and, like bridegrooms going out to meet their brides, went out into the fields to receive the Sabbath. Rabbi Isaac Luria and his disciples expanded this ceremony and would recite hymns and songs they had composed for the service as well as selected psalms. Eventually, this ceremony moved from the mountains and fields into the synagogue, where it became the first segment of the Shabbat Maariv service.

In order to contextualize the meaning of the Kabbalat Shabbat service, we must understand the notion of spirituality which motivated the mystics in Safed to create it.[8] According to the Kabbalists, human beings have a role to play in the continuing creation of the world, an obligation to function as God's "partner" in the *tikkun* (repairing) of the Universe.[9] God and human beings work together to bring redemption to the world, as Max Arzt shows in this concise explanation of Jewish mystical philosophy, drawing from Scholem's major work on Jewish mysticism (1941:283–86). Arzt writes:

> The Kabbalists taught that every man is in a state of exile because he has shrunk in spiritual stature to become immersed in a morass of moral corruption and pollution. The people of Israel is in *Galut* (exile), and it can achieve its *Tikkun* (redemption)[10] by returning to God from whom it became alienated when it ignored His commandments. To speed the end of the *Galut*, the Jew needs to find his *Tikkun* through a life of prayer, piety, and good deeds. By fulfilling the commandments of the Torah, the individual Jew can wend his way back to the original splendor which was his when he had *D'vekut*, continuous adhesion to God. He needs to lift his life out of the *Klippot* (shells) that cause confusion and disorder and that disturb the harmony of Creation. By this *Tikkun*, the individual Jew not only reclaims his alienated self but also liberates the *Shekhinah* (Divine Presence) from its state of exile, thus accelerating the arrival of the Messianic era of Israel's restoration to the Holy Land (1979:20, 21).

The mystics of Safed did more than develop esoteric philosophy delineating the relationship between God and Israel. They believed that human deeds had an effect upon the upper worlds and so they labored to create communities in which the values of love, honesty, piety, and charity permeated human relationships. Indeed, there is a genre of Jewish ethical literature from the period known as *Hanhagot* (Guidelines for Behavior) which presented practical directives on how to conduct oneself in daily life, control one's anger, and give and accept criticism.[11] While the Kabbalist Moses Cordovero (1522–1570) attained prominence for his commentary on the Zohar and systematic synthesis of mystical literature up to his time, his practical directives concerning personal life and interpersonal interactions had a tremendous effect upon his students and disciples.

Cordovero's student Isaac Luria, known as the Ari (Lion) (1534–1572), developed into the most influential Kabbalist of Safed in the sixteenth century. Fine notes that: "At the heart of [his] mythology stands the radically Gnostic notion that sparks of divine light have, in the process of God's self-disclosure or emanation, accidentally and disastrously become embedded in all material things. According to Luria, these sparks of light yearn to be liberated from their imprisoned state and return to their source within the Godhead, thus restoring the original divine unity. The human task in the face of this catastrophic situation is to bring about such liberation through proper devotional means" (1984a:62). This tikkun was to be brought about by all of one's actions—how one treats fellow human beings, eats, studies, celebrates rituals, prays, and sings. Functionally, the rituals and practices developed by Luria and his school were understood to hasten Israel's redemption and the coming of the Messiah. Luria describes the Friday evening ritual as follows:[12]

> This is the order of Kabbalat Shabbat: Go out into an open field and recite: "Come and let us go into the field of holy apple trees"[13] in order to welcome the Sabbath Queen. . . . Stand in one place in the field; it is preferable if you are able to do so on a high spot, one which is clean as far as one can see in front of him, and for a distance of four cubits behind him. Turn your face towards the West where the sun sets, and at the very moment that it sets close your eyes and place your left hand upon your chest and your right hand upon your left. Direct your concentration—while in a state of awe and trembling as one who stands in the presence of the King—so as to receive the special holiness of the Sabbath. Begin by reciting the Psalm: "Give to the Lord, O Heavenly beings" [Ps. 29], sing it entirely in a sweet voice. Following this, recite three times: "Come, O Bride, Come O Bride, O Sabbath Queen." Next, recite: "A psalm, a song for the Sabbath day" [Ps. 92] in its entirety, followed by "The Lord is King; He is robed in majesty" until "for all time" [Ps. 93]. Then open your eyes and return home. Enter and wrap yourself in a fringed prayer shawl. . . . Circle the table—prepared with the Sabbath loaves—walking around it several times until you have repeated everything which you had recited while in the field. (Fine 1984a:74, 75)

Except for the recitation of psalms, most of Luria's personal customs and practices were not followed by subsequent generations. However, in his directions we see the rubrics of the Kabbalat Shabbat service in their nascent state as they were to develop and take hold among Jewish communities throughout the world.

In time, Kabbalat Shabbat was standardized to consist of six psalms, corresponding to the six days of the week, and the hymn *Lekhah dodi*. The service opens with the Sabbath psalm, Psalm 29, followed by Psalms 95–99.[14] Following *Lekhah dodi*, Psalms 92 and 93 are recited. Shabbat is referred to in rabbinic literature as a "taste of the world to come," and thematically these psalms stress messianic redemption, salvation, and the coming of the Kingdom of God on earth.[15] In many traditional congregations, the hymn *Ana bekhoah* (Please, with the strength of your strong, right hand) is said before *Lekhah dodi*, and chapter 2 of Mishnah Shabbat, *Bameh madlikin* (With what do you light [the Sabbath candles]) is intoned after the hymn, before the beginning of the Maariv service.[16]

The Kabbalists' innovations to expand the celebration of Shabbat were influenced by the directive in the Talmud "to add from the weekday to the holy day" (Babylonian Talmud, *Yoma* 81b). In accord with this sentiment, they started the service before the start of the Sabbath, an hour and a quarter before the appearance of the stars.[17] The leader begins the Kabbalat Shabbat prayers standing on the *bimah* (raised platform, stage) and, in many traditional synagogues, moves to the shaliach tsibbur's regular place at the reader's stand only at the *Barekhu* (Bless [the Lord who is blessed!], the call to prayer) the formal beginning of the Maariv service. This change of location indicates that Kabbalat Shabbat is an innovation, not included in the original order of prayers. During the singing of *Lekhah dodi*, it is customary to turn around when the last stanza is recited (*Boi veshalom* . . . [Come, in peace . . .]) to face the entrance of the synagogue and bow. In this way the worshipper symbolically welcomes the "Sabbath bride." The custom of bowing to the door is also a commemoration of the custom of walking outdoors to greet the Sabbath (Elbogen [1913, 1972] 1993:92).[18] After Kabbalat Shabbat, the service continues with the Sabbath Maariv service, which is based on the weekday evening service, as described above.[19]

2

The Meaning of a Tune

The Sabbath Hymn *Lekhah dodi*

The Concept of Tune in Jewish Worship

Many worshippers, especially during the High Holidays, do not feel they have been to services unless they hear their favorite tunes for certain prayers.[1] The tune, separate from the words, serves as a portal to the past, a connection with ancestors, real and imagined. The "right" tune grounds one in history and becomes an assurance of authenticity. The tune is a vehicle for transcendence. For many Jews who do not understand much Hebrew, the tune *is* the prayer. Cantors, rabbis, and lay leaders who do not understand this point are forever at odds with their congregations. Every year, freshmen who come to services for the first time at our Hillel Foundation tentatively approach me and say, "Rabbi, I enjoyed services but you know, you sing all the wrong tunes here." "What are the 'right' tunes?" I ask. "The ones we sing at home!"

Judit Frigyesi differentiates between nusach, which she calls "flowing rhythm," and "metric tunes," which she sees as "insertions" in the service (1993):

Essentially, metric tunes . . . suspend momentarily the basic flowing-rhythmic music; they highlight sections of the text; and they enliven and articulate the form of the service. These metric insertions can be omitted or replaced, new tunes may be composed or adopted from the Jewish or non-Jewish folk repertoire. The precentor is expected to know when, how many, and what kind of metric tunes to use in a given service, and his taste and creativity to bring new melodies into practice are appreciated. Of course, metric pieces are not entirely free of the bonds of tradition. Some melodies have come to be associated with a given function and text, almost codified in local custom. The congregation often insists on particular tunes which are seen as the token of loyalty to local tradition, as the mark of the identity of the community.

But from a purely liturgical point of view, these tunes are not necessary; the service may fulfill its religious function even if the entire metric material is eliminated. (Frigyesi 1993:69)

While Frigyesi is correct, from my experience few of the worshippers in the services examined here would feel that the service had been conducted properly without the singing of specific tunes. This is especially true on Shabbat, when congregants have more time and it is considered praiseworthy to embellish the service. Congregants treat their favorite tunes with considerable reverence. In my previous research, many cantors and lay leaders described the resistance, or even hostility, they encountered when attempting to change favorite tunes or introduce new tunes into the service (Summit 1988:103–6).

Mark Slobin characterizes these metric tunes as the "music of participation" (1989:195–212). In many conversations, worshippers spoke about the power of singing together and saw these tunes as one of the few ways that a community can actually experience unity. They allow an individual to hear and feel what it means to blend voice and breath, to create, though only temporarily, a transcendent community of palpable beauty and harmony. Thus, participatory singing becomes a transformative occasion as well as an opportunity to experience community on a deeper level.

The repertoire of participatory tunes is continually evolving. Certain tunes from Western Europe that have become standard fare in Ashkenazi worship date back to the famous cantor/liturgical composers of the mid-nineteenth century such as Salomon Sulzer, Lewandowski, and Abraham Baer. Other tunes are drawn from various Mideastern communities, such as Yemenite or Moroccan. Tunes also come from the youth movements and summer camps of the Reform, Conservative, and Orthodox movements, traditional and popularized Hasidic songs, Israeli folk, and popular music (Slobin 1989:196; Schiller 1992). There is also a large modern Orthodox music network producing both popular and religious music that finds its way into the service (Kligman 1996). So too, a growing number of singer/composers associated with the Jewish renewal movement are producing and distributing their music. This is a creative time for contemporary Jewish music and, in addition to well-known contemporary composers of liturgical music, it is not unusual to find tunes that are composed by congregational leadership or members in individual congregations.

Lekhah dodi: The Central Tune in the Kabbalat Shabbat Service

Lekhah dodi developed from the liturgical tradition of the *piyyut* (Jewish liturgical hymn). From the talmudic period onward, each generation incorporated additional prayers and meditations in the siddur. By the sixth and seventh centuries more and more of these complex metrical poems had been added to the service as creative worshippers were influenced by Arabic poetry and the desire to inject free expression into the set prayers.[2] While much of the Hebrew and Aramaic language of these poems was difficult and often obscure, *piyyutim* (pl.) became extremely popular, and eventually many were adopted as standard prayers in the liturgy. Their popularity was attributed to the varied popular tunes used for their recitation (Shiloah 1992:111–29; Landman 1972:9).[3] *Lekhah dodi* was one of the last piyyutim to be included in the siddur and is found in both Ashkenazi and Sephardic services (Ydit 1972:5; Elbogen [1913, 1972] 1993:92).

The following are two English translations of *Lekhah dodi*. The first is by Lawrence Fine (1984a:38–40). I also include his notes (4–8) to the text.

"Observe" and "Remember," in a single command, the One God announced to us. The Lord is One, and His name is One, for fame, for glory and for praise.[4]

Chorus: Come, my Beloved, to meet the Bride; let us welcome the Sabbath.[5]

Come, let us go to meet the Sabbath, for it is a source of blessing. From the very beginning it was ordained; last in creation, first in God's plan.

Shrine of the King, royal city, arise! Come forth from your ruins. Long enough have you dwelt in the valley of tears! He will show you abundant mercy.

Shake off your dust, arise! Put on your glorious garments, my people, and pray: "Be near to my soul, and redeem it through the son of Jesse, the Bethlehemite."[6]

Bestir yourself, bestir yourself, for your light has come; arise and shine! Awake, awake, utter a song; the Lord's glory is revealed upon you.[7]

Be not ashamed nor confounded. Why are you downcast? Why do you moan? The afflicted of my people will be sheltered within you; the city shall be rebuilt on its ancient site.

Those who despoiled you shall become a spoil, and all who would devour you shall be far away. Your God will rejoice over you as a bridegroom rejoices over his bride.

You shall extend to the right and to the left, and you shall revere the Lord. Through the advent of a descendant of Perez we shall rejoice and exult.[8]

Come in peace, crown of God, come with joy and cheerfulness; amidst the faithful of the chosen people come, O Bride; come, O Bride.

Many English translations have rendered the text in English poetically, so that it can be sung in translation. Such is this version, translated by Joel Rosenberg (Teutsch 1989:48–54).[9]

O, come, my friend, let's greet the bride,
the Sabbath Presence bring inside.

"Keep" and "Remember" in a sole command
the solitary God did us command
"I AM!" is one, the Name is one,
in name, in splendor, and in praise.

Toward the Sabbath, come, make haste,
for she has every blessing's taste,
ordained at first, and long ago,
the last thing made, the first in mind.

O, Sovereign's abode, O, holy regal crown
rise up, emerge, where once cast down,
enough of sitting in the vale of tears,
God pities you, yes you God spares.

Be stirred, rise up, throw off the dust,
my people, don your clothes of eminence,
by hand of Bethle'mite Jesse's child,
draw near my soul, redeem it, too.

Arouse yourself, arouse yourself,
your light has come, arise and shine,
awake, awake, pour forth your song,
on you now shines the Glorious One.

Don't be abashed, don't be ashamed,
why be downcast, why do you sigh?
In you my people's poor find shade,
a city rebuilt where her ruins lay.

Your robbers shall be robbed themselves,
all your devourers will be removed,
your God rejoices at your side,
the joy of a bridegroom with his bride.

To right and left you shall burst forth,
revering God, to south and north,
by hand of one from Peretz's line,
we shall rejoice and find delight.

O, come in peace, O divine crown,
with joy, rejoicing, and with mirth,
amid the faithful, loved by God,
come in, O bride, come in, O bride!

The Talmud mentions various song texts that express the joyous welcome of the Sabbath (Babylonian Talmud, *Baba Kama* 32a, b). These texts form the basis of the personification of the Sabbath as bride. The Talmud

Figure 2.1. A Jewish Yemenite bride in a wedding procession, escorted by women holding lit candles. Photo: Debbi Cooper.

quotes Rabbi Hanina as saying, "Come and let us go forth to welcome the queen Sabbath" (Babylonian Talmud, *Shabbat* 119a). So too, the Talmud reports that before Shabbat, Rabbi Jannai would dress in his best garments and say, "Come, O bride, come, O bride!" This imagery was developed by Shelomo Alkabetz HaLevi (c.1505–1584) in his piyyut *Lekhah dodi*. In accordance with a common practice of that time, the first letter of each of the hymn's eight verses formed an acrostic of the author's Hebrew name, Shelomo HaLevi.[10]

Shelomo Alkabetz was a Kabbalist, a mystical poet and prolific author who wrote biblical commentaries, prayers, and sermons. He was a brother-in-law of the Kabbalist Moses Cordovero, who was a pupil of Joseph Caro, the author of the most widely accepted code of Jewish law, the *Shulchan Arukh* (The Prepared Table). Alkabetz's text of *Lekhah dodi* was known to be the favorite of his student, the Kabbalist master Rabbi Isaac Luria.[11] Helped by Luria's influence, this hymn was eventually adopted by Jewish communities throughout the world.

While the messianic themes of *Lekhah dodi* reflected older talmudic concepts that associated redemption with the observance of the Sabbath, these sixteenth-century mystics in Safed went considerably further in their interpretation of its male-female imagery. For them, the Kabbalat Shabbat service, and *Lekhah dodi* in particular, were seen as a wedding between the female and male aspects of God, thus the stress on the imagery of the Sabbath as bride. The mystics saw the six days of the week, the realm of the profane, as dominated by a spirit of disjunction. On Shabbat, God's feminine aspect, the Shekhinah, rejoins the male aspect of God, the King. This renewing of cosmic marital vows was understood as the first step in the coming of the Messiah. The Kabbalists applied this idea to their own lives, and the act of marital intercourse on Friday night was imbued with special significance and understood to mirror the cosmic union of these divine elements.

Reuven Kimelman describes how *Lekhah dodi* addresses another aspect of the role people play in bringing about ultimate redemption. By observing the Sabbath, Jews pave the way for the messianic rebuilding of Jerusalem. He explains that the hymn's concentration on the Sabbath and Jerusalem "is a focus on the sacred in time and space":

> Both the Sabbath and Jerusalem are the centers of their respective categories of the sacred. Although human reality understands them as distinct, kabbalistically, or from the divine perspective, they are one. Simply put, Jerusalem is the spatialization of the holy as the Sabbath is its temporalization. Therefore were one to profane the Sabbath by treating it like one of the six days of the week one could be ejected from the sacred center in space to the periphery of the exile. In the same vein, were one to properly observe the Sabbath in time, one could be restored from the profane periphery to the center in space, namely Jerusalem. Thus the rebuilding of Jerusalem is dependent upon Sabbath observance. (1998:xxi–xxii)

Kimelman explains that the singing of *Lekhah dodi* was in itself an act of unification.[12] Stanza by stanza, the performance of this ritual hymn was structured to bring together God and the exiled Shekhinah, functionally hastening the coming of the Messiah.[13]

We know that music in general played an important role in the spiritual lives of the Safed Kabbalists. Elbogen states that the songs sung at their communal meals "gladdened the participants and aroused in them ecstasies like those of spirits participating in the pleasures of Paradise." Elbogen quotes Solomon Schechter, who reports that Israel Najara, one of the most talented poets of the age, knew "how to charm even the angels with his songs" and would "dazzle his comrades with melodies that made them feel themselves transported to heaven" ([1913, 1972] 1993:292, 93; also cf. Schechter 1908).[14]

Customs and Melodies

Bathja Bayer writes that while *Lekhah dodi* was meant to be sung, no information exists that preserves its original melodies. She reports that the earliest printed version of the text, found in a Sephardic prayer book (Venice, 1583, 1584), says, "To the tune of *Shuvi Nafshi li-Menuhaikhi* ("Return, my soul, to my rest")" (1972:6). While we have no record of the melody of this particular piyyut, here we see an early example of the application of various tunes to this hymn, a practice that continues today. Cantorial manuals of the eighteenth century already contain hundreds of melodies that often reflect the style of the gentile environments, such as "Menuetto" or "Polonaise" (ibid.). Idelsohn estimated that there were more than 2,000 melodies of *Lekhah dodi* (1929:116).

It is common to find seasonal variations of *Lekhah dodi*, linking the tune to signature melodies or motifs of the respective Sabbath or holiday season. There are special melodies for *Shabbat Shuvah* (the Sabbath before Yom Kippur), for *Shabbat Sefirah* (the Shabbat preceding the beginning of the counting of the Omer, the period between Passover and Shavuot), and for the Sabbaths during the three weeks before *Tisha B'Av*, the commemoration marking the destruction of the First and Second Temples. There are also special versions sung on the Sabbaths before Hanukah and Passover. The use of these various tunes is determined by local custom and differs greatly from congregation to congregation. Since the singing of *Lekhah dodi* technically precedes the beginning of the Sabbath, some communities, as in seventeenth- and eighteenth-century Prague, accompanied its singing with musical instruments (Idelsohn 1929:508–9).

There is also the custom, found among the Hasidim today, of setting each stanza to a different melody, or at least distinguishing the fifth verse, *Hitoreri* (Arouse yourself!) by an energetic melody, and the last verse, *Bo-i veshalom*, by a lyrical one (Bayer 1972). It is also common to find that the tune changes at the sixth verse, *Lo tevoshi* (Do not be ashamed), such as in the tune recorded at Tufts Hillel (also cf. Slobin 1989:199, ex. 3) and the tunes recorded by *Rav* (Rabbi) Mayer Horowitz, the Bostoner Rebbe's son, as will be discussed. According to the Rebbe, the reason for this switch is to emphasize the theme of joy in the hymn's last four verses.

The application of various tunes to *Lekhah dodi* was stressed in the late 1960s as the havurah movement sought to renew the intensity and relevance of Jewish worship. In his article on "Music" for the first *Jewish Catalog*, George Savran writes: "New songs are everywhere waiting for the proper setting and time for their use as niggunim. For anyone involved in leading group tefillot, prayers, the introduction of a new niggun[15] can be a momentous event that can transform an entire service." Savran comments that a new version of *Lekhah dodi* "removes an air of 'tiredness' from oft repeated prayers" (1973:215). He goes on to suggest many possible tunes for *Lekhah dodi*, among them Simon and Garfunkel's "Scarborough Fair." While this may strike some as inauthentic, one has only to listen to collections of local variations of *Lekhah dodi* to see the extent to which local style has influenced the performance of this popular liturgical hymn.

In his examination of "the music of participation," Mark Slobin collected "favorite tunes" of *Lekhah dodi* from members of the Conservative Cantors Assembly. The assembled results from 93 cantors showed tremendous variation, representing 184 variants of this hymn. The distribution of the tunes showed "a couple of heavy favorites, some common tunes, some rare and others only sung by a single hazzan" (1989:198). The first of the most common melodies was by Salomon Sulzer, with a companion version by Louis Lewandowski. The second most frequently cited tune is in a Hasidic style and of unknown origin. Slobin says, "The fact that the two most popular tunes are of different geographic and musical orientation, and that one is by a known composer and the other is anonymous, typifies the variety and the layered sense of repertoire in the music of the liturgy" (1989:199).

The fact that *Lekhah dodi* offers Jews so many opportunities to make musical choices that reflect their worship community's style, history, and interests makes the singing of this hymn a defining musical moment in the Kabbalat Shabbat service.

Lekhah dodi in Five Worship Communities

B'nai Or: "The Special Gift That You Guys Have Is Your Music"

After a communal, potluck Shabbat dinner, about eighty people drift upstairs to the Masonic Hall, where B'nai Or's Friday evening service is held. Other members skip the dinner and come directly to the service. The leader, Lev, sits in the center of a circle, cradling his guitar on his lap. He smiles and greets people by name as they fill in around him, some on the floor, some in chairs. People are dressed festively but informally. Tonight one couple is celebrating their *ufruf* (Yiddish, literally, "calling up" [to the Torah on the Shabbat before one's wedding]). This evening the group is large, and some of the older members and visiting families take seats on the permanent benches built into two sides of the room. The atmosphere is relaxed; children play in the center of the circle before the service begins. Friends visit. Members pass out prayer books while Lev schmoozes with the crowd: "Have you met my wife? Aren't you supposed to be in Philadelphia? It's nice to see your face! Are you going to stay in touch with us somehow?" He strums his guitar; the crowd quiets down and joins him in a niggun (CD #1). After singing together, he invites people to look around the room, recognize who is there, say hello to one another. He gently requests that parents keep rambunctious children under control and then leads the community in singing a version of the chorus of *Lekhah dodi*, without the verses, composed by Mordechai Zeira (CD #2). After this tune, he encourages the assembled to "take one big collective deep breath and let go of some of the week." After a chorus of deep sighs, he laughs and says, "I guess you need another collective breath." People laugh in return and sigh. Lev then encourages people to find someone they do not know, introduce themselves and wish each other *Shabbat shalom* (Sabbath peace). People turn to those sitting next to them or behind them and engage in a few minutes of animated socializing that gives way to singing as Lev leads a second niggun (CD #3). The group moves to the side of the room to light Shabbat candles, after which Lev gives a short talk, a meditation about the meaning of Shabbat as a time to refrain from creation, from making, from doing. Explaining that he just bought a new computer and is thinking in computer metaphors, he invites the group to think of Shabbat as a time when "all systems are down." He speaks of Shabbat as a time when we strive not to control or destroy anything in the natural world. After this introduction, he asks people to divide into groups of three, take about five or six minutes, and talk together about how they use time and what gets

Figure 2.2. Lev Friedman leading prayer at B'nai Or. Photo: Bethany Versoy.

done in a day. He asks if there is any time that people set aside for holiness. These young professionals take the question seriously. They talk about their busy lives and their struggles to balance work, friends, and family. After a few minutes of group discussion, Lev prepares to start the service.

Before he begins the full version of *Lekhah dodi* (CD #4), Lev smiles and addresses guests and new participants, explaining, "Here it's a *requirement* to sing!" Both the leadership and members of B'nai Or recognize that music plays a central role in the community's worship. When I spoke to Lev, he noted, "People who've come in, like you or Zalman [Schachter-Shalomi], who've observed, have all said, 'The special gift that you guys have is your music.' . . . people love to sing and they really get into it and I'm always saying, 'Harmonize! God loves harmony.' So people try." Lev is not alone in these sentiments: members also recognize and appreciate the importance of music to B'nai Or's worship. One long-time member observed, "I think that music plays a very central role [in B'nai Or]. . . . How are we going to transcend if we don't have music?" Liturgical experimentation is encouraged, and members have developed high expectations that worship should be moving and transformative. This member further noted, "I'm a . . . much more intuitive person than an intellectual person, so I find that music sound gets me to a spiritual plane more than words. I have a hard time with word prayers and I don't speak Hebrew or read Hebrew. And in English . . . when you put things into words sometimes it minimizes, whereas sound has a sort of infiniteness. I have to say there are certain melodies that take me [snaps fingers] 'out there.'"

Figure 2.3. Children lighting Shabbat candles at B'nai Or. Photo: Bethany Versoy.

This member's husband stressed that the atypical willingness of their congregation to become immersed in a tune helped facilitate his religious experience. He explained that good religious music involved "the freedom to stay with something." He continued, "We may start with a niggun and there's no worry that [people will be thinking] 'What time is it?' One thing that works for me in terms of achieving something similar to a meditative state has to do with repetition . . . fully immersing into a melody . . . it resembles at times a mantra." He said that when he was fully involved in the singing, "There's a tremendous sense of community" and "It feels like true talking to God."

BACKGROUND AND HISTORY   Members and outsiders alike have referred to B'nai Or as "New Age" Judaism: services incorporate meditation, storytelling, singing, chanting, musical instruments (guitar, percussion), extended silence, group discussion, dance, and creative movement. Many of the group's members have been involved with Eastern spirituality and have explored Sufi traditions, Buddhism, yoga, and meditation before returning to their "Jewish spiritual roots." The group's eclectic neo-Hasidic style grew out of the interaction of this small local group with Rabbi Zalman Schachter-Shalomi in the early 1980s. B'nai Or, a term taken from one of the Dead Sea Scrolls, can be translated either as "Sons of Light" or "Children of Light." Now B'nai Or of Boston is one of the largest havurot affiliated with the national movement called ALEPH: the Alliance for Jewish Renewal.

B'nai Or has its roots in the havurah movement, which developed at the end of the 1960s and the beginning of the 1970s.[16] While the concept of fellowships and the existence of small, participatory communities can be traced back throughout Jewish history (Neusner 1972:1–49), two new forms of havurah developed in the late 1960s and early 1970s: independent havurot and those based within larger synagogues. Havurat Shalom, founded in Cambridge, Massachusetts, in 1968 and now located in Somerville, has been described as the "movement's model independent havurah" (Hecht 1993:43ff.; Prell 1988a:92–93). Havurot were also founded in New York and Washington and in association with universities in East Lansing, Ann Arbor, and Madison, as young Jews active in the counterculture established communities centered on prayer and study. These communities were understood to be alternatives to organized religion, which was seen to be irrelevant and insensitive to the needs of youth. These havurot developed as small, intense, highly participatory, informal worship communities in which groups of friends came together in living rooms, communal houses, Hillel foundations, and rented church basements for study, prayer, and often political and social action. Influenced by Martin Buber's neo-Hasidism and by Eastern philosophy, they strove to re-create communities that felt Jewishly authentic, spiritual, and antimaterialistic. Shira Weinberg Hecht writes that these havurot shared countercultural values, including "an attitude toward organization which opposes hierarchy, elaborate structure and professionalism; concomitant goals of active and broad participation in community and in religious practice; and gender egalitarianism in prayer" (1993:vii). Gender equality was not an original value of the early havurot, which like the early civil rights movement stressed "free rights for all men." Originally, "egalitarianism" meant that there was no difference between teachers and students, who were all spiritual searchers together. Only later did the term apply to gender.

Since their inception, havurot have become minor organizational fixtures on the American Jewish landscape. One can find various alternative Jewish communities in both urban and rural settings throughout the country. The havurah movement has been loosely coordinated by the National Havurah Committee. Summer Havurah Institutes, organized as weeklong family retreats, provide opportunities for study, worship, resource sharing, reunion, and fellowship on a national level. Yet many havurot are either indifferent to or unaware of the national group.

The Boston area has many such small fellowship groups that meet in members' homes or rented spaces for Shabbat and holiday worship. They tend to be egalitarian and informal. They seldom have a rabbi or professional staff: members lead services and share organizational duties. B'nai Or is atypical. It functions as a participatory havurah where members plan and lead services, but it also employs an engaging and charismatic leader who leads services once a month.

This study will focus on the service led by Lev Friedman, B'nai Or's founder and spiritual leader. While he is not a rabbi, he was ordained as a *maggid* (teacher, preacher, storyteller) by Zalman Schachter-Shalomi at the group's inception in 1982. Originally formed as a community to celebrate the High Holidays, B'nai Or, like many alternative Jewish communities, has continued to evolve as members have grown older, had children, and moved from graduate school to professional lives. Early in its history the havurah described itself in the following manner in the *Guide to Jewish Boston:* "B'nai Or is concerned with the individual and collective Jewish experience as well as the healing of the planet Earth. Davening happens both in English and Hebrew (simultaneously) and we sit in a circle on the floor. We are more concerned with the esoteric than the exotic, so if your background is limited or non-existent, don't let that stop you" (Feldman 1986:60). B'nai Or has grown to more than 175 unit members, including single members as well as traditional families and gay and lesbian couples, with or without children.

"IF PEOPLE DIDN'T HAVE A GOOD SPIRITUAL EXPERIENCE, IT ISN'T MY FAULT. YOU GET OUT OF IT WHAT YOU PUT INTO IT" Neither the members nor the congregation's leader takes the transformative aspect of B'nai Or's music for granted. Lev invests time and thought as he plans the musical aspects of the service. While he was conscious that he played a large role in shaping the community's Shabbat experience, he stressed that he has cultivated a shared responsibility for the quality of the worship at B'nai Or. He asserted, "Everyone knows, at least the old-timers, who have been coming for a while, that *everybody* needs to sing . . . and help with the energy for the evening. While I can be the focus for it . . . it is everybody's responsibility to keep things going. . . . If people didn't have a good spiritual experience, it isn't my fault. You get out of it what you put into it."

Lev was conscious of the dangers of being a strong leader, and he tried to address those issues through his own spiritual practice before the service. He said, "Before every service, I do a meditation in which I ask that I get my ego out of the way. [Then] . . . I can be a lot more receptive. Something can happen." He described how he would put on his *tallit* (prayer shawl) and *kippah* (skullcap) and go into a room by himself before the service. "I ask that each part of my being can be a vessel for the community. . . . The most specific thing I say is, 'Just help me to get out of the way.'"[17] He saw his role more as that of a facilitator of group experience through the use of music. In discussing the centrality of music at B'nai Or, he observed, "I suppose it has just evolved by the simple virtue of the fact that [as the leader, I am] . . . mainly a musician, not a rabbi. My expertise seems to be moving group experience. I mean 'moving' in a double entendre. I can move it along and I can make it moving. I seem to have the skill of knowing, not always but most of the time, knowing where the group needs to go. . . . I seem to have a good feeling for what kind of melody will work, where and when. I don't know how to articulate that so much because that's very much intuition."

However, it is not only Lev's musical intuition in choosing particular tunes that shapes the nature of music at B'nai Or. He also leads the group in musical and spiritual exercises that focus the way the group both sings and listens to one another during song. He said:

I suppose we've attracted a number of people who are just really musical because that is so much of what goes on in our group. . . . I think also the fact that the music flows so freely is that it took me a while but eventually I was really encouraging people to sing, even if they believed they couldn't sing. Every once in a while, when it looks like there are a lot of new people, I will say, "How many people here don't think they can sing?" Inevitably, five or six hands will go up and I'll say, "Well, anyone can sing. *You* can sing and don't worry about what you sound like because the person next to you is not listening to you. They are listening to themselves." And then, on occasion [I'll ask:] "Who do you hear when you're singing?" Often people say, "I hear myself." [If so] I'll tell them that they are singing too loud. . . . We need to be able to sing so that we can hear everybody else in the room. . . . All of this comes from my musical background. One of the tricks I learned when I was in a musical group was to sing out of someone else's jaw. . . . [I'll say] "Pick somebody across the room and imagine that you're singing out of their mouth." The difference between the singing before I said that and after I said that is very substantial. . . . It's a much rounder sound. It's a much more sympathetic sound.

This sensitivity is cultivated for a greater purpose. Lev spoke of singing as a means to create a feeling of group cohesion where God's presence can be manifest through song. He explained:

I think that singing that way also sets up more of what I like to call a "Shema consciousness feeling," you know, that everybody is *ehad* (one) and that everybody is connected.[18] I will sometimes do a meditation where [I ask people to imagine] . . . as we breathe out, the breath goes out from the heart in the form of light and it goes around the circle from heart to heart connecting the hearts. We imagine it going around to the right and then going around to the left, and so when you combine that with singing as a group, some kind of deep experience happens.

B'nai Or is the only worship community I examined that did such spiritual/musical exercises in the course of worship. They are seen as important ways to elevate the congregation's music and, through it, to facilitate spiritual experience. Lev explained, "There's some kind of intimacy that happens when you sing. Take that a step further and obviously the object of singing in shul is to sing to God. . . . We're not only singing together, we're praying together, through song."

When describing tunes that "really take you out there," the woman quoted above spoke specifically of one of the tunes B'nai Or used for *Lekhah dodi* (CD #2). She was aware of the tune's questionable authenticity. Because this version of the hymn consisted only of the chorus without the nine Hebrew verses, she said, "It's not the *real Lekhah dodi.*" Still, she stressed, "I just really love that and I could spend the whole night singing that song and that would be a fine service."

In fact, another member reported, once the congregation did just that. "There was one service where we did this [CD #2] entirely, instead of a niggun." B'nai Or is atypically flexible in this regard. The community is relatively unconstrained by the observance of traditional Jewish law that dictates a set order to the prayers. A general supportive atmosphere, coupled with the community's dedication to spiritual exploration and experimentation, allowed such a service to happen.

Another member reflected on this flexibility, contrasting B'nai Or with the Newton Center Minyan, a more traditional worship community in the area. This member observed:

[Going to the] Minyan is like going to the symphony or some other classical performance. The nice thing is everybody gets to perform at some time. You know what's there, you can appreciate the nuances . . . five different people can get up and do the *Kedushah* [the Sanctification, the third section of the *Amidah*] for Musaf, and you never know what [tune] they're going to pull out of their hats.[19] That's the fun part, but the words are always the same, and you know within a range of five or six [musical] choices what they're going to do. Everyone brings their interpretation to that, so the Minyan is like the symphony. Going to B'nai Or is like going to the Grateful Dead. You *never* know what's going to happen. What are they going to do next? Which song is it going to be? How are they going to sing it? How long is it going to go on? It's a totally other experience, and I enjoy both, so I'll go to both.

B'nai Or was not the only worship community examined in this study that used this tune (CD #2) for *Lekhah dodi.* This tune is also popular at Temple Israel, although there it was not used as a warm-up but rather as the actual tune for this hymn as it occurs in the service. It is common for the Reform movement to shorten or simplify prayers, and the absence of the more complex text of nine Hebrew verses does not trouble either the leadership or the members of the Reform congregation. On occasion I have also heard the Conservative service at Tufts Hillel use this tune. However, in that setting a stricter adherence to traditional practice necessitates that the hymn's verses be sung, and so the melody for the simple phrase *Shabbat shalom umevorakh* (a blessed and peaceful Sabbath) is applied to the verses.[20]

While this tune was used flexibly in the service at B'nai Or, its use was purposeful and strategic. Lev described how he used the tune to create a mood for the beginning of the service and to help people make a transition to the peaceful atmosphere he wanted to create on Shabbat. He explained, "I find that tune to be very soft and soothing and there's something you can do with the harmonies that's very . . . like a sigh, and that things have shifted mode into holy time." Other members also saw the song as transitional, moving the group into the mood of the Sabbath. Another member observed, "I find [this tune] to be extremely centering and calming. It sort of brings energy that might be flying all over the place. Transitions are being made and that *Lekhah dodi* to me is . . . grounding, it's centering, and it's . . . making one more leap of a transition away from what I've done all day." Another member spoke about the effect that the simple and accessible Hebrew lyrics had upon her when she first learned this tune: "I think saying 'Shabbat shalom' with a tune makes me *feel* peaceful, makes me appreciate the sweetness of Shabbat and experience that sweetness."

Lev also used this tune, and an interpretation of its text, as a way to welcome and integrate new members. He explained, "One of my sweetest hits [favorite interpretations] on *Lekhah dodi* is that when we say, *penei Shabbat nekabelah* [Let us welcome the Sabbath; literally: let us receive the face of the Sabbath] that we're really supposed to be receiving *each other's* face. Giving each other permission to have a Shabbos face, which means to be different from how we are when we're strained and stressed during the week. One of the things I have attempted to get people to do at that particular moment is to look around the room and to see who's there and to smile at each other and to open up." B'nai Or draws visitors and new potential members every week. Lev used *Lekhah dodi* to encourage newcomers to introduce themselves to other people in the group. He elaborated, "Sometimes after [looking at one another around the room], I have begun the custom of having people introduce themselves to one another. That grew out of newcomers being not quite comfortable. . . . Like any group, there are cliques, and people who like each other stick together, so it was hard to know who is new. This is a way of doing that."

In general, members of this havurah were much more concerned with how the song worked than with where it came from. People were unclear about the origin of this tune. Lev reported that he learned it from a tape in the Jewish bookstore that he owns and manages in Brookline. Other members assumed that Lev wrote it. One member stated that she didn't really know its origin, mistakenly characterizing it as Hasidic. She liked the tune, saying that it was "calming" and "a good focusing melody" marking the beginning of Shabbat. The member who said that she could "sing the tune all evening" described it this way: "It's fluid, it's gentle, it's soulful. It's not marching music and it's not insipid and it's not sitting around the campfire."

Not everyone in the community felt so positive about this tune. One woman related that when she first heard it, "it was such a sweet thing and now it's passé for me, it doesn't do it for me anymore. I can intellectually say it's a pretty song but it *used* to be, 'Oh, yeah!! We're doing this song!'" Another woman simply said, "I don't like that song at all. Some people absolutely love that song. It doesn't go anywhere for me. It's lighter, it's very melodic, but it doesn't have much variety and range." This member felt that B'nai Or needed to learn more Hebrew and liturgy, knowledge that she called "hard skills." Because this tune lacked the Hebrew verses, she thought less of it, calling the tune "a nice little introduction."

"YESHIVA ROCK": AN AMERICAN LEKHAH DODI On the other hand, this same member loved the full version of *Lekhah dodi* composed by Lev and experienced it as transformative (see Example 2.1). She did not know the origin of this tune and attributed it to older, authoritative sources. Through this tune, the palpable presence of the Sabbath entered her life and her being. Speaking of Lev's composition, she declared:

> It's beautiful. I love that. It's very joyous. . . . I don't know where it comes from, I think it's an old melody. I know that Zalman [Schachter-Shalomi] does the same one, [Lev] might have learned it from Zalman. but I'm not sure. . . . It really lifts me up. It takes me from wherever I am and I can kind of join the flow of life and feel very transported and I also feel like I'm being really prepared to bring in the Shekhinah, and when we open the doors and use the movement of *bo'i khalah* [enter, O bride!], I really *feel* this awesome moment. I really love that. It's like foreplay. I feel like the whole song is like preparation to this moment to where we're consciously opening ourselves up to receive Shekhinah.

Lev described how he composed this tune: "It just came to me one day. I may have been taking a shower . . . [and I thought], 'This is a hit! This

Ex 2.1. *Lekhah dodi*, B'nai Or, CD #4. Composed by Lev Friedman.

sounds good.'" He continued, "I see it as Yeshiva-rock. It's an American *Lekhah dodi*. It's definitely American and it's rock'n'roll. It's folk music, it's all the influences. It's probably Jewish, musically, only to the extent that it follows an A minor. . . . It's definitely American. I don't really think about these things when I come up with them, but Debbie Friedman[21] and that whole genre, Camp Ramah, that's where I'm getting the Yeshiva-rock."

The use of the minor key is more common in Hasidic and Israeli folk music than in rock and roll.[22] On the last line of the verse, Lev plays an E chord and uses a walking bass up the E string that contributes to the "bluesy feel," as described by another worshipper, who echoed Lev's description of this tune. This member stated, "To me, [CD #4] . . . is more American. It's got kind of an . . . upbeat bluesy feel to it." Another member also saw the nature of the tune as an aid to group participation in services. She said, "You can clap to it, you can snap to it, and that's why people like it . . . even if they don't sing, they can still participate."

DANCING DURING LEKHAH DODI There is no set choreography for the dancing at B'nai Or during *Lekhah dodi*. Many people dance by themselves, swaying their arms over their heads. Groups of friends put their arms around each other's shoulders and dance around the room. Some members see the dancing as "family time." One mother noted, "Usually some of the women go off . . . with kids and dance on the side." Dancing is voluntary, and many people simply move in place to the music as they sing the hymn. Another member was conscious that the dancing was unfamiliar to newcomers, who rarely participated. He said, "It's also a time where I see all these people dancing and all the new people just sitting there staring."

Lev views the dancing positively. He remarked, "I think of *Lekhah dodi* as such a joyous hymn and I've always thought of *Lekhah dodi* as a time to dance. When we go out to greet the Shekhinah, one ought to dance her in. Years ago, before Joyce and I had kids and things got a little too *mishug* [his slang for the Yiddish *meshuggene*, crazy], we used to always dance in the house on Friday night to welcome in the presence of Shekhinah and Shabbat. It was a tune that came to me and I said, 'Wow, this is great! People will dance . . . and move to this!'"

As leader, Lev is conscious of the boundaries of free expression in services. He said that he "loves" the dancing during *Lekhah dodi* and stressed, "I've always felt that B'nai Or should be a place where people could have a spiritual experience; however, they needed to have it, [without] . . . disrupting the group." B'nai Or was the only worship community examined in this study where parents were asked to keep their children under control during services. Perhaps this was necessary because the bounds of acceptable behavior are looser in this congregation. Congregants are free to move throughout the worship space; people sit on the floor and occasionally engage in extemporaneous dance. Personal expression through music, prayer, and dance is allowed and encouraged.

For some worshippers, this approach to prayer stretched the limits of acceptable behavior in synagogue. Not everyone had positive reactions to the group dancing that took place on Friday evening. One woman said, "I like that tune [CD #4], [but] I often don't like what happens in the group dynamic. That's like 'play time.' . . . I come to services one Friday night a month to have my jolt of mysticism and . . . people get silly. That's the only way I can put it." She continued, "[People are] . . . throwing teddy bears in the air, doing the can-can, stuff like that. I sound very 'stick-in-the-muddy' . . . I find it breaks the unity. I find usually what happens in the service is that it's got this . . . soft glow to it and this is like . . . people get frisky." She had these issues with other experimental aspects of the service as well and felt that these diminished the seriousness and intensity of prayer. "There are certain melodies where I feel like we're singing camp songs and it doesn't work. . . . People will bring in these little songs . . . sometimes we'll do little dances . . . and it feels too workshop-y, it feels too campfire-y. And it's fine to have a campfire and it's fine to have a workshop but I want my prayer space to be just mystical and full of grace." While asserting that she was "not a puritan," she explained, "I don't like blueberries in my yogurt and I don't like frivolity in my spirituality." For this worshipper, the service walked a thin line between meaningful spiritual expression and a hodgepodge of experiential exercises.

Another congregant expressed that he wanted *Lekhah dodi* to be a spiritual preparation "as opposed to party time." At one point the community's ritual committee addressed the manner and purpose of the dancing during *Lekhah dodi*. The woman who often teaches and leads dance discussed some of the realizations that emerged from those discussions: "The dance can get so wild that we have to remember *why* we're dancing and *who* we're dancing before [i.e., God]. . . . Lev has said . . . that [dancing] was great, but if people scream at the end, maybe that's not containing the sense of holy energy, of spark, and so [it's better to] contain it rather than to give it off like you're at a rock concert." This member also discussed the feeling she wished to facilitate when she led the community in dance: "[The dancing] was sort of out of control and I wanted people to feel the spirit of it and the ecstasy of it but not forget what we're doing and why we're doing it and not get involved in the dance because it feels good without connecting to the kavanah." This balance between structured and free religious expression was thoughtfully, and continually, negotiated.

Even the most spontaneous religious expressions have a tendency to become regulated and institutionalized. My own teacher, the liturgical scholar Jacob Petuchowski, often said, "The kavanah [in this sense, spiritual creativity] of one generation becomes the *keva* [fixed liturgy] of the next." Members of B'nai Or struggle to create a worship service where, in the words of one member, "it feels like true talking to God." In their creative efforts to achieve that goal, these Jews push the limits to explore how music, dance, and meditative exercises can help them transcend regular prayer and transform the worship experience. However, this experimentation requires careful monitoring. If it crosses the line and is seen as silly or out of control, its power is diminished. Both music and language in worship are chosen carefully, to open deeper possibilities for spiritual experience while maintaining a tether to Jewish tradition and history. For the majority of their members, they have succeeded in creating Shabbat prayer in which music is authentic, moving, and transformative.

Temple Israel

The atrium of Temple Israel is an unlikely place for Shabbat services. This Reform temple's main sanctuary seats 900 and is both imposing and impressive. The stationary seats are arranged in rows, and congregants look from a distance at the rabbis and cantor, who are seated on the raised bimah. The attractive smaller chapel is comfortable and will easily accommodate over 200 worshippers. The atrium is a large, sunny hall outside the main sanctuary. Whereas the chapel and main sanctuary have beautiful arks that hold the Torah scrolls, the atrium on Shabbat is set up with folding chairs and a small podium standing opposite a portable ark. To the right and the left of the podium, the two sections of chairs face each other: when you sit or stand, you are looking at other members of the congregation. During the week the atrium is empty. Sometimes the walls are hung with an art exhibition.

Light streams into the atrium from above as a mixed generational crowd gathers at 5:45 P.M., atypically early for a Reform Friday evening service. Grandparents sit with grandchildren. Several clusters of high school students sit together. Some families come dressed casually and mention they are on their way to Cape Cod after services. Other men and women come to the service directly from work; they meet and sit with friends or family. A *tsedakah* (charity) box is placed on a table near the door, and some

Figure 2.4. Cantor Roy Einhorn and congregents at Temple Israel. Photo: Richard Sobol.

Figure 2.5. Worshippers begin to gather in the atrium at Temple Israel.
Photo: Richard Sobol.

people make contributions as they enter the room. Members of the congregation who serve as ushers greet worshippers and hand out prayer books. At one time Temple Israel ran two Friday evening services, and the service in the atrium was often called "the early service." Now that it has become the main Friday evening service, it is simply referred to as "Kabbalat." Some participants so love the singing that they refer to it as "the music service." Before worship begins, the cantor stands informally at the podium in the center of the room. His guitar hangs on a strap over his shoulder as he chats with some children in the front row. Two of the temple's three rabbis stand in the crowd and greet congregants by name as they walk into the atrium.

HISTORY AND BACKGROUND Temple Israel is sometimes referred to as the "Brahmin shul" in Boston: many venerable, prestigious Jewish families are among its members. Its impressive building is on Longwood Avenue, not far from the hospital district in Boston. Temple Israel is the second oldest synagogue in Boston, established by German Jews who split off from Congregation Ohabei Shalom in 1854. Late in the nineteenth century, Temple Israel affiliated with the Reform movement, and it is now the largest Reform congregation in New England, with more than 1,500 member families. The Temple employs three rabbis, a cantor, and a staff of administrators and religious school teachers.

Motivated by their aesthetic sensibilities, early Reform leaders in America were strongly committed to making changes in the worship service such as the introduction of both prayer and a sermon in the vernacular, the elimination of the repetition of certain Hebrew prayers, and the use of choral singing with organ accompaniment in the Sabbath service (Sorin 1992:170ff., also cf. Petuchowski 1968:105–27).[23] They created a form of worship, with prayer books, hymnals, and professionalized clergy, that more closely resembled American Protestantism than the *shtiblakh* (small synagogues, Yiddish) of Eastern Europe (Schiller 1992). Unlike Judaism in Germany, Reform Judaism in America was neither under government control nor greatly affected by traditional elements that limited and criticized the early reformers in Europe.[24]

The radical character of early Reform Judaism was somewhat mitigated after more than 2.3 million Eastern European Jews emigrated to America between 1881 and 1929 (Sorin 1992:12–37). Growing anti-Semitism in Russia, coupled with economic opportunities created by rapid industrialization in the northeastern United States, set the stage for this period of Jewish immigration to America. As these Jews attained higher economic and social status in the 1920s and 1930s, many joined the Reform movement both as laity and clergy. Their emotional attachment to traditional ritual both in the home and the synagogue caused a shift toward traditional practice, and over time, Reform's rejection of Jewish law and ritual softened. After the Second World War and into the 1950s, upward economic mobility and the move toward the suburbs strengthened affiliation with the Reform movement. It was the first movement in America to ordain women as rabbis, in 1972; now approximately half of the rabbinic class at HUC–JIR is composed of women. The movement began to invest women as cantors in 1976, and now women make up a majority of students in the School of Sacred Music's cantorial program.

In the nineteenth century, composers such as Sulzer and Lewandowski drew from traditional Jewish sources while harmonizing them to make them more modern and Western. Continuing this approach, composers such as Binder, Freed, and Weiner produced new music for the synagogue; their compositions remained formal and performance centered. From its early history into the 1960s, the choir and organ dominated the music in the Reform movement. While some Reform congregations had a cantor, or more commonly a cantorial soloist, the rabbi was the central liturgical leader in Reform worship. Strongly influenced by the model of Protestant worship, the rabbi functioned as preacher and "reader" of the service.

Congregational music consisted primarily of the singing of hymns, set congregational responses to key sections of liturgy, and inspirational performances of synagogue art music. The music of the Reform movement changed considerably in the 1970s as congregations were influenced by the more informal and participatory style of the havurah and the music of the Reform youth movement, both in turn having been influenced by the folk boom and counterculture. So too, after the 1967 Israeli war, Israeli folk and popular music had an increasing impact on the Reform service (Schiller 1992:205–9). Some of the most influential music came from Israel's Hasidic Song Festival, a popular commercial event that introduced many Hasidic and "neo-Hasidic" songs to both Israeli and American Jewish cultural and religious life. Since the late 1960s the role of the cantor has become increasingly influential in Reform worship. It is common for Reform cantors to accompany themselves on guitar.

HOW THE ATRIUM SERVICE DEVELOPED For years the Friday evening service at Temple Israel was "classically Reform." It was held in the large sanctuary, where the rabbi, cantor, and choir conducted the service from the bimah. When the early reformers made changes in Jewish liturgy in the last century, they sought to restore a sense of beauty, decorum, grandeur, and spiritual edification to worship.[25] These early changes were reflected in this service at Temple Israel. Men and women dressed up and the rabbi delivered a formal sermon. While key prayers were retained in Hebrew, most of the service was translated into English.

In Conservative and Orthodox synagogues, the Shabbat morning service is the most important service of the week. However, the Reform movement found it increasingly difficult to draw large crowds on Shabbat morning. Businessmen often kept their shops open on Saturday, and many activities competed for the attention of these less ritually observant congregants. The Reform movement addressed this issue by placing more stress on the Friday evening service, which became longer, more elaborate, and started after the Sabbath dinner. A Torah reading was often included, as was a sermon by the rabbi, elements that traditionally were part of Shabbat morning prayer. In keeping with the increased formality of this expanded service, music was frequently provided by a professional soloist or large choir, accompanied by the organ. While this later service allowed more people to attend Sabbath worship, it precluded the celebration of a leisurely Shabbat dinner in many Reform households.

The concept of an early service, though standard in traditional circles, was seen as innovative in a Reform congregation. Yet the time was just one of the factors that made the new atrium service unique. Rabbi Bernard Mehlman explained how the atrium service started in the summer of 1979. Shortly after he began at Temple Israel, he learned, to his surprise, that the temple did not hold Friday evening services during the summer. He reflected, "It didn't sound right to me. . . . There's something bizarre about this congregation being closed on Shabbos. . . . We saw it as an opportunity. . . . We wanted to [start a service] that was appealing to families, that was in an upbeat, accessible mode, something that people didn't have to put a jacket and tie on to come to." He also wanted a more participatory service: "I wanted a community that had access to the music, that could sing together." The Temple's beautiful glassed-in atrium, without fixed seating, provided both the informality and the flexibility the rabbi desired. The congregation responded so favorably to this summertime innovation that they gradually increased the number of early services conducted in the atrium, including holiday and vacation weekends during the year. Soon more people were attending the atrium services than the 8:15 P.M. service.

At this point, a disagreement arose in the congregation. Some of the older members wanted the later service to continue, while the younger members favored the early service. For a while, the rabbis conducted parallel services. During that period there was a certain tension between members in their 60s, 70s, and 80s, who loved the more formal, classically Reform service, and the younger members, who expressed a preference for more participatory worship. As one participant in the atrium service said, "[At the later service,] there are people who turn around and give you dirty looks if you read along aloud in the Hebrew or try to sing with the choir." Eventually this issue was decided simply by attendance. It was difficult to get a minyan for the later service, while more than 200 people came to the early service. At that point the atrium service became the regular Friday night service at Temple Israel.[26]

Rabbi Mehlman stressed, "The whole religious sensibility is one that wants involvement and participation and community. It's in the air, in a society which is so fragmented, like a discharging of atoms in so many different directions, the synagogue can really provide that one place where [these Jews] can sense themselves as a community. They find some common ground, and something of the divine. . . . This generation is not going to find that by coming into the sanctuary and have the lights go dark and [rabbis] . . . walk out onto a bimah in black robes and declaim." Instead of a formal sermon, the rabbis give a short *devar Torah* (informal, educational talk). The rabbis and cantor pride themselves on finishing this service right on time so that "families can go home and celebrate Shabbat together." This approach has proved successful. Even with some of the generational differences, this service draws large numbers and appeals to diverse groups within the congregation.

The congregation has assembled and printed an attractive prayer book of its own for the early Friday night service, called *Qabbalat Shabbat: A Liturgy of Learning.*[27] The introduction states, "The Jewish worship service contains a series of liturgical rubrics which are very much like the movements of a symphony." After describing these sections, the siddur goes on to emphasize:

> Singing plays a significant role in our service. Many of the melodies were traditional in European Jewish communities, while others are modern compositions. The full participation of the congregation in

each prayer, reading and song reflects the Jewish view of worship as a responsibility we all share." (ibid.)

This introduction reflects the philosophy of the congregation's professional and lay leadership, who see their Temple as innovative and flexible yet grounded in authentic tradition. The stress on congregational participation and personal responsibility for the worship experience can be seen as a polemic against the performance orientation of many large congregations. In accord with the service's subtitle, "A Liturgy of Learning," all prayers were both translated into English and had full English transliteration of the Hebrew text. Short meditations and explanations accompany the text throughout the service.

"I LOVE THE INTIMACY, I LOVE THE SUN, I LOVE THE ATRIUM, I LOVE THE GUITAR." The cantor described the spectrum of people who attend this service: "It crosses the generational lines. We've got young people that come, we have college kids that come, . . . kids that come with their parents, and then we have single adults, moving into middle age, and then senior citizens." Congregants are drawn to this service for a variety of reasons. One woman said, "It's . . . my favorite service, because I love the setting, I love the intimacy, I love the sun, I love the atrium, and the relative informality of the . . . participation . . . the feel of a community again, rather than a huge sanctuary. I *love* the guitar." She continued, "It's partly my favorite service because I have young children, and [because of the children's schedule] I'm effectively barred from going to later services." She also stressed that it helped that this service was short, under an hour. It was just the right length for a busy person with children.

For many worshippers, the music at Kabbalat Shabbat served as an emotional and psychological transition from the week into the Sabbath. This same worshipper described how the music of the service had a physical effect on her, helping to set the tone for a peaceful Shabbat after a hectic week. She explained:

> I can just start to feel the tension draining out of my body as the music starts and as the liturgy starts and as the voices are raised. . . . It is a physical reaction, and to me that is so wonderful. It's a gift because when I come home from work on Friday night *everything* is late. . . . Did the baby-sitter stick the chicken in the oven? . . . Did my daughter set the table? It doesn't stop. . . . But when I make the transition at Temple Israel at Kabbalat Shabbat, it just sets the tone for the rest of the weekend . . . the rest of Shabbat.

A former president of the congregation spoke of her visceral reaction to the tunes used for this service: "Every song of the Kabbalat service makes me decompress a little more. . . . [In Temple] nobody interrupts me, and when I finally get there and then I have the music, there's a catharsis about it."

In developing this service, Rabbi Mehlman wanted the music to do even more than make a transition from the week to Shabbat. He wanted to undermine the sense of performance, of theater, that he felt was found too often in large synagogues. He said, "For me the music is that bridge that enables [worshippers] to enter into the spiritual moment, the transcendent moment . . . that's one direction. The other direction is to . . . make a sacred community of the moment. If music can't do that, we've created a moment in theater, and that's certainly not what I'm striving to do."

The members with whom I spoke do not see themselves as an "audience" and do not experience this service as theater. Before services begin, people chat, laugh, and visit. Members say that they are drawn by the sense of community, a feeling so strong that it is palpable for many worshippers. One member emphasized how different this was from other worship experiences, where people's attendance was motivated by guilt or obligation: "It's a group of people who really want to be there!" Another member observed, "It's like worshipping in your own home. . . . You look around and you feel a community. People have come from all different places. . . . They really have gone out of their way to be here. They're committed to it."

One member contrasted this service with the later service that for years had been held in the main sanctuary. She described why she was originally drawn to the early service:

> We participate as a community in a much more direct way in the atrium service. The liturgy is very accessible. . . . It's . . . very comfortable, warm, . . . there's just something about sitting next to your friend, putting your arm around a friend and singing *Oseh shalom* ([God who] makes peace) (CD #5) that you don't do in the big sanctuary, and you don't do on Friday night at 8:15 when you're exhausted and everybody has already been home and had dinner, . . . and Roy [the cantor] makes the music very accessible.

In the large sanctuary, the leaders conduct the service from the bimah and are physically separated from the congregation. In the atrium, leaders and congregants are so close they often touch. One woman said, "I do feel much more . . . connected to the rabbis and cantor . . . because you're on the same level with them. . . . I feel like *I'm* leading the worship service as well. . . . Nothing has been preplanned, that's what it feels like."

In fact, the rabbis and cantor have thought long and seriously about the nature of this service. Together congregants and clergy have created worship that has eliminated many of the barriers commonly experienced in more formal worship settings. Members feel that their active participation is noticed and valued, and they are correct in their assessment. Rabbi Elaine Zecher excitedly described how these worshippers have become knowledgeable participants: "One thing that I can't stand [in most formal worship] is when rabbis have to tell people to stand up and sit down. I think the 'arms up and down' is *so* hierarchical, so antithetical to what worship is supposed to be. It was so thrilling to me, at some point in doing Kabbalat Shabbat services, that we realized we didn't need to tell people to stand up. They rise without being told!" Congregants feel very much at home, but the informality of this service does not belie a lack of seriousness or reverence. Rather, it has developed because these worshippers have become increasingly knowledgeable about, and subsequently more comfortable with, Jewish prayer.

The cantor also stressed his commitment to community participation: "I think the familiarity and the ability for them to participate makes it theirs, and I think that anyone who pays dues and comes to a synagogue should have the expectation that it *is* theirs and they don't want the picture turned and turned and turned all the time." He explained that as much as he is the professional, the music and musical repertoire belong to the congregants. Members feel a connection to particular tunes. If he changed or eliminated a specific tune, a typical comment would be, "What happened to the melody that *I* know, Cantor? " He continued: "I like people to walk out of here feeling like they've sung the melodies that they wanted to sing, or they've heard me sing something that's nice, or provocative in some way, and gives them something to think about. . . . But by and large, I want them to feel that the music is familiar and they're able, if they want to, to sing."

For many members, the use of guitar, as opposed to the organ in the main sanctuary, helps to create a more relaxed, personal setting for worship. One member said that the guitar "creates a more informal atmosphere, so people become more comfortable. . . ." Another member explained that she was a "sixties person," and the guitar symbolized her generation—personal expression and a commitment to social justice. With the guitar, she said she felt that the cantor was specifically "singing for me."

In fact, this service begins with a song session. The cantor plays the guitar and leads the congregation as everyone sings shortened versions of popular Hebrew songs, including "standards" from the Hasidic festivals of the 1970s and 1980s (CD #6). The cantor described this singing as a "little warming up of the engine to get into *Lekhah dodi*." When asked why he sings those particular songs with the congregation, the cantor stressed the importance of choosing a repertoire familiar to a broad range of ages. He explained, "[We sing them] because the little kids know them and the older people know them. In that service, everyone sings. They sing everything. That's the beauty of this service. . . . It's for them to use and have and they like me there to lead it, but frankly I can just cut back on volume and they can carry it."

One congregant believed that the warm-up song session conveyed an important message about the current philosophical direction of Temple Israel. She explained that the congregation's younger generation had inherited a legacy of formal worship, complete with organ, choir, and clergy who wore black robes as they officiated from the grand bimah in the sanctuary. This was now changing, and the change in the style of the congregation's music conveyed this new direction with immediacy and intensity.

Younger leaders, now in their 40s and early 50s, spoke of how the older members of Temple Israel originally "hated" the early service. In the words of one younger member, it "drove the other half of Temple Israel crazy." These older members thought that the early service had too much Hebrew and simply felt "too Jewish." For example, there is quite of bit of traditional chant in this service, which the older members associated with Conservative and Orthodox prayer. Many older members found this service to be "too involving, too participatory, absolutely without decorum." Too many sounds had changed. The guitar had displaced the organ. The temple choir no longer sang. On a practical level, it was also difficult for many of the older members to hear the service in the atrium. According to Rabbi Zecher, the acoustics in this glass-ceilinged room "sounded like a handball court." Eventually this problem was solved with strategically placed wall speakers, but until it was fixed, the older members felt isolated and excluded. Even the accepted dress code was different. Congregants came to the early service dressed informally. As one younger member laughingly reported, even this was "a revolution! In the old days, you'd come in hat and gloves!"

Still, the changes in style were no laughing matter for the older generation. They wanted a service primarily in English so that it would be intelligible and understandable. Very much Americans, they were embarrassed by what they perceived as the disorderliness of traditional Jewish prayer. Everything in their grand sanctuary, from the choral music to the rabbi's formal sermons, reflected order, class, and style. However, this was a style that many of the younger members experienced as decidedly "un-Jewish."

In an anti-assimilationist slur, one younger member said, "The setting that is most comfortable for [the older generation] is to go to Trinity Church, where the choir is disembodied and up high." This member believed that her parents' generation had experienced more overt anti-Semitism and had therefore learned to shy away from particularistic expression. She thought that many of the old guard at Temple Israel had a "great need for assimilation." This view of the temple was held by people on the outside as well. This member continued, "When we held interviews for a new rabbi [in 1979], the Union [of American Hebrew Congregations] told us that we were the 'cathedral congregation' and we needed a 'cathedral rabbi.' We said, 'We don't want a cathedral rabbi, we've already done that.'" When they hired Rabbi Mehlman in 1979, the younger members got what they wanted, and the new rabbi understood that he was hired, in part, to move the congregation in a new direction.

LEKHAH DODI AT TEMPLE ISRAEL The stress on communal participation influenced the cantor's choice of tunes throughout the service. He emphasized, "I don't see a service as being successful when I walk into a synagogue and see a cantor up there just performing and having the congregation sit around and watch. So that's a part of who I am and what I do. I don't switch the music around a whole lot."

His approach to choosing tunes for *Lekhah dodi* was studied and thoughtful. At Temple Israel I recorded several tunes to *Lekhah dodi*. The first was also sung at B'nai Or (CD #2). The second was a variation of the tune composed by Louis Lewandowski (CD #7). The cantor is also conscious of generational connections to specific melodies. In describing how he chose a tune for *Lekhah dodi*, he said, "I like to blend . . . for instance, I'll use [sings tune, CD #2] but I like to throw in [sings tune, CD #7]. The younger kids don't know that as well, but anyone who's over 30 or 35—*that's Lekhah dodi.*" He went on to explain, "I use four [versions of *Lekhah dodi*] and there could be a special one that I'll introduce, but I use the [Salamone] Rossi [from the Isadore Freed collection]. . . . I use the Davidson Yemenite . . . I use a tambourine for that . . . and there might be others." The cantor recently returned from a sabbatical in Israel and had brought back the signature tune for *Lekhah dodi* used at Congregation Kol HaNeshama, a liberal synagogue in Jerusalem (CD #8).

Congregants appreciated his relatively conservative approach to change. One worshipper commented, "I like the new one [CD #2]. I don't like it when they change music. I get resentful. The music has memories, when I hear it, it just touches something inside of me." This member expressed a desire to be transported by the tune of *Lekhah dodi*. For her, this meant that a melody should not be too challenging. This is how she viewed the tune (CD #2): "I like melodies that are melodic, that flow. I don't like things that are jarring. When they are easy, it becomes like a mantra, it's a vehicle to take you to another place."

While this congregation's enthusiastic embrace of participation is clearly a source of pride for the cantor, there are times when this "success" amuses and frustrates him. He laughed and said, "In fact . . . if I want to sing something myself, without them, I've got to adjust my tempo in the *Hatsi kaddish* [half Kaddish] [CD #9]. When they sing Barekhu [CD #10], I start singing really before they're done because some of them insist on singing everything I sing, which bothers me sometimes." In traditional worship, there is a clear understanding that the shaliach tsibbur chants the *Barekhu* and the congregation responds with the Hebrew phrase that translates, "Blessed be the Lord who is blessed forever and ever." At Temple Israel, not all congregants are familiar with this distinction, and some enthusiastically join with the leader in all the Hebrew chanting. There are also times where the cantor wishes to set his role apart from that of the congregation and perform. He noted, "There are some things that I think are a little more cantorial, where I just want to interpret it my way instead of having to be lockstep with everybody. . . . I generally have several pieces within the service that cannot be sung by the congregation." He described the verses in *Lekhah dodi* (CD #7) as one of the opportunities for him to sing by himself and said, "They wanted to try [to sing with me], but for the most part they listened to me for that."

In this transcription of *Lekhah dodi* (Example 2.2), unstemmed notes, without bar lines, indicate the free tempo of the cantor's recitative.[28] The larger the note, the longer its duration. By varying the tempo of these sec-

Example 2.2. *Lekhah dodi*, Temple Israel, CD #7.

tions, the cantor can more or less preclude congregational participation and sing these verses solo. The cantor said that there was more at stake here than his desire to perform in a worship setting. He explained, "In fact, there's a message that's important. There's something that's here that requires a little more expertise than anyone else [has]. Otherwise, the cantorial position starts to become, in times of economic troubles, expendable. And I don't do that thinking about it, but I actually do it because it gives me a chance to express myself and to use my voice a little more than just singing along with everyone else." Even in this congregation where participatory singing has been encouraged and embraced by staff and members alike, these factors cause the cantor to balance participation and performance to a limited extent. This tune of *Lekhah dodi* is a good example of this purposeful balance.

Worshippers noted that they were not put off by the cantor's solo singing but rather saw it as an integrated element in the music of the service. One woman declared, "[When the cantor sings the verses] I love that. It's counterpoint . . . it's a persona. . . . It doesn't feel like [performance] when he does it." The personal warmth that these congregants felt for their cantor mitigated the feeling that he was setting himself apart from the congregation, even when he wished, by his own admission, to perform a bit. A member stressed that congregants felt this way "because we like Roy. . . . He's not a star. He's not so apart from us. He's just a wonderful person and whatever comes out, he's one of us." It should be stressed, however, that cantorial performance is viewed negatively by most of these members. One member recalled another synagogue she had recently attended in which the cantor was primarily a "performer." She said, "The whole service [was] his chanting . . . and I felt *so* isolated from the worship." This style of worship stood in marked contrast to her experience at Temple Israel, where, she said, "everybody [gets to] have a piece of the service."

"A COUCH THAT'S COMFORTABLE TO SIT ON" Rabbi Zecher is presently involved in Synagogue 2000, a national program to develop new models for Jewish worship. This project is directed by Rabbi Lawrence Hoffman, professor of liturgy at the Hebrew Union College–Jewish Institute of Religion. Rabbi Zecher spoke about Hoffman's concept that in order to be meaningful, all of the details of the worship experience must reflect back the worshipper's conception and understanding of God. Hoffman calls this process "the theological feedback loop." Rabbi Zecher explained: "When you ask people what's their image of God, they say that it's intimate, it's connected, it's being touched, it's human relationships. Then they go to these [huge sanctuaries] where they're anonymous, where they can't participate, where it's performance oriented and the theological feedback loop doesn't feed back. They're not *experiencing* their own view of the spiritual." She continued, "That's why I love Kabbalat Shabbat, because the loop closes. There is no part where, 'The reader speaks! You be quiet!' [Rather], there's a rising sense of community feeling in the room because people feel that they're connecting spiritually to one another, to something beyond themselves, to the community as a whole."

Another member described the nature of religious experience to which she aspired in services, stressing, "To me, prayer and song come from the heart and should be spontaneous and flowing. . . . I love the momentum. You keep praying, you keep singing, you keep moving. I just want all songs to be participatory. I don't come here to listen to other people sing. *I* come here to sing, and to sing a lot." This feeling of transcendent experience, which she went on to describe as "a catharsis and a release and a reconnection," was brought about through the music of the service.

The cantor also understood that the purpose of familiar music was not only to facilitate community participation in the service. It also created the possibility for a transcendent experience in prayer. If the music was unfamiliar, too difficult to sing, or organized so that some performed while others listened, it could not fulfill this goal. He explained, "I have an inner struggle [because part of me wants to present] more esoteric, difficult, ambitious pieces of Jewish music . . . on the other hand, I want to provide a couch that's comfortable for them to sit on, and when they walk out they feel like they've lost themselves a little bit in that . . . service. When people sing and they're singing something familiar, you start to let go in layers what you came in with from the street."

While most of the members I spoke with at Temple Israel did not discuss their feelings about this service in religious terminology, their observations reflected increased appreciation of certain traditional Jewish values. Jewish law designates Shabbat as *kodesh* (holy, separate), differentiated from the other six days of the week. Jews are traditionally obligated to create and recognize a *havdalah* (distinction) between the sacred and the ordinary. When these liberal, Reform worshippers speak of "letting go in layers what you came in with from the street" and "decompressing" from the week, they are speaking about making this transition from *hol* (profane) to kodesh, from the ordinary to the sacred. When a member of the congregation describes Shabbat services as "the one place during the week where no one interrupts me," she is recognizing the importance of creating and preserving sacred space.

Worshippers spoke of how meaningful it was, even momentarily, to step out of their harried lives to join with friends and family. As another member emphasized, "The ultimate goal, I think for us, is that we want community. We want to feel connected to each other, and the music allows that . . . to happen." When these Jews describe how important it is for them to celebrate with their friends and family at services, they are affirming the centrality of *klal Yisrael,* the Jewish community, in their lives. These core values are realized in the details of the worship: movable chairs set so that congregants see one another, a closer physical connection between clergy and congregation who all pray on the same level, and the music that undergirds the experience of prayer. This music allows them to step out from their busy schedules, establish a brief but powerful oasis of peace, situate themselves in their history, and join together in shared community.

For the older generation of Reform Jews at Temple Israel, making prayer meaningful meant bringing Jewish worship in line with modernity. An inspirational sermon, organ, and choir contributed to their experience. They appreciated the order, the esthetic beauty, and a certain grandeur that marked their service. The men and women, lay and clergy, who have established the atrium service had a different sense of the prerequisites for meaningful worship. Empowered by the counterculture of the 1960s to question authority and in search of a less hierarchial service, they worked to construct prayer that was informal and participatory. Their service draws much from American culture: the guitar and the music of contemporary Reform composers shape their worship. Still, a climate favorable to ethnic and cultural expression, coupled with a low level of overt anti-Semitism, fostered increased particularistic expression in prayer. More Hebrew was introduced and the congregation selectively embraced aspects of worship once rejected by classical Reform, such as traditional chant. They have created a style of Reform worship that, to them, feels both contemporary and increasingly traditional, a synthesis that reflects their desire to be more deeply engaged in their culture and religion.

The Conservative Service at Tufts Hillel: Kabbalat Shabbat in a College Congregation

Tufts recently completed construction of a new Hillel Center. Prior to 1995 the Conservative service at Tufts Hillel met in the former chapel of Tufts' now-defunct Crane Theological Seminary. Students were thrilled to move into their own worship space when the Hillel Center opened. Conservative services meet in the Center's large chapel, a hexagonally shaped room with polished wooden floors and simple white walls. About a hundred movable chairs are set up in a modified semicircle, facing east toward large windows that look out at ground level onto a meditative garden. To the left of the windows, a striking ark holding two Torahs is build into the wall. Before services begin, students wheel out a book cart with copies of *Sim Shalom*, the Conservative prayer book. This service is designated as "egalitarian": both men and women fully participate in the service and its leadership.

It is common to have two students share the leadership of the service, with one person leading Kabbalat Shabbat and the second leading Maariv. Often the student co-chairs try to pick a man and a woman to split these two sections. The Conservative service draws from fifty to a hundred students weekly. Services last approximately an hour and are followed by a Shabbat dinner that is attended by Reform, Conservative, Orthodox, and unaffiliated members of the Tufts Jewish community.

Students come to services late. Even though a core group attends regularly, there are always many new faces in the crowd. Newcomers invariably arrive on time and are disturbed to find so few people there. I usually reassure them and tell them not to worry, explaining that services run on "Jewish Standard Time." Most students dress up for services: Men wear ties and jackets, women wear skirts or dresses. The student co-chairs of the Conservative Committee at Hillel approach potential leaders a few minutes before services and ask if they would like the honor of leading. If a student is leading services for the first time, he or she knows in advance

Figure 2.6. Student-led service at Tufts Hillel. Photo: Richard Sobol.

Figure 2.7. Students socializing before services at Tufts Hillel. Photo: Richard Sobol.

and prepares the leader's solo sections with the help of a cassette tape and tutoring by experienced students or Hillel staff. Some years, students vie for the honor of leading services. Other years, they must be encouraged or coerced into assuming leadership. If the Conservative co-chairs are not there on a specific Shabbat or if no one volunteers to lead, I will encourage students to do so. In a pinch, I will daven part or all of the service. Before Kabbalat Shabbat begins, students sit in groups, talking and visiting with their friends. The leader calls the group to order: "Shabbat shalom! Welcome to the Conservative service at Tufts Hillel. We begin with *Yedid nefesh* (Beloved of [my] soul) on page 14 of our prayer book" (CD #11).

BACKGROUND AND HISTORY The Hillel Foundation serves the religious, cultural, educational, and social needs of the Jewish community at Tufts University, one of the private universities in the greater Boston area (4,500 undergraduate, 1,500 graduate). Approximately one-third of the undergraduate student population is Jewish. The majority of Jewish students at Tufts could be classified as liberal Jews, affiliating with either the Conservative or Reform movement. Modeled on many communal, social service, and religious organizations in the Jewish community, Hillel encompasses a wide range of committees that plan the community's religious and cultural life. In addition to my own position as rabbi and director, Hillel employs five full-time staff members for programming, development, and administration.

Students often describe the Conservative service as being in the style of Camp Ramah, the summer camp of the Conservative movement. The vast majority of the service is conducted in Hebrew with the exception of a psalm occasionally read responsively in English. Much of the liturgy is sung to tunes that are popular at Ramah camps around the country. Other sections are chanted to tunes that worshippers consider traditional and that are familiar both from their synagogues at home and from camp.[29] While the leader introduces and closes the psalms using Kabbalat Shabbat nusach, the worshippers basically read through the prayers almost silently, often joining in as the leader chants the prayer's hatimah. The rumbling undertone of worshippers davening quickly through the prayers at their own pace, common in Orthodox prayer, is absent from this service. Students' facility with Hebrew is mixed: some participants speak Hebrew fluently and are conversant with both the liturgy and nusach of the Friday night service. Other students are able to read Hebrew phonetically and have memorized key sections of the liturgy but do not understand the meaning of the text. Even among the students who are facile with Hebrew, many would be embarrassed or self-conscious to daven out loud, afraid they might be seen as overly pious.

In addition to regulars, certain students attend occasionally or when they want to say *Kaddish* on the observance of the anniversary of a relative's death. These students are less familiar with the service but view the Conservative service as "more authentic" than the Reform service at Tufts. There is no instrumentation in the Conservative service. Even though few of the members of this service are strictly ritually observant, the students feel that the lack of a guitar and the fact that most of the service is in Hebrew define this service as "traditional."

At the end of the nineteenth century many of the philosophical and liturgical changes supported by the Reform movement proved to be too radical for certain American Jewish leaders and congregations. Thus the stage was set for the founding of the Conservative movement.[30] The early Reform movement's formal rejection of ritual practice, such as traditional observance of the Sabbath and the dietary laws, motivated a group of rabbis to break off from the Reform movement. In 1886 their leaders established the Jewish Theological Seminary, the current rabbinic school of the Conservative movement.

Upon its founding, the Seminary represented a loose confederation of congregations. However, the infamous May Laws in Russia in 1882[31] prompted a massive Eastern European Jewish immigration, increasing the Jewish population in America to three million by the early 1920s. Unlike the early German Jewish immigrants who formed the mainstay of the Reform movement, these Russian, Polish, and Rumanian Jews were predominantly Orthodox and were drawn to more traditional practice. Many eventually joined, and influenced, the developing Reform movement. Others sought out a form of Judaism that while more American, still maintained a traditional orientation. Strengthened by the affiliation of these immigrants and their children, Conservative congregations grew. Their association, the United Synagogue, was formed in 1913. This body was a counterpart to the Union of Orthodox Jewish Congregations (1898) and the Union of American Hebrew Congregations of the Reform Movement (1873).

Between the 1930s and 1950s, the Conservative movement founded teaching institutes, youth programs, summer camps, and a publishing house. By the 1960s, when Jews had entered mainstream America economically, socially, and politically, the Conservative movement was the largest branch of American Judaism. It began to ordain women as rabbis in 1985 and has invested women as cantors since 1987.

As part of the move to modernize and innovate, the Conservative movement shortened some prayers, added more decorum to the service, and often had a synagogue choir accompany the cantor in prayer. Few early Conservative congregations used the organ; one does not find much instrumentation in Conservative worship. The cantor was maintained as a central liturgical figure in the synagogue, though in the interest of shortening the service, the intricate florid performance common during the "golden age" of *hazzanut* (cantorial performance) was less acceptable. During the High Holidays one can still hear this style of hazzanut in many congregations. Since the 1970s, the Conservative leadership, concerned about a passive laity, has moved toward a more participatory service (cf. Kligman 2000:922). In this area, Conservative congregations have been influenced by the music of their youth movement, United Synagogue Youth, and their summer camp, Camp Ramah, where Israeli, Hasidic, and contemporary Jewish songs are used in the liturgy.

Jewish students come to Tufts University from fifty states and many countries around the world. They represent tremendously diverse congregations: large and small, formal and informal, with and without cantors. Many students have been involved in United Synagogue Youth (USY) or attended one of the Ramah camps. Yet others have no affiliation to the Conservative movement and are drawn to explore their religious and cultural identity when they enter college. A student's choice of which service to attend is influenced by many factors: an existing affiliation with a particular movement, past experience with Jewish worship, a desire to explore new approaches to prayer, or simply a wish to be where their friends go.

From year to year, continuity is provided by the professional Hillel staff, a few faculty members, and the small group of students who stay active throughout their four years at Tufts. Yet the college community is constantly changing, and the transitional nature of this population is especially pronounced at the beginning of each year as freshmen arrive on campus. In addition, it is common for seniors to become very active in the leadership of this service, and their loss is felt acutely when they graduate and leave the community. Tufts encourages students to study abroad during their junior year, and many students who are active in Jewish life attend the one-year or one-semester programs in Jerusalem or Tel Aviv. When they return in their senior year, they have broadened their experience with Jewish worship and often learned new tunes. Some return from Israel more ritually observant than before they left. These factors conspire to keep this worship community in constant transition, an ironic fact since so many students come to this traditional service looking for community and a sense of belonging.

"IF YOU GO SOMEPLACE NEW AND THE TUNES ARE THE SAME, YOU FEEL LIKE YOU BELONG" When asked why they participated in this service, many students stated that they looked to Hillel for a ready-made community, free of the uncertainty and social tension that marked so many arenas in university life. One student explained that during the week he socialized with other students in a variety of casual or academic activities. He might know someone from team sports or from class, but ultimately those activities told him little about that person's values and deeper interests. This student explained that going to services on Friday evening was different: "You go to Hillel and you meet everyone because of one thing, because they're Jewish, because you have a common bond and they all share the same values as you. It's kind of nice to be in that haven [and] . . . not to worry about, . . . 'Gee, what's that person like?' . . . They're interested in Judaism. . . . The people that choose to go want to be there and . . . they're all nice people . . . they're going to talk to you. A lot of people that are involved in Hillel are like that. I feel really close to them. I can talk to them and they're very friendly. It's kind of like home. . . . I can just relax."

Many students stressed that the tunes used at Friday night services were an important component that made them feel comfortable in this new community. One student commented, "Part of going to a service on a Friday night is that you get a warm feeling of camaraderie. You're all there together. You all have a common heritage, and when you go someplace new you don't feel that as much as when you go someplace that you're familiar with, but if you go someplace new and the tunes are the same, you do feel a little bit more like you belong." This student continued, "If I went someplace halfway across the country, and they happened to use the same tunes, I would feel very comfortable in that place." Through this music, students have developed ties to one another that nurture and sustain them throughout the week. The singing during Kabbalat Shabbat creates a connection, whether real or imagined, that transcends many of the social boundaries regularly experienced by students on campus.

Many students participate fully and enthusiastically from the first moment they walk into the large chapel. Yet for the most part, the music at Hillel on a Friday night is quite different from in their home congregations. Conservative synagogues across the country display a broad range of worship styles, often influenced and shaped over the years by cantors who have left their particular musical signature on their congregation. Conservative cantors take pride in using the proper nusach for Shabbat and holidays. In the best cases, they are also educators whose davening exhibits the breadth, depth, and complexity of Jewish liturgical music, nuances that are increasingly lost on their congregants. Except for a few "superstar daveners," most Conservative students do not come to college with a developed appreciation and knowledge of daily, Shabbat, and High Holiday nusach. In camp and youth group they have learned a simpler, group-oriented style, a common musical tradition, forged through the Conservative movement's youth organizations; Camp Ramah, United Synagogue Youth, and to a lesser extent the Solomon Schechter day schools. When they come to Hillel, they find—and strive to maintain—this style of participatory, peer-led prayer.

Camp Ramah is the strongest influence in standardizing musical and liturgical traditions. A nationally coordinated program of staff training and education has built this common tradition of tunes, nusach, and a particular stylistic approach to davening, according to the camp's national director, Rabbi Shelly Dorf. Ramah currently runs seven overnight camps and three day camps across the country and in Canada. While including all of the regular activities found in a summer camp for suburban children and teenagers, Camp Ramah also teaches Jewish traditions, values, texts, and prayer. Spirited daily services with highly participatory singing and the creation of a special appreciation for Shabbat are religious hallmarks of the camps. At staff training seminars, participants not only daven together and share new songs, they learn creative approaches to teaching and involving their campers in communal prayer. They also work on their own liturgical skills, learning nusach and refining their davening before returning to their individual camps. Recently music teachers from all the camps came together to explore the best way to use and teach from a new songbook produced by Ramah. Through these national and international gatherings, according to Rabbi Dorf, staff is able to develop and pass on "a common set of songs, tunes, and nusach."

While youth group settings do not allow for an experience of total immersion in Jewish culture as does camp, United Synagogue Youth conventions and weekend retreats bring high school students together region by region, as well as nationally, to study, socialize, pray, and sing. One has only to listen to two college students playing "Jewish geography" ("You're from Chicago? Do you know . . . ?") to realize the extent and importance of the social connections forged throughout the country by these camps and youth groups. These students share more than friendship: they share a tradition of liturgical music that differs considerably from that in their home congregations.

Not all students attending the Conservative service have participated in camps and youth groups, and it is often easy to spot these students in services. Students related that when the music was unfamiliar, they felt that they did not belong. One student stressed the anxiety he felt upon first attending Hillel services, especially when he heard new music. He explained, "I didn't feel comfortable coming the first time . . . even though I've been around Judaism for quite some time, and I've been to lots of different services . . . even if you're totally into Judaism . . . it's just always weird going to a new service and especially hearing new tunes." Even a knowledgeable Jew can feel alienated in worship if everyone else seems to be fully involved, singing the prayers, and one is unable to join in. Thus a significant part of a student's initial connection with, or alienation from, the campus Jewish community rested on his or her relationship to the music at services. I have found that students use their reaction to the music as a "quick read" on the nature of the campus Jewish community as a whole. On the basis of the style of music in worship, they often form opinions about the kind of students who participate in organized Jewish life and whether or not they will fit in with the campus Jewish community.

I like the fact that students come to the traditional service "prepped" by Camp Ramah and USY. However, I do not want the service to feel too much like a clique or an exclusive club. I have tried to address this issue in several ways, with mixed results. One year I met with the students who were to lead Kabbalat Shabbat and discussed the tunes we should use for the first service of the semester. While using the Ramah style service as a base, we decided to broaden the music selections and added some Conservative congregational favorites, a Debbie Friedman song, a new Hasidic niggun, and some contemporary Israeli material. Some people liked this; others said that by trying to please everyone, we ended up pleasing no one. I have had the best results, both on Friday night and during the High Holidays, by simply naming the problem as I welcomed new students to the first Shabbat service of the year: "Welcome to Tufts Hillel. We come from many different congregations and many different traditions. For better and worse, this is not the same congregation that you grew up in, with parents, relatives, and friends. Some songs will be familiar, some will be new. It's great to welcome you here and I hope that, if you come back several times, this service will feel more and more like it belongs to you." Students have told me that hearing this helps. Still, I regularly meet students in their junior or senior year who tell me, "I tried out services when I was a freshman, but I didn't know the tunes you use at Hillel. I felt too uncomfortable and just never came back."

"THE MUSIC WAS A MAJOR REASON FOR STAYING" Cultural and religious identification on a college campus is primarily voluntary expression. Jews constantly choose how, when, where, and how frequently they will participate in Jewish life on campus. I know from hundreds of conversations that many Conservative students feel strongly about the importance of Judaism in their lives. They proudly identify as Jews. Yet they do not assume that these strongly held personal beliefs have to translate into action, activism, or religious observance. Friday evening worship is voluntary, and so attending services is considered and evaluated against all the other seductive options that a campus offers on a Friday night. In general, Conservative students do not feel the same sense of *hiyuv* (religious obligation) that determines the choices made by Orthodox students. A practicing Orthodox student does not decide to attend Kabbalat Shabbat because of the quality of the music. While the Orthodox student will ask if there is a minyan for prayer and care that the davening is accurate and proper, the student is obligated to pray on Shabbat. Besides, other campus activities, such as a movie, dance, or basketball game, are outside of normative Orthodox practice on the Sabbath.

Conservative Jews, for the most part, approach religious activity from a different perspective. Because participation in cultural and religious activities is understood as a personal choice, the kind of music used in worship is a significant factor that these students consider when deciding whether or not to participate. One student stressed how much he liked the tunes and said that he probably would not come to services if the music was "all dull and boring." Students sometimes feel confused when they find that their participation, especially connected to music, is fun. One student said that sometimes he felt guilty that he was having such a good time singing in worship. He justified himself by saying, "I don't think there's anything *wrong* with enjoying something as serious and spiritual as prayer." Another discussed his regular attendance at service and explained, "For me . . . the music was a major reason for staying."

For some students, the tune does more than provide an enjoyable community experience and a comfortable feeling of familiarity. The tune is not the vehicle for spiritual expression; it is religious expression itself. A Tufts senior explained it in this way: "One of the main reasons I like [services] is because of the music and the melodies. [When I returned from studying in Israel] I sort of synagogue-hopped for a couple of weeks to find out which synagogue had the best melodies for Friday night services, and that was the one I stuck with. I didn't know much about the liturgy, but I knew what melodies were good for me, and that's what was pretty much the most important thing because . . . I read Hebrew but . . . most of it I don't understand, so the way I get most of what I get from services is through the melody." This student continued, a bit nervous about revealing that for her, the tune was more important than the text of the prayer. She said, "When everybody's singing well together—one of those melodies—it really makes me feel . . . unified. This might be heresy, [but I get even] more from the melody than from the words."

"PRAYER SHOULDN'T BE A SPECTATOR SPORT!": STUDENT OWNERSHIP OF SERVICES Spirited singing, student leadership of services, and a thoughtful consideration of the meaning of the liturgy shape this Conservative service. Many students wish to continue a style of prayer from camp and youth group where they first encountered the heady experience of leading prayer themselves. One student quoted his counselor from Camp Ramah, emphasizing that "prayer shouldn't be a spectator sport." While many students expressed affection and respect for their cantors at home, the majority were unequivocal about their preference for student-led services at Hillel. One student described the distance he felt between the clergy and congregation at home: "[In my synagogue] . . . you've got a leader up there and people are literally and figuratively lower down and you're just sitting there looking up [at them]." He explained that at Tufts "It was different. I felt like people in the audience [sic] really took more of a part in it." This student's use of the word "audience" rather than "congregation" is telling. In many synagogues, students say that they feel like passive spectators, members of the audience. This feeling is reinforced by the architecture of most synagogues, where the rabbi and cantor conduct services from a raised bimah. At Hillel, students feel that the leader and worshippers are on the same level, literally and figuratively. The term shaliach tsibbur, the *representative* of those gathered for prayer, implies connection between the leader and congregation, a dynamic that is reinforced and enhanced in this peer-led service.

In addition to feeling a stronger bond between the leader and the congregation, students appreciate being in control of the experience of worship. They are invested in decisions, large and small, that shape the service. One student explained, "When people have an argument over what melodies you use, they have a stake in it. It's really neat!" It is not unusual for a friendly disagreement to break out as members of the congregation call out suggestions before the leader chooses a tune for *Lekhah dodi* or, more commonly, before one of the two possible closing hymns, *Adon olam* or *Yigdal* (Praise [the living God]) (CD #12). Such active involvement is supported by the informality of the service and the sense that student participation, and constant input, are welcome.

While the Conservative service at Tufts Hillel always had strong participatory singing, most current students do not know that this service was not always student led. For my first five years on campus, when I was fresh out of rabbinical school, I jealously kept the role of leader for myself. I had just finished five years of graduate training and had much that I wanted to teach. When I first came to Tufts, I did not give much thought to who would lead services: I simply assumed that I would. So did the students. Besides, I had a clear idea of the kind of service that I wanted to create at Tufts: warm, welcoming, informal yet serious, a place for friends to gather after a busy week. I wanted a setting that had great music and yet enough silence for personal reflection. My only problem was that I had never really led a traditional Kabbalat Shabbat service; this style of worship was not taught at Hebrew Union College, the rabbinical school for the Reform movement. I had recently returned from a year in Jerusalem, between my fourth and fifth year of rabbinical school, and had regularly davened there with the Bratslav Hasidim on Friday night. However, their service was too traditional, and their wonderful tunes were too complex to use with relatively assimilated American college students. So that summer I turned to a friend who was a rabbinical student at the Conservative movement's Jewish Theological Seminary and asked him to make a tape of nusach and tunes for Kabbalat Shabbat. This friend had always been active in Camp Ramah, and so from the beginning the traditions and melodies I brought to this service were influenced by Camp Ramah, though I had never been a camper or counselor there.

Services started out small. There were many weeks when we were lucky to make a minyan: now it is not unusual to have a hundred students at services. I functioned both as cantor, leading the davening, and as rabbi, speaking at the service. It took a full university cycle of four years for that service to become established, and when it finally was, it seemed a natural step for me to begin to hand over the reigns to members of our community. I enjoyed leading but felt that too many people focused on me during prayer. I began to think in depth about the role of an enthusiastic leader and how that leader can block the davener's line of vision in worship. In good prayer, the rabbi, cantor, and congregation are all "performing" and the "audience" is God, however one defines holiness or the focus of one's prayer. Too often in contemporary worship, the rabbi and the cantor are the performers and the congregation becomes the audience. An accomplished leader can run a service smoothly and "correctly," but I did not want to deprive the worshipper of the experience of praying for him- or herself. It became much more satisfying for me, and ultimately more in keeping with my educational goals for Hillel, to help create an empowered, knowledgeable community, to teach others the Hebrew, the tunes, and the nusach, how to lead prayer.

There was also a personal, spiritual aspect to my decision to move away from the role of sole leader. As leader, I was always "on" come Friday night. I loved the Kabbalat Shabbat service but had little opportunity to daven for myself. I was constantly focused on the logistics of the service. Are there enough chairs? Is the heat set too high? Does that new person have a prayer book? I hoped that as an occasional leader, I could recapture my own kavanah and become a better role model as a serious davener.

I stepped out of the role of sole leader gradually and with a certain ambivalence. First I started breaking the service into two parts: Kabbalat Shabbat and Maariv. I would lead one part and a student would lead the other. I began announcing at services that I was happy to teach students how to lead services, and I began to make tapes of tunes and nusach to pass out to interested students. Eventually a cadre of students emerged who were comfortable and enthusiastic about leading services; most of them had led worship at Camp Ramah or in USY. Many others learned how to daven by regularly participating in our service at Tufts. By the time we moved into the new Hillel Center, it was taken for granted that this service was student led.

Over time, a strong Reform service developed at Hillel, and I felt that it was important for me to spend time with both communities. Now, every Shabbat I give the same brief sermon at each service. I still occasionally lead the Conservative service or teach a new tune there, but my primary role is that of teacher. I enjoy sitting in the congregation, praying and singing next to my students. It is also deeply satisfying to see them become competent, knowledgeable leaders, actively shaping their Jewish experience. In the words of Rabbi Lawrence Kushner, I believe that the Jewish community would be a healthier place if rabbis treated regular Jews more like rabbis and Jews treated rabbis more like regular Jews (1984).

In developing this style of participatory, peer-led service, I have learned that no good deed goes unpunished. It is not uncommon for new students to come to Kabbalat Shabbat and express their disappointment that the rabbi is not leading services. In addition, student-led services come with a certain price. While many are accomplished and skilled leaders, some make jarring mistakes in the Hebrew, others do not appreciate or convey the subtleties of traditional nusach. For example, it is common for leaders to use Shabbat morning nusach for the Friday night *Barekhu* or to mix up the tunes for the various forms of the Kaddish used throughout the service. My task then becomes educational, but when we encourage many new leaders, we invariably trade a uniform, controlled quality of davening for student ownership and participation.

LEKHAH DODI AT TUFTS HILLEL: "IT'S NOT THE ORIGINAL FOR EVERYBODY BUT FOR ME IT'S THE ORIGINAL" In discussing the role of specific tunes in the service, one student described how *Lekhah dodi* was the pivot point, a major transition in Kabbalat Shabbat. She related, "Everything builds up from the beginning [to *Lekhah dodi*]. At first people are still stressed out about the week, and then after we do *Lekhah dodi*, people are much more into singing . . . it's just really nice for going into Maariv."

The most popular *Lekhah dodi* at Tufts has been CD #13, the second most popular tune collected by Mark Slobin (1989:199). The origin of this tune is unknown. While recognizing that musical authenticity was subjective, one student still asserted that for her, this tune was the "real" tune for *Lekhah dodi*. She observed, "I think of that as the original, maybe because I've heard it so many times. Of course, it's not the original for everybody but for me it's the original . . . it's the real one." Occasionally a student will request or sing the Lewandowski tune for *Lekhah dodi* (CD #7). A number of years ago I taught the tune I learned in Jerusalem at Congregation Kol HaNeshama (CD #8). Increasingly students will sing the tune recorded at Shaarei Tefillah (CD #15), discussed later in the chapter. Still, tune CD #13 has remained by far the most popular choice. Slobin describes it as having unknown origins but suggests that the extended second section resembles many Hasidic tunes, and the minor key suggests that it may have developed in Eastern Europe (1989:198). Davidson too could not trace the origins of the tune. He calls it a "folk song" and presents his own arrangement (1987:No.7).

One factor that "drew people in" is the call and response pattern in the chorus. Another student explained, "I like . . . where you can split it up [into call and response] I think it makes it sounds a lot nicer . . . it's more harmonious." Another commented, "That verse or chorus repeats itself so much that . . . even if I don't know the parts in the middle, I could always participate with [the chorus] because I've heard it so much."

The Tufts community has developed three options for singing this tune. Option one is to sing it through all nine verses, without changing the melody at verse six, *Lo tevoshi*. The second option is a variant of option one: The congregation sings the first three verses and then davens the middle three verses silently; worshippers then conclude the last three verses using the same tune as the first three. The third option is to sing all nine verses but to switch tunes at the sixth verse, *Lo tevoshi*. This version is transcribed in Example 2.3.

While many students stressed that this was their favorite tune for *Lekhah dodi*, they expressed different preferences in regard to how the hymn is sung. Some favored switching to a different tune after verse six.

As one student expressed it, the change in tune "fits the words better and also I think it's such a long song that . . . [the change of tune] keeps the interest up." Another student said that while she liked the change of tune in verse six, she preferred not to switch because she was "not so familiar with the last few verses."

Other students did not like the tradition of singing the first three and last three verses and letting the congregation daven the middle verses silently. These students came from congregations where the hymn was sung in its entirety. As one student said, "When you have a song that people like . . . I think you should just do it all. It's only a few more verses. I think continuity is better than just cutting the middle." However, other students held the opposite opinion. One worshipper said that if you sing all of the verses, "it gets long and repetitive [and] by the last verse, everyone would be bored with it." This practice at Hillel dates back to the time before there was no separate Reform service and worship had to address the needs of both Conservative and Reform Jews on campus. Many of the Reform students found this hymn's nine verses of difficult Hebrew intimidating, and so I tried to introduce an option that would satisfy both populations. Since Hillel has been holding two services, *Lekhah dodi* has increasingly been sung in its entirety.

Many students connected specific settings with particular tunes. One student explained that he had learned tune CD #13 for *Lekhah dodi* in Israel, and it reminded him of that important trip that influenced his Jewish identity. He said, "I like that particular melody . . . it could be because I associate it with . . . some shul in Israel that I really liked. They used that melody. I think that's what I associate it with, when I was on Pilgrimage [a trip to Israel for high school students run by the Conservative movement]." He contrasted it with the Lewandowski tune that he learned in his home synagogue and said, "I always thought that was boring. It's so repetitive." Another student commented, "[Tune CD #13 is] what I'm used to because that's what I learned at [Camp] Ramah. I tend to like the things I learned there the best because . . . I learned it in a very comfortable and nice atmosphere."

THE TRANSITION THAT NO ONE KNOWS At the chorus of *Lekhah dodi* following the sixth stanza, *Lo tevoshi*, many members of the community are unclear about the correct melody. This confusion does not stop the community from choosing this tune, nor did it elicit much comment when worshippers discussed this hymn. The community is clear about the melody from the seventh verse to the conclusion of *Lekhah dodi*. However, I often exchange glances with a music professor who regularly attends services, and we cringe when the congregation arrives at the invariably cacophonous chorus between the sixth and seventh verses. At that point it sounds as if the entire congregation is improvising unsuccessfully. I was not able to transcribe this chorus from the first tapes I recorded of this tune: worshippers were singing too many variations to distinguish among them. Members of the community are conscious of this discordant sec-

Example 2.3. *Lekhah dodi*, Tufts Hillel, CD #13.

tion of *Lekhah dodi*. When I announced that I wanted to make a recording of that section, a group of students burst out laughing. Someone said, "You want that part on tape?!" In a short discussion that followed, another student said that if people would only pay attention and follow the leader's tune, that chorus would not be so jarring. In fact, that was what happened in the recording session, and the transition was smoother than I have ever heard it in worship. Many students in this service had no idea what the correct tune was at that point in the hymn. They try to muddle through by listening to the leader or the people sitting next to them. As one woman said, "I just listen to whoever's leading the service and I try to pick it up."

Many tunes in the service are passed as oral tradition from one generation of students to another. Although the first part of this tune has been transcribed and published, I found no written versions of the tune from the sixth verse to the end. Even if written versions exist, none of these students consult written sources for *Lekhah dodi*. They learn it through their participation in services. When I lead davening, I sing my own version, which differs from that sung by other leaders of this service.

In an effort to explain why the tune breaks down at this point, I recorded several solo renditions of this transition. Example 2.4 shows two versions. The first is from a student who often leads services. The second version is my own best guess of the transition between the sixth and seventh verses as I sing it when I lead this hymn. These two versions differ considerably. In fact, I listened to a number of other versions, and no two were close to identical.

A quick comparison confirms the difference between these two variants. The student begins his version on the fourth above the tonic, C. He also introduces two new accidentals, D♭ and G♭, both not found in the key of Cm.[32] While I include the same accidentals, I begin on the tonic and basically sing a different tune. While this accounts for the congregational discordance at that point in the tune, it does not explain why there is no standard version of this brief section of this *Lekhah dodi* tune. One possible explanation can be found in the Hasidic practice of applying various tunes to the verses of *Lekhah dodi*. This in fact is the case here, where one tune is applied to the first five verses, another to the sixth verse, a third to the seventh and eighth verses, and yet another to the last verse. While a certain amount of care is taken in fitting the borrowed tune to the verse, less attention is placed on the transitions from one tune to the next. Although standard transitions develop in some congregations, this is not the case in all communities. As a result, worshippers are left to struggle as best they can from one verse to the next.

There is another possible explanation why members do not seem to be bothered by the brief musical dissonance in the transition. During the metric tunes in Jewish prayer, worshippers sing together, but when people daven in nusach, there is a general discordant murmur of voices in the synagogue. Each worshipper has a slightly different variation of nusach. Furthermore, people proceed at their own pace. Musical discordance has

Example 2.4. Transitions between the sixth and seventh verses of *Lekhah dodi*, Tufts Hillel, CD #13.

a place in communal worship, and worshippers may simply contextualize the lack of a clear melody at that point in the hymn in the "messier" tradition of congregational davening.[33] This brief moment of unresolved musical conflict should be put in the context of a tradition that has raised verbal argument to a high art. The Talmud not only preserved conflicting opinions, it occasionally says that opposing traditions are both "the words of the living God" (cf. Babylonian Talmud, *Gittin* 6b). While the mix of different musical traditions is not esthetically pleasing, it underscores the stubborn insistence of individual worshippers on bringing their own musical traditions into the room, even at the expense of group unity.

In the complex, multicultural atmosphere of the campus, these Jewish students come to Hillel looking for a welcoming and supportive community. Familiar melodies, learned at camp and youth group, signify shared values and experience. Students enjoy the control and power of leading worship for themselves and have created a service marked by enthusiastic, participatory singing. They continue to daven in the style learned at Camp Ramah and USY, a simpler style than their home congregations, where knowledgeable professionals control the liturgy. Away from their families and home congregations, these students affirm the importance of Jewish tradition not by trying to re-create the traditions of their home congregations but by actively assuming the leadership and ownership of their own Jewish community.

Congregation Shaarei Tefillah: A New Tune Becomes an Anthem of Identity

Early Friday evening and Saturday morning, well-dressed families walk down Commonwealth Avenue on their way to Shaarei Tefillah. Women are stylish, and it is not obvious that a dress code ensuring modesty exists in the synagogue. Women's shoulders and legs are covered, and married women generally wear hats. Suits, or ties and jackets are the norm for both men and boys, although some follow the Israeli modern Orthodox style and wear nice slacks and white shirts. All men cover their heads, and most wear *kippot serugot*, knitted Israeli yarmulkes, favored by the modern Orthodox.

Shaarei Tefillah is located in an attractive split-level house on a shady street in suburban Newton. It looks very different from Congregation Beth El, literally around the corner, the synagogue from which this newer breakaway congregation separated in 1984. From the front, one cannot tell that this house is a synagogue, except for the bulletin board announcing the congregation's name and times of weekly and Shabbat services. The entrance to Shaarei Tefillah is down the driveway, in the back of the house. When you enter, you see that the building was gutted to create a large, airy sanctuary, separated into men's and women's sections. Men and women come into the foyer together but then split off to their separate sections. Many women say that they like the synagogue's *mehitsah*, the separation between the men's and women's sections. Unlike in many Orthodox synagogues, women are not seated behind the men or upstairs in a balcony or hidden to one side behind a curtained partition. The shul is divided down the middle. A five-foot-high wall separates the sections. The ark holding the Torahs is on the men's side, yet the women have a fairly good view of the bimah and the ark.

Before Kabbalat Shabbat, early attendees daven Minchah, the afternoon service. Friday evening is attended primarily by men, with a sprinkling of young unmarried women and a few married women present to say Kaddish in memory of a deceased relative. Even though many of the women in this congregation are professionals, most tend to be home on Friday evening preparing Shabbat dinner and readying the house for the Sabbath. After Minchah, men joke and chat with one another. Regular members are rarely out of touch: attendance at Sabbath services is a defining aspect of membership in the community. On Friday evening one of the two *gabbayim* (pl.) might welcome an unfamiliar guest. The gabbai also looks for someone to lead services. While leading Kabbalat Shabbat and Maariv on Friday evening is an honor, it is a simpler job than leading services on Shabbat morning. There is a greater pool of qualified leaders from which to choose. The gabbai might ask a knowledgeable guest or a student who is home from college or recently returned from studying in Israel. This week the shaliach tsibbur is a college student home from Princeton. He puts on a large tallis and steps up to the bimah. The congregation joins with him in singing *Yedid nefesh*, the hymn they use to begin the Kabbalat Shabbat service (CD #14).

HISTORY AND BACKGROUND This modern Orthodox congregation began in 1984 when it broke away from Congregation Beth El in Newton. While members described the split as "generational," religious, social, and musical factors also figured in the formation of this congregation. In addition to

Figure 2.8. Joshua Jacobson in front of the ark at Shaarei Tefillah.
Photo: Richard Sobol.

being younger than the population at Beth El, the core members of
Shaarei Tefillah tended to be more Jewishly knowledgeable and more traditional in their religious observance. They were also interested in a more
participatory and spirited approach to prayer. Congregation members
share in the obligation to lead davening during the year.

The congregation grew quickly and now numbers approximately 140
families. Initially they met in members' living rooms before moving into
their own building. The congregation now employs a full-time rabbi and
is governed by lay officers and an executive board of approximately fifteen
members. The liturgy is overseen by two gabbayim, who help in the organization of the congregation's religious life.

In addition to services on Shabbat and holidays, weekday morning and
evening services are held every day. Most of the members send their children to the Maimonides School, a large Orthodox day school in Boston.
Their children attend the best secular universities, but the families encourage them to study at *yeshivot* (pl.), academies of traditional learning,
in Israel for a year before going to college. Both the men and women of
this congregation work in business, professional, and academic jobs in
Boston, and their professional lives provide their primary interaction with
American culture. In almost every other aspect of their lives they turn in-
ward toward their community. Membership in this community assumes
active and regular attendance and participation in the synagogue. Members observe the Jewish dietary laws, and many families will not eat at a
nonkosher restaurant. Members are also *shomrei Shabbos*, observant of
the laws of the Jewish Sabbath, neither driving nor using electricity on

Shabbat. They are studied and meticulous in the performance of sacred and liturgical text.

The term "Orthodoxy" was initially used to label traditional Jews in contradistinction to the Reform movement in Judaism at the end of the eighteenth century.[34] Orthodoxy stressed the immutable authority of halakhah and the divine origin of both the written and oral Torah as interpreted through the *Shulchan Arukh*, and it condemned any changes in traditional practice. Orthodox leaders in Germany such as Isaac Bernays (1792–1849) and his disciple, Samson Raphael Hirsch (1808–1888), supported strict traditional practice while formulating an approach that was friendly to secular culture and the Enlightenment.[35] Through his influential writings[36] and famous dictum *Torah im derekh erets* (Torah with a worldly occupation), Hirsch stressed the relevance of Jewish law and sanctioned the importance of secular education for the traditional Jew. This movement was termed neo-Orthodoxy and in many ways reflects the approach of the modern Orthodox community, in both Europe and the United States.[37]

Samuel Heilman and Steven Cohen divide the contemporary Orthodox community into three groups; nominal, centrist, and traditionalist (1989). It is important to stress that this is a sliding spectrum and all of these categories blur at the edges. Nominal Orthodox claim they recognize Orthodoxy as the only authentic Judaism but they do not in fact continue to follow halakhah. Centrist Orthodox, including the group who call themselves modern Orthodox, are professionals and college graduates who deal with modernity by compartmentalizing their lives, functioning in two worlds simultaneously. The third group, traditional Orthodox, separate themselves more fully from American culture. They are also called yeshiva or "Black Hat" Orthodox. To their right are the ultra-Orthodox Haredim—the Hasidim and the members of Agudath Yisrael, who continue to stress separatism not only from American culture but from other Jews and Jewish organizations (ibid.).

The Young Israel movement, initiated in New York in 1912, is an American Orthodox movement that has special relevance to this study. Its particular mission was to make modern Orthodoxy more appealing to young American Jews and, in doing so, to initiate esthetic changes in the prayer service. They introduced congregational singing and eliminated the auctioning of communal honors (cf. Nulman 1985:91–92; Slobin 1989:195–96). Modern Orthodox congregations don't usually have professional cantors except on the High Holidays. During the year, male congregants take turns serving as shaliach tsibbur. The leader is expected to chant the service with the appropriate nusach and, according to the particular synagogue's custom, lead the Israeli, Hasidic, or other tunes that are used for certain sections of the liturgy.

"WHO WE ARE AND HOW WE GOT STARTED" The men of Shaarei Tefillah look prosperous and conservative, very much members of "the establishment." Yet in discussing the relatively recent formation of their congregation, one worshipper described them as "the younger generation" that "cut its teeth in the 1960s." In fact, their separating from Beth El to found their own synagogue was somewhat of a revolutionary act. These knowledgeable and ritually observant Jews wanted a more participatory worship environment where control of the davening was more in the members' than in professional hands. To achieve this, they had to create their own alternative institution. One member characterized the congregation by saying that "there's a certain independence, almost a revolutionary, New England type of mentality." Another member, speaking of the separation from Beth El, explained, "[We] groped our way toward an institution [in which we] . . . were trying to be more open and informal, but at the same time somewhat . . . more Orthodox. [We were] . . . trying to be creative and different and traditional at the same time." He continued, "[This] resulted in certain interesting anomalies, and one of these anomalies manifested itself in . . . the attitudes toward music."

A member described how the professional leadership of the old synagogue set a staid tone for communal worship, a tone that was inconsistent with the excitement, commitment, and communal dedication that many of these younger Orthodox members were feeling about their lives. Many had grown up in synagogues where professional cantors had determined the style of davening. One member described the cantor in the synagogue that he belonged to before moving to Boston: "[At] that synagogue . . . the hazzan, although many of us thought very highly of him as a scholar and as a person, was *exceedingly* dull as a hazzan. Even for a hazzan he was dull! He sang everything—no matter how happy—as though it were a dirge. His *Hallel* (joyous collection of psalms sung on festivals) was enough to bring tears to your eyes!" In forming Shaarei Tefillah, members wanted to exercise more control over the nature of worship, infusing it with life and energy.

This member continued, "I . . . remember that the first couple of weeks of the congregation, when everybody was in a frenzy of enthusiasm, we sang a tune which wasn't new, it was one of the tunes that is sung in all the congregations for *Lekhah dodi*. It was sprightly and it sort of signified the enthusiasm and energy [we were feeling] [CD #15; see Example 2.5]. This was a new generation that was . . . striking out on a new and vigorous path. . . . One of the ways this new generation identified itself, in contrast to what we came from, was by singing a tune that was more lively, more modern sounding than the . . . more traditional tune before." He thought of this tune as an "anthem of identity," associated with the exciting and conflictual events surrounding the formation of the congregation.

It is not unusual for a particular *Lekhah dodi* tune to be connected to a congregation's essential identity. Because of its centrality in Kabbalat Shabbat, this hymn is a central moment in any Friday night service. While some worship communities rotate four or five favorite tunes for *Lekhah dodi*, it is common for a congregation to have a "signature melody" for this popular hymn. Furthermore, *Lekhah dodi* is one of the few "junctures of choice" in a modern Orthodox service where it is possible for the leader,

Example 2.5. *Lekhah dodi*, Shaarei Tefillah, CD #15.

Le - khah do - di li - krat ka - lah, pe-nei Sha - bat ne - ka - be-lah.

Le - khah do - di li - krat ka - lah, pe-nei Sha - bat ne - ka-be-lah.

Verse one:

Sha-mor ve-za-khor be-di-bur e - chad hish-mi-a-nu El ha-me-yu-chad.

A-do-noi e-chad u-she-mo e - chad le shem ul-ti-fe-ret ve-lit-hi-lah.

within an accepted context, to innovate. One member explained, "*Lekhah dodi* would be the opportunity for people to introduce various folk tunes, pop tunes into the service, where it's sanctioned by custom that one doesn't have to use nusach—that it's not out of line. So although Orthodoxy never perceived such a thing as change, basically doesn't pay attention to change or pretends it doesn't happen, pointing to everything that stays the same as being what's significant, there are certain opportunities within the service that allow Orthodox people to innovate just a bit."

Although this member said that he could not remember the tune that was used for *Lekhah dodi* at Beth El, other members said that the Lewandowski tune was commonly sung at that shul (CD #7, without instrumental accompaniment). The contrast between these two tunes is considerable. The Lewandowski tune is in three-quarter time and is sung slowly. Its lilting melody ascends and descends in intervallic steps. The tune CD #15 moves at a quicker tempo, propelled by intervallic jumps, syncopated rhythm, and lines of descending eighth notes. The worshippers' associations with the tunes are also very different. The Lewandowski tune has strong Old World connotations and was very popular in America in the 1940s and 1950s. The generation of the 1960s sees it as part of their parents' repertoire. On the other hand, Shaarei Tefillah tune CD #15 is seen as an Israeli tune, often learned on a first trip abroad during the period following the Six Day War in 1967.[38] Members described that period in Israel as heady and exciting. During those years, many young Jews from all denominations studied, traveled, and volunteered in Israel, engaging in their first independent explorations of their Jewish cultural, political, and religious identities.

"THAT TUNE WAS THE WAY TO START SHABBOS" As another member related, "My strongest recollection [of CD #15] is in *Yerushalayim* [Jerusalem]

. . . probably after college that summer . . . going to Hillel in *Beit Hastudent* (the Student Center [and dormitory]) and that [tune] was *it*. There were 300 or 400 people, it seemed like a thousand people in that room, . . . and the place rocked and [singing that tune of *Lekhah dodi*] was the way to start Shabbos. That was the *on* button."

As a former rabbinic student in Jerusalem, I also remember attending Kabbalat Shabbat at Beit Hastudent in 1973. In fact, I lived there for several weeks while I was looking for an apartment in Jerusalem. I carry vivid memories of that crowded room, packed with knowledgeable, traditional young Jews from all over the world, joyously and enthusiastically welcoming the Sabbath. Much of our social and religious life was organized around music. We would prowl the alleys of the Yemenite, Hasidic, and Syrian sections of town, looking for the shul with the best *Lekhah dodi*. I remember gathering in student apartments for potluck dinners, packing tape recorders and bottles of cheap Israeli brandy for "zemir-ins" (after "sing-ins," from the Hebrew *zemirot* [Sabbath table songs]). A few years before, we had organized and participated in sit-ins, as we occupied campus buildings during the late 1960s; now we came together with a different purpose. Wanting to learn more about our history and traditions, we met to trade and record as many melodies as we could collectively assemble. The tunes that I and many other American Jews learned at that time still make up the staple of our favorite liturgical repertoires.

WHAT MAKES A "GOOD" TUNE FOR LEKHAH DODI Shaarei Tefillah's initial choice of tune CD #15 was purposeful; there were other popular Israeli tunes, but they did not fill the congregation's needs as well. One member criticized the tune used in many other congregations, including Tufts Hillel (CD #13) and explained why it was not a "good tune" for this hymn. He said, "The problem with that [tune] is the chorus. It's kind of redundant, and it requires a certain range of voice too, that everybody doesn't have. I think it's a more difficult one to sing." In addition to being more difficult to sing, this member noted another problem with this tune. It keeps repeating phrases of the hymn. He explained that he learned from his cantor that one should not repeat words when praying.[39] He continued, "I've come to . . . feel it in my gut that it just feels better to do stuff that keeps you going. It's like you're traveling . . . a train isn't a bad analogy. You don't go and then come back and then go and come back. You're kind of on your way emotionally and spiritually. Trying to get to a place. . . ." For this worshipper, tune CD #15 fulfilled those requirements and kept the service moving, both "spiritually and emotionally."

His cantor was also citing a specific halakhic restriction; music should not obscure the meaning of the text of the prayers. There is a danger of doing so if certain words and phrases are repeated. Yet this member added a personal interpretation to this prohibition. He felt that the energy and momentum of the davening should be maintained by every means possible. Furthermore, he valued enthusiastic communal participation, as he had experienced in Jerusalem, and was concerned that if a tune was too musically complex, it would limit involvement.

There were additional, practical reasons why some members of this congregation did not like other tunes. A number of people criticized the Lewandowski *Lekhah dodi*, and the gabbai reported that tune was used very infrequently. When asked why, he replied, "I think that's because it takes too long . . . people are rushed to get Shabbos in—maybe they're more rushed to finish davening [and] go home. . . ." He added, "It's not just that people don't like [that melody]—it's that it's too slow." For many members of Shaarei Tefillah, davening was not seen as an "experience." While prayer was a serious obligation, it was not necessary to linger over the service. A graduate student commented that he liked tune CD #15 for several reasons, speed being one of them. He said, "I would say everyone knows it. It's pretty quick. I like to daven fast, I *layn* (chant Torah) quickly. Like when I layn, I daven quickly but I do it clearly. I make sure everyone can hear it but I like to do things fast."

Shaarei Tefillah exhibited a limited range of tunes for *Lekhah dodi*. In fact, tune choice in general was limited. Members trace this tendency back to the founding of the congregation. One member recalled an incident at a Shabbat morning service in which the congregation's old guard rigidly enforced their conception of proper musical tradition. This member explained that when the congregation was formed, some worshippers attempted to introduce a greater variety of tunes in the service. He related, "People would get up and sing the Kedushah, instead of doing Shabbat nusach, would sing a different [Israeli] pop tune to each section . . . like *Erev shel shoshanim* [Night of roses], that type of song which is actually done in many [modern Orthodox] Young Israels [synagogues]. It wasn't an innovation to hear, but this particular fellow—I no longer remember exactly what tunes they were—but he [sang some of] . . . the pop tunes of the time. This did not sit well with [a prominent professor of Judaica who was among the founding members of that congregation] because [he viewed these as] . . . 'frivolous, little *tunelach*' [Yiddish diminutive of 'tunes']. This was not what you were supposed to do! . . . [The professor] went over to him afterwards and said, 'I thought the tunes you sang, or the way you sang them to the Kedushah, were inappropriate,' or something quite uncompromising . . . so, it's kind of tough to take that from a man of his stature, but that's what he used to do. Now, nobody else would have the nerve to say that." This story was repeated by several members. They explained that this legacy of enforcement, coupled with the members' tendency to simplify the davening and shy away from performance, had restricted both the choice of tunes and the level of congregational singing at Shaarei Tefillah.

One knowledgeable worshipper contextualized the very use of any tunes in the service and explained their origin. He said, "That style of congregational participation . . . in America goes back at least to the Young Israel movement, which goes back to the early part of the century. . . . It's hard to believe now, [but this was] innovative, introducing English into the sermons, which was at the time unheard of, and singing certain tunes, which in Europe would have been considered ridiculous and frivolous and not traditional. . . ."[40] He stressed that over time, the use of these tunes was ritualized and they became standard features in the liturgy. He continued, "But of course these 'new tunes' were new about seventy years ago and are now quite traditional in their own right."

Many people now find it difficult to imagine such strong opposition to congregational singing, especially when the liturgy is set to a noncontroversial Israeli tune. It is instructive to consider a story told by the cantor and musicologist Macy Nulman when he was engaged as cantor in a large synagogue in Brooklyn. He attempted to introduce some congregational singing into the service and was summoned to a board meeting. The chairman of the board exclaimed, "We pay you a salary and you ask us to help you in singing!" (Nulman 1985:92). Nulman relates that many considered the participatory style of "Young Israel nusach" to be equivalent to a church (ibid.). At least, for some in that generation, congregational singing felt Christian, a dangerous move toward assimilation and away from proper, traditional nusach.

Even in this breakaway shul, the tendency to preserve ritual was stronger than the tendency to innovate. The member who described how tune CD #15 was chosen as an "anthem of identity" commented, "It will come as no surprise . . . that this 'radical innovation' rapidly became institutionalized. . . . This tune is sung, at present, 95 percent of the time. . . . Almost everybody sings it almost as though they have to, even though nobody said they have to. . . . Now occasionally . . . people do sometimes add other tunes, but it's remarkably uniform, to a greater extent than it is at other congregations."

NARROW PARAMETERS FOR CHOICE At Shaarei Tefillah the possibility for tune choice does exist, but parameters are more limited than in the other congregations examined in this study. These Jews live within stricter boundaries and, as is discussed in chapter 3, consciously decide to limit choices in many aspects of their social, communal, and religious lives. In accepting the mitzvot, the commandments of the Torah as interpreted by modern Orthodox tradition, they affirm the importance of close attention to detail in their religious observance. This attitude is also seen in the care they apply to the public performance of sacred text and to the musical choices they make during worship. A number of worshippers described how they treated the juncture of choice that occurs after the fifth stanza of *Lekhah dodi*. One member explained:

There's a kind of traditional break between the first five stanzas of *Lekhah dodi* and the last four. . . . If you listen very carefully, there is a minute extra pause of about three nanoseconds before *Lo tevoshi*, because everybody knows that that's when . . . if the hazzan's going to make a change [in tune], that's when he's going to do it. So everybody stops for a second, even though they know the tune has been going along, to see whether he's going to change or not. Now in our synagogue very few people do, but every now and then somebody does. But people's experiences at other synagogues have led them to expect that this may be the point, so you don't want to embarrass yourself by plunging into a new tune only to have the hazzan trump you with a new tune that he's entitled to change to . . . but that's the only change you're entitled to make, if you're going to make any. If you do *Lo tevoshi* to the same tune as the first five, that means you're going through to the end. So again, the degree of freedom is significantly stylized and limited.

Many members discussed this juncture of choice in *Lekhah dodi*. The graduate student noted, "I know a lot of people go up to *Hitoreri, hitoreri* [the fifth verse] and they finish that and then they change the tune and go through the last four stanzas with a different tune." Later in this chapter the Bostoner Rebbe discusses his theological and textual imperatives for a melodic switch at the sixth verse of *Lekhah dodi*, a fact that was not recognized or acknowledged by any of the members I interviewed in other congregations. In fact, another member of Shaarei Tefillah stressed that he did not like to change tunes in the middle: "I like continuing on. I don't like the transition. It's like, Shabbos is moving along, you're into *Lekhah dodi*, and I like the original tune, and then suddenly you go to this [different tune]. . . . It just has the word 'Lo' ['no' or 'don't'] too much. Then it seems by the next paragraph . . . it's switched back." This member was unclear of the reason for the switch, but he believed that it was purposeful and he mentioned the name of a knowledgeable member of the synagogue who must know the reason. He assumed that the system is rational, that there are explanations for ritual acts, even if he is ignorant of them.

Members of Shaarei Tefillah discussed how *any* attempts at liturgical innovation were risky for the hazzan. One can count on the community response in a standard tune. When switching a tune or introducing a new one, a leader takes a risk that the congregation will not participate. The gabbai observed, "If people know [a new tune], they'll sing along immediately. If not, [the hazzan] . . . just slugs it out. You do the best you can." Another member believed that this difficulty was not unique to their congregation and observed, "It takes guts to introduce a new melody, knowingly, into the congregation—whether it's Orthodox, Conservative, Reform, or havurah, or whatever. At least, when you're at a summer camp you have the possibility of having a music class during the week where you get to teach everybody the new melody and then you sing it, but otherwise people resist a new melody all the time. If it's real catchy and if it's real simple, you can take a chance and go with it and it might work."

In general, worshippers agreed that there was not a great deal of experimentation with tunes at Shaarei Tefillah. The gabbai said that one of the few times different tunes were encouraged was on the Sabbaths before certain holidays. Then *Lekhah dodi* was sung to the signature melody of the holiday to foreshadow the approaching festival. The gabbai stressed that this was a "specialized skill," and one of the gabbai's jobs was to "set up" the leader, reminding him to use that particular tune. He said, "Like around Hanukah time [when *Lekhah dodi* is often sung to *Maoz tsur* (Fortress Rock), a popular hymn sung on Hanukah] . . . you have to set up the hazzan. [That's] . . . the only time that people really sort of experiment with a couple of different tunes [for] *Lekhah dodi.*"

"SPIRITUALITY? IT DOESN'T SOUND LIKE ANYTHING WE DO" As was described earlier, at the havurah B'nai Or, members chose particular tunes to facilitate religious experience in prayer; worshippers expressed preference for tunes that could "take them out there," that offered the possibility of transcending ordinary experience. At Shaarei Tefillah these ritually observant Jews understood the role of music in prayer very differently. For example, both groups sang niggunim during Kabbalat Shabbat. At B'nai Or these wordless tunes were often sung for long periods of time. Worshippers said they would "lose themselves" and feel as one with their community and with God as a niggun would build in volume and intensity. Members of B'nai Or sing niggunim much the way that Hasidim do. During the extended periods of singing, some members hope to achieve a state of *devekus* (the desire to cleave to and become one with God, Ashkenazi pronunciation), something to which a Hasid might aspire in music and dance.

However, when I asked about the use of the niggun sung after *Yedid nefesh* at Shaarei Tefillah, one worshipper stressed that even though it was a niggun, it did not necessarily carry the Hasidic associations of a niggun for that congregation (CD #14). This member contrasted the joyous revelry of the Hasidim to the more controlled singing at Shaarei Tefillah and observed, "But what's happened in modern Orthodox settings, which is primarily a *misnagdic* [anti-Hasidic; Ashkenazi pronunciation][41] type of setting, is that the tunes are there but they're really not free and open. They've just become rituals of their own." He continued, "For a misnagdic crowd, it's about as free as it gets. We come from a tradition . . . of emotional restraint, and people from our part of the world just don't let it all hang out. The congregational singing is a socially sanctioned way for letting *some of it* hang out." While this response does not represent everyone in this congregation, one can generalize and say that there are Jews who want to know about God and there are Jews who want to know what God wants them to do. I met many more of the latter at Shaarei Tefillah.

That is not to say that music does not play an important part in congregational life or add joyous celebration to certain religious occasions at Shaarei Tefillah. There are evenings regularly when members come together to sing Jewish songs. However, when worshippers discussed the use of music in prayer, spiritual elevation was not their stated goal. This member continued, "There are times—I think for me . . . they come more at weddings, bar mitzvahs—you're dancing around. It's an emotional occasion to begin with, or at least parts of it are, where the song clearly adds to it. Most singing is rather stodgy and routine, and it's different at certain sections, particularly solemn sections of the High Holiday davening. But again, it's the song adding to an already emotionally charged occasion. It isn't common, in fact it's almost nonexistent in my experience, for a song in an ordinary routine context to elevate the situation beyond the routine." Phrases like "religious experience" or "transcendent music" were not part of the vocabulary of this synagogue. This member continued:

> Spirituality does not compute in Orthodoxy. That is to say that the term "spirituality" simply doesn't come up. It has a *goyish* [non-Jewish] ring to it. That sounds rather bizarre to say, but I think it's true. That doesn't mean that Judaism has no spirituality, but if you're not used to thinking in that category, you have to ask yourself—what does that mean? . . . [You] go through the motions and you know what you're supposed to do, but you never really think about how it touches your soul. I have to preface my remarks by saying that spirituality sounds Reform or maybe Protestant or something. But it doesn't sound like anything we do.

"A PERSNICKETY INSISTENCE ON ACCURACY" A number of members offered explanations for the relative dearth of communal singing in this modern Orthodox service. One member of Shaarei Tefillah concluded that it simply was not necessary: people already knew how to pray.

> Now, I think one of the reasons you don't find as much group singing in an Orthodox service as you do in a Conservative and Reform is that in Conservative and Reform large congregations—I'm not talking about havurot or camp or seminaries—by and large, the people don't know how to read Hebrew, people are not familiar with the service, and they don't know how to daven, and so the natural solution is to make up songs.

This was echoed by another member who had grown up in a Conservative synagogue and since become more traditional. He said that the introduction of additional tunes into the service would be "a distraction." He explained, "[If you're going to New York] . . . the train is on the track and if we have to stop by Stamford, Connecticut, along the way, it kind of slows things down. You don't get to Grand Central . . . in the same heat of arrival as you would otherwise." For this knowledgeable worshipper, too many tunes were unnecessary. Davening supplied the rhythm and energy necessary for prayer, an experience that is both personal and communal, fixed and creative.

While "spirituality" is not stressed, there are other values that are held as extremely important in this community. One member of Shaarei Tefillah discussed the value put on the correct performance of sacred text, in this case in regard to chanting the Torah.

Our community places an unusually high premium, for even an Orthodox shul, on accuracy in Torah reading. And the standards are very rigid or very high, depending on your point of view. People are expected to be expert, whether they're kids—at whatever level—to get the words all right, to get the notes pretty much all right, and to be very, very careful. . . . Apparently, in many parts of Europe, people didn't care about trop [signs for biblical cantillation], that wasn't something you paid any attention to. . . . So the trop is really a resurgence in America. It's traditional, but it's neo-traditional because there were parts of Europe where it was simply not paid attention to. So . . . we teach our kids trop and we want them to layn well. . . . it's clear to me that to some extent it's an American innovation. Although it may seem like tradition going back to Sinai, in fact it's not. It's a self-conscious kind of recapturing of something. There's always been trop, but never has it been paid so much attention to. We have . . . a persnickety insistence on accuracy.[42]

Accuracy is an important value for this community. In certain venues congregants disregard this community value at their peril. This member continued, "If somebody gets up there [and makes mistakes while chanting the Torah] . . . it's like open season—they smell blood in the water—and everybody goes after him." In chanting Torah, music provides the framework for a careful, well-prepared, serious performance of sacred text. Attention to detail is essential to an authentic presentation of the tradition. So too, in all aspects of their lives, these Orthodox Jews pay attention to details—in the labels of the food they buy, in the clothes they wear, in the social and communal obligations that bring them together for prayer and religious celebration.

At Shaarei Tefillah these modern Orthodox Jews are committed to preserving the Jewish tradition according to their best understanding of its proper interpretation. "Losing yourself through music" holds little appeal for this group. In their own terminology, these Jews already "know how to daven." They read Hebrew easily, and many speak it competently, if not fluently. While tunes are important in Shaarei Tefillah's service, their use is limited. Too much singing is seen as frivolous and unnecessary. Members look to other criteria to define serious participation in worship. They value a natural, understated approach to the performance of nusach and a knowledgeable, accurate performance of sacred and liturgical text.

Congregation Beth Pinchas (The Bostoner Rebbe's)

On Shabbat the Hasidim who attend Beth Pinchas dress in their finery. Many men wear *shtreimels* and *kapotahs*, the fur-trimmed hats and long black frock coats once worn by the Polish gentry, adopted by the Hasidim as a symbolic statement of their dignity and importance in the eyes of God. Men rush into services, their long beards and *payot* (corkscrew side curls) wet from the *mikvah*, the ritual bath visited by many Hasidim for immersion and purification before Shabbat. About forty men gather for the later minyan. The New England Chassidic Center holds two *minyanim* (pl.) for Kabbalat Shabbat. The early minyan finishes in time for worshippers to arrive home for an earlier dinner. While some Bostoner Hasidim attend this service, the majority attend the later service, which begins at sundown. This is the "Rebbe's service," and he attends whenever he is not with his extended community in Israel or Switzerland. Not all of the worshippers at this minyan are Hasidic: there are a number of modern Orthodox men, clean-shaven, who wear dark suits and fedoras. Their *tsitsit* (ritual fringes) are wrapped around their belts, not as exposed and obvious as the free-hanging fringes showing from under the shirts of the Hasidim. A number of college students, as well as some Israelis who live in Boston, also daven "at the Rebbe's." The Chassidic Center runs several outreach projects; visitors are both common and welcome at Beth Pinchas (The House of Pinchas), named in honor of the first Bostoner Rebbe, Grand Rabbi Pinchas Dovid Horowitz, the father of the current Rebbe, Grand Rabbi Levi Yitzchak Horowitz.[43]

The shul is filling up as I arrive for Kabbalat Shabbat. Men drift into the sanctuary. A few women sit behind the mehitsah; it is almost impossible to see them behind the high partition tucked at the far end of the room. Men and women are always separated in this shul, for prayer, dancing, and eating. However, as in all Orthodox congregations, it is permissible for younger daughters to remain with their fathers during prayer, and mixed groups of three or four children surround several of the young fathers. An older Hasid with an impressive white beard stands alone and davens Minchah. He prays quietly but his nusach is strong and distinct, tuneful and melodic. A young man to my right finishes davening Minchah, gathers his children around him, and chants *Shir Hashirim* (The Song of Songs). This short book, allegorically interpreted to portray the love between God and Israel, is chanted by many traditional Jewish communities before Kabbalat Shabbat. Among Yemenite, Moroccan, and Syrian Jews the entire book is chanted in unison by the congregation before every Shabbat (cf. Summit 1979). At Beth Pinchas the community does not chant Shir Hashirim together; rather, some individuals read it as a preparation for the Sabbath evening service. Some members study Talmud or review the week's Torah reading to themselves, rocking over the large books cradled in their laps. Many men chat with their neighbors. Soon about fifty men are there, making up the congregation for evening prayers.

A man in his 30s sitting in front of me turns around to welcome me and check me out. "Good Shabbos! Welcome! Are you visiting Boston? Is this your first time at the Rebbe's?" It is common for visitors to undergo a friendly examination in most traditional synagogues. *Hakhnasat orhim* (welcoming guests) is an important mitzvah. If I happened to have nowhere to eat Shabbat dinner, or to spend the entire Sabbath for that matter, I would most likely be invited to eat or stay with a family. I explain that I live locally and that I am there both because I am interested in the music and because when I was in college I occasionally davened here. The man

Figure 2.9. The Bostoner Rebbe, Grand Rabbi Levi Yitzchak Horowitz. Photo: Micki Keno.

introduces himself and tells me that he is not really a Hasid, but Rav Horowitz is his rebbe (spiritual guide and teacher). This has been his regular shul for the past ten years. He encourages me to participate in the study sessions and says that it is really too bad that the Rebbe and his son are away that week.

At that point a young man acting as gabbai walks around to "finger"

Figure 2.10. The sanctuary at Beth Pinchas. Photo: Richard Sobol.

someone to lead davening. When one member turns him down, he offers some friendly admonishment, telling the shirker that he should "Take it like a man!" The gabbai asks another young man, who accepts the honor. I happen to know this man's family; he is related to our veterinarian, who davens at Shaarei Tefillah. This leader is self-assured and has a good voice. His nusach is very similar to my own. He chooses a complex tune for *Lekhah dodi*, one that is actually three or four different tunes strung together. While the community participates in the tune and a few people clap along during the last verses, the singing is not as spirited as it was the following week when the Rebbe returned from Israel and joined his Hasidim in prayer.

I returned for services the following week and found that while the Rebbe did not lead services, he did start the tune for *Lekhah dodi*. As he explained to me later, choosing the tune for this hymn is a special prerogative that he reserves for himself. When he is away, the honor falls to his son, Rav Naftali. The Rebbe said, "[Among Hasidim in general,] it's not the minhag of the Rebbe to start *Lekhah dodi*. [But] . . . if you leave it to the congregants, they are going to come up with some tune, some melody that no one knows, and it's going to kill the service. So in order to avoid that, I've put down a rule, that was fifty years ago, that *I'm* going to do *Lekhah dodi* and what happens is . . . , I make *my* decision." In this way he could ensure the quality of the tunes for this essential part of the service, which he saw as influencing the entire Friday evening experience. Both the Rebbe and his sons think carefully about how to maximize involvement in worship. Rav Mayer said, "There are groups that change their niggunim all the time. We prefer that the whole congregation join in, so we don't change the songs too frequently, so everyone will get to know them. So every once in a while, we'll add a new one as it finds favor in the eyes of the Rebbe."

This week the singing was spirited, worshippers swaying and clapping as they sang. The Rebbe led a rather complex tune, which was actually a compilation of several tunes separated by various niggunim. The davening seemed stronger in the Rebbe's presence. It felt as if people were concentrating harder on their prayers. At the end of services an older man hit the *amud* (reader's stand) and announced, "*Shaharit* [morning services] at 8:45!" Worshippers crowded around the Rebbe to welcome him back, exchange a few words, and wish him good Shabbos. While I spoke to many people in the community about music and prayer, I will concentrate here on the comments of the Rebbe as well as some observations by his sons, Rav Naftali and Rav Mayer.

HISTORY AND BACKGROUND Although the American Hasidim are a part of Orthodox Jewry, in many ways they function as a separate group of Jews in America. The term "Hasidism" is derived from the Hebrew word *hesed*. From biblical times the term connoted both piety and saintliness.[44] In modern times it generally suggests followers of Rabbi Israel ben Eliezer (d. 1760), known as the *Baal Shem Tov* (Master of the Good Name [of God]) and referred to with the acronym *Besht*. He stressed that common Jews could approach and serve God through love and joy. In addition, Hasidism emphasized the importance of sincere and intense prayer, in which one strove to bind oneself to God (*devekus*) and achieve a state of spiritual ecstasy (*hislahavus*). Singing and dancing were important aids to prayer and religious experience.

Reb Hillel of Parichi, Byelorussia, is reputed to have said, "Whoever has no sense for music has no sense for Hasidism" (Nulman 1975:96). Music plays a central role in Hasidic life. As a movement, Hasidism developed in seventeenth-century Poland after the bloody persecutions of the Chmielnicki massacres and the false messianic promises of Shabbetai Zevi (1626–1676) and Jacob Frank (1726–1791).[45] Persecuted by the non-Jewish population, dismayed by promises of unfulfilled redemption, and disenfranchised from the wealthy rabbinic leadership of Poland, the Jews of Poland and Eastern Europe flocked to this populist, revivalist movement. Hasidic worship developed as a reaction to the stress on elite scholasticism in Eastern European Jewish culture; the opportunity for full-time Talmud study was the privilege of the rich and well married. Although today Hasidim take Talmud study and the role of Jewish law very seriously, at the movement's inception the Hasidim taught that there were several ways to approach God, and music and dance provided even the poorest, uneducated Jew a way to praise and rejoice with the Holy One.

During the nineteenth and early twentieth centuries Hasidism spread rapidly throughout Eastern Europe and Russia, dominating Jewish life in many places. The movement was initially carried to America with the massive Jewish immigration of the late nineteenth and early twentieth centuries, together with the political turmoil of World War I. Then World War II and the catastrophic destruction of the Holocaust scattered and annihilated Europe's Hasidic dynasties and brought surviving Hasidim to settle in the New World. The first Hasidim in America established shtiblakh, small synagogues, in the New York area, specifically in the Williamsburg section of Brooklyn. Grand Rabbi Pinchas Dovid Horowitz arrived from Eastern Europe to the West End of Boston in 1915 and proceeded to create what is, according to the Bostoner Hasidim, the first American Hasidic dynasty (Axelrod, n.d.). A descendant of a series of renowned Hasidic masters, going back to the Baal Shem Tov, Rabbi Horowitz chose an American designation, called himself simply "the Bostoner," and established the New England Chassidic Center in 1916. After conditions deteriorated and anti-Semitism increased in the West End, the first Bostoner Rebbe moved to New York, settling in Williamsburg in the late 1930s. Following the Hasidic practice of dynastic succession, after the Rebbe's death in 1941 his eldest son, Rabbi Moshe, assumed leadership of the Bostoner Hasidim in New York. The Rebbe's younger son, Rabbi Levi Yitzchak Horowitz, returned to Boston to serve as the community's Rebbe in its new location in Dorchester. The Chassidic Center eventually moved from Dorchester to Brookline, its location since 1960. The Center runs projects providing temporary housing, social services, and psychological support for Jews in need, especially in the area of health care. They also run programs that bring college students to celebrate the Sabbath together with Hasidic families and the Rebbe.

From the 1960s onward, Hasidic and neo-Hasidic music influenced synagogue and youth music in all the major branches of American Judaism as well as in Israel. Hasidic music had special influence in the havurah movement of the late 1960s and early 1970s.[46] Neo-Hasidism, as introduced in the work of Martin Buber and Abraham Joshua Heschel, and later writers on spirituality such as Zalman Schachter-Shalomi, Lawrence Kushner, Arthur Green, and Arthur Waskow, together with the music of Shlomo Carlebach, influenced all of American Judaism's mainstream movements in the past thirty years in their institutional attempts to find relevance and meaning in Jewish worship and ritual.[47]

In an informational pamphlet written for the Chassidic Center in the mid-1980s, Rav Naftali Horowitz, the Bostoner Rebbe's son, writes, "Chassidic faith is based on experiencing your religion . . . the ritual and the ceremonies, the song and the dance and the joy—that is part of the Chassidic philosophy." Both visitors and Hasidim experience this exuberant rejoicing at the Rebbe's *tish* (table), for the Sabbath meal on Friday evening following services and for *seudah shelishit* (the third meal) ushering in the conclusion of the Sabbath. These community events are held on special occasions in the Chassidic Center. Here, as in services, men and women are seated separately, a practice the Rebbe does not suggest that families follow in their home for Shabbos dinners. Over chicken, kugel (noodle pudding), tsimmes (sweet carrots), wine, and schnapps (whiskey), participants listen to the Rebbe teach Torah and sing zemirot and niggunim. The niggunim are introduced by the Rebbe or his sons and often can go on for fifteen or twenty minutes, accompanied by spirited dancing around the tables in the crowded room. The Rebbe's presence is also felt in the Kabbalat Shabbat service. While he sometimes leads the davening, more often a congregational member is asked to be shaliach tsibbur. While the leader chants the majority of the service to Kabbalat Shabbat nusach, *Lekhah dodi* is a musical focal point of this service. Various niggunim are interspersed between the verses of text. The congregation is familiar with four or five melodies for this hymn.

I remember as a college student attending the Rebbe's and being swept up by the crowded intensity of their singing, dancing, and Torah study, so different from the ordered decorum of my Reform temple in Connecticut. When I was in college, the only other place where I experienced such religious intensity and individual participation in Jewish worship was on my occasional visits to Havurat Shalom in Somerville in 1970. In fact, the havurah B'nai Or and the Bostoner Rebbe's shul share a unique relationship. On one hand, these two communities represent opposing extremes in regard to participation of women in religious life, a commitment to the unchanging nature of Jewish law, and the willingness of their members to integrate with the American superculture. On the other hand, both communities stress the importance of music and dance in achieving a spiritual union with God. Indeed, it is only on these "edges" of the Jewish community that one hears God discussed much at all.[48]

"MUSIC BRINGS OVER AND CLEAR ACROSS TO THE SOUL, THE FEELING OF THE MOMENT" Rav Naftali discussed how music conveys the emotions that are at the core of Jewish prayer. He said that music was able to express feelings such as joy, longing, awe, and sadness with immediacy and intensity:

> The role of music basically is to uplift the spirit. Sometimes the spirit asks to be uplifted, like when you have a melody to bring in the Kabbalas Shabbos, . . . you sing the *Lekhah dodi* when you greet the Sabbath, so it's more on a point of joy. Then you have certain situations where . . . the music will talk about the longing of the bringing of *Moshiach* (the Messiah). You have music where you talk about longing. . . . Sometimes you have a type of song that deals with awe . . . sometimes you have a prayer where the type of trop sing-song is of mourning, like on Tisha B'Av . . . so the music can get the words across, and your kavanah in tefillah, your intentions in prayer, is much stronger.

The Rebbe addressed the place of *Lekhah dodi* in the Kabbalat Shabbat service: "There's no question that *Lekhah dodi* is the center of the musical segments." He described the position and meaning of the hymn in the service, explaining that the journey through the week toward the Sabbath was one moving from exile to redemption, from this world to the postmessianic World to Come. Thus, arriving at the Sabbath is an occasion for joyous celebration, best expressed through music. As the Rebbe explained, it is "an occasion of song, it's an occasion of festivity." The Rebbe explicated the specific textual connections of the Kabbalat Shabbat liturgy to the rhythm of the week. He said, "Of course, the *Lekhah dodi* represents the Shabbos." He described a particular custom of the Bostoner Hasidim: "We introduce the *Mizmor leDavid* [Psalm 29, A Song of (King) David] [before *Lekhah dodi*] in the Bostoner nusach by quoting the Gemara [here, a specific teaching in the Talmud], *Bo'u venetse hasadeh likras kalah,* 'Come, let's go out [to the fields] and greet the kalah" [Babylonian Talmud, *Shabbat* 119a], [the bride] which is basically the *Lekhah dodi.*"[49]

In most cases, when teachers refer to the kabbalistic interpretation of the psalms preceding *Lekhah dodi* as corresponding to the six days of the week, the final psalm (29) is simply thought of as corresponding to Friday. The Rebbe explained that in fact this psalm is actually related to Friday evening. Therefore it should be sung in a manner that emphasizes the joyous and triumphant entrance of the Sabbath. He added, "And the Mizmor leDavid, which represents Friday, but the Friday which is the *erev Shabbos kodesh* [evening of the holy Sabbath], is said with much more fervor than the other prayers." In many non-Hasidic communities worshippers recognize this psalm's importance by standing for its recitation. However, the Rebbe pointed to a deeper, mystical meaning to be found in this psalm: "And there is, in it, you have the seven [references to] *kolot* [voices, pl. of *kol*]: " *kol asher bekoach, kol asher behadar, kol asher berazim*, all of these representing kabbalistically . . . the seven *middos*."[50] These *middot* (character traits) include such qualities as justice, mercy, majesty, and endurance, divine qualities that human beings should strive to develop and emulate.

In the early 1980s a group of the Rebbe's Hasidim moved to Israel and established a community in Har Nof, a new neighborhood of Jerusalem, under the leadership of the Rebbe's son, Rav Mayer. The Rebbe described a minhag followed by his Hasidim in Israel that emphasized these seven middot: "There are some communities, including ours [in Har Nof] . . . that for each one of the 'kolos' the shaliach tsibbur stops, or the people stop and they do it in unison with the shaliach tsibbur, *kol asher bekoach, kol asher be hadar*, everything is done in unison, almost like Kedushah. Again, in order to get into the mood, into the feeling." By musically emphasizing these sections of text, they experience the very act of welcoming and escorting in the Sabbath on both a personal and cosmic level. The journey of personal spiritual perfection mirrors the progress of the world as it moves from *hol*, the six profane days of the week, to *kodesh*, the holiness of the Sabbath, from *galut*, exile, to *geulah*, redemption. The davening at Beth Pinchas intensifies during Mizmor leDavid. Not only do worshippers stand but they sing louder, faster, and with more fervor. By the time they arrive at Mizmor leDavid, they are in unison. It feels as if the energy in the room is literally ratcheted up several notches as we approach *Lekhah dodi*.

In contrast to the other worship communities in this study, at Beth Pinchas *Lekhah dodi* was the only prayer that was sung to a metric tune in the Kabbalat Shabbat service. Rav Naftali explained that the main time for singing in the service was during *Lekhah dodi*, that "Everything else basically is nusach." Both the Rebbe and his sons understood this hymn to be composed of two distinct sections. The first section, comprising the first five stanzas, creates a sense of expectation. Rav Naftali explained, "[In] the first part, the type of music . . . is like a type of song where it's not real, real happy, but you . . . liven up to the point of greeting Shabbos. . . . In the secular world, [you have] 'Hail to the Chief.' [Just so] the first part [of *Lekhah dodi* is the] type of song where you're talking about anticipation." According to Rav Naftali, just as "Hail to the Chief" creates anticipation that an honored personage is about to enter, so too the first section of *Lekhah dodi* creates anticipation for the Sabbath Bride. In regard to the second section, beginning with the verse *Lo tevoshi*, he said, "It's basically a song of pure joy."

The Rebbe describes these two sections of *Lekhah dodi* in a somewhat different manner:

> The *Lekhu nerananah* [Come, let us rejoice, referring to the part of the service where singing is indicated] [introduces the] two sections [of]

. . . *Lekhah dodi,* which is the highlight of . . . the musical part. It has the first section, up to *Lo sevoshu,*[51] which is usually a more somber tune, and then *Lo sevoshi,* which talks to *klal Yisroel* [the community of Israel] after going through the previous parts of *Lekhu nerananah,* which discusses the galut in Yerushalayim [where] klal Yisroel [is] not in good shape [referring to the first five verses of *Lekhah dodi*]. Then comes the pep talk: *Lo sevoshu! Velo sikalmu!* Do not be ashamed! Do not be embarrassed! And then [the hymn goes on to describe] the great events that are going to take place.

The Rebbe does more than apply two separate tunes to these two sections of the hymn. He describes them as two separate songs. According to his explanation, this approach emphasizes the transition from somber anticipation to joy, key elements in welcoming the Sabbath.

HOW THE REBBE CHOOSES A TUNE FOR LEKHAH DODI For the most part, the Bostoner Hasidim adopt tunes from Hasidic dynasties famous for their music. The Rebbe said "[Most of our tunes come from] Modzhitz[52] and Ger.[53] [But there are] . . . some that goes back to our own stock of a hundred years ago in Jerusalem." Describing his process in choosing a tune, he says that often he tries to connect this central moment in the Kabbalat Shabbat service with important events that might have occurred during the week in his community. He first thinks in practical terms, considering events that have happened in the shul and with his congregants. For example, he said, "If there would be a *hasanah* [wedding, Ashkenazi pronunciation], . . . even among the somber melodies you would choose one that has more feeling of joy rather than being all serious."

As important as this concern was, there was an even greater issue. He wanted to facilitate his community's involvement in services and not bore them with stale tunes or repetitive melodies. He explained, "The main point, though, is that when I choose a tune, I choose a tune that I want people to know, that they'll be able to help, that they get involved in it. And we have, I would say, four, five tunes that we rotate, . . . somewhat depending on the moods, but in order not to have people feel monotonous in having the same tune, even though each one of them, they're all gems, they're all really special."

The Rebbe felt that for a tune to be successful, it has to have movement. He made fun of the Lewandowski tune and noted in amazement, "For the love of me, I can't understand, whenever I go to a shul outside of [our] shul and they start the 'national' *Lekhah dodi* [sings Lewandowski tune]. It's as dead as could be! . . . it [just] continues on! [sings, making fun of the tune] . . . Do something! Change! Nothing at all. People go through it and it's lifeless."[54] Being forced to sing a "lifeless" tune for *Lekhah dodi* diminishes the entire worship experience, in his opinion. He explained, "And of course, it sets the tone, it sets the mood. There's nothing to it, so you just go through the motions, some join, some don't join, but there's nothing to get you excited!" One of his Hasidim concurred with the Rebbe's assessment of the tune as being "dead" and even characterized it as "a funeral dirge." The Rebbe spoke personally, as he projected himself into the place of other worshippers who would be "subjected" to such a tune on a regular basis. He said, "I don't see how they can stand it! [tunes that stay the same throughout for the entire hymn]. *Lo sevoshi* is not as bad because it's only four stanzas, but with *Lekhah dodi*, where there's six [including the chorus], it just becomes monotonous, when you do the same, no matter how nice the tune is. It's nice for one, two. . . ."

I asked the Rebbe if I could record one of his melodies of *Lekhah dodi*, a tune that was a regular staple of the congregation. We met in his study and he recorded his rendition of CD #16 and #19 for *Lo tevoshi*. When I asked if I might include this recording on the compact disc for this book, he expressed his support for the project but preferred that I not include his recording. He explained that it was simply not something that a Rebbe did. He said that his son, Rav Mayer, was known as a singer and composer and suggested that his son might record this and some other Bostoner tunes. Rav Mayer agreed and recorded two versions of *Lekhah dodi* (CD #16, #18) and two versions of *Lo tevoshi* (CD #17, #19).

Regarding the tune of the first section of *Lekhah dodi* (CD #16), the Rebbe explained that in general, tunes are not composed specifically for *Lekhah dodi*. Therefore, unlike the other tunes examined earlier, these Hasidic tunes do not have verse and chorus with a repeating chorus for the refrain. He said:

We've been doing, off and on, a Modzhitz melody [for] thirty-five years but as I say, we switch, we alternate, and it's a melody that's not the usual one in . . . the Hasidic way of Hasidic melodies. The Hasidic melodies that you do for *Lekhah dodi*, you *take* the melody, it's not *made* for *Lekhah dodi*. There's no melody that's really made for *Lekhah dodi*. You use the melody if it would be fitting to *Lekhah dodi*. And therefore, when it comes to repeating the *Lekhah dodi* at the end of the verse, at the end of the stanza, you just continue with the tune, there's nothing special about the *Lekhah dodi* in its repetition.

He continued, "This tune that we do [has] a refrain . . . where the *Lekhah dodi* is repeated, which is unusual. Even when I do all the other tunes for *Lekhah dodi*, [they] do not have that refrain for *Lekhah dodi*. You sing, but you sing the end part of whatever the tune is." When Rav Mayer recorded this melody, he said that even though it was a Modzhitz tune, it was now regularly sung at Beth Pinchas: "We are the ones that have been singing it as an accepted niggun within Boston Hasidus [Hasidism]."

The Rebbe described the melodic pattern of the verses in this way: "The first verse is by itself, that's the refrain. The first and the second are the same, the second is a repeat of the first. . . . Then you have *Likras Shabbos* is the second, *Mikdash* and *Hisnaari* is the third, and *Hisoreri* goes back to the second; and for *Lo sevoshi*, we change again." I see the structure of the tune in a somewhat different way, with the chorus and the first verse standing alone. The second and fifth verses are basically the same, as are the third and fourth verses. The tune is in G major throughout.[55] Rav Mayer pointed out deeper significance in the tune's structure: "It's actually made up of four sections, and many people have told me that it's parallel to the name of God, which has in it four letters. If you'll notice, the first, second, and third are different but the fourth one repeats the second, which is just like [the four Hebrew letters that make up God's name]." Here Rav Mayer teaches that when we examine this music closely, we see God's presence revealed in the very structure of the tune. The Rebbe understands that the purpose of the tune is to help convey the meaning of the hymn. In describing verses in which God entreats Israel to strive toward redemption, he stresses the connection between the music and text: "It [the tune] really represents the words. It's very important there. You switch over and you're talking to Yerushalayim. [Sings in a plaintive, requesting manner:] *Kumi, Tse'i,* Come get up and go out! *Metokh hahafekha,* from the darkness . . . [literally, 'from among the upheaval']. Basically, it represents the words."[56]

The Rebbe described the tune that he chose for the second part of *Lekhah dodi, Lo tevoshi.* In this tune, the sixth and eighth verses stand alone while the seventh and the ninth verses are basically the same melody. In this tune, or more accurately, compilation of tunes, each chorus of *Lekhah dodi* is unique with the exception of the last chorus, which is a repeat of the ninth verse. The Rebbe explained how he borrowed and adapted the melody from the wedding blessings: "That's Ger" [i.e., a melody of the Ger Hasidim]. It's taken off, I switched it from the original which is for the *Sheva Brakhos* [the seven blessings following a wedding], [sung to the text] *Asher boro* [(God), who has created], I believe, and we switched it to *Lo sevoshu* and that's been our tradition for a long time." He explained that at this point in the hymn, the aspect of joy is so pronounced that "By *Lo sevoshu,* there's some Hasidic situations where they actually do a *rikkud* [dance], they dance at *Lo sevoshu.*" He went on to explain, "Vizhnits[57] does the dance. By us, it's maybe each one in his place getting some sort of action. In Israel we do a dance Friday night at the completion of the service. The whole shul joins, which is an extension on the prayer, but again trying to get a mood of festivity, song being part of it."

When Rav Mayer recorded the Modzhitz tune for *Lekhah dodi,* he paired it with a different tune for *Lo tevoshi* (CD #17), which he said was a "march" of the Gerer Hasidim. This choice of tune underscored the Rebbe's comments that *Lekhah dodi* is composed of two separate sections and one may mix and match tunes. In fact, in the second rendition of *Lekhah dodi,* Rav Mayer used the Sheva Brokhos tune for *Lo tevoshi* that the Rebbe had matched to the Modzhitz tune. Still, Rav Mayer preserved the same approach to *Lekhah dodi* that the Rebbe discussed. He follows the Rebbe's view that because the first section refers to the destruction of the Temple and the Jewish people's desolate past, tunes for that section should be "more somber" and "slower." The second section, which points toward Israel's future messianic deliverance, is more joyous and "lively."

Rav Mayer described the first section of the second tune he recorded as "a real Bostoner niggun" (CD #18). This tune was composed by Rav Moshe Horowitz, the Rebbe's older brother. Rav Mayer explained that his uncle had composed this tune when he "came back to Israel for the first time since he left it with my grandfather in the thirties, . . . that was in 1963–64."

Rav Mayer described how special he believed this tune to be: the music for each verse was written to maximize the emotional impact of the text. He saw the tune beginning with a waltz-like invitation, "Come O Bride," and then moving from the somber and serious toward enthusiastic, joyous rejoicing. He said that it was difficult for "people coming from the outside to appreciate [that] . . . the song changes tempo and feeling according to the interpretation of each stanza, so the first time you hear it, it's nice but you don't appreciate it as much until afterwards you begin to see the relationship [between the text and the music]."

The Rebbe's philosophy, as well as his singing, have great influence in his community. One of the Rebbe's Hasidim (in the sense of "followers") related a well-known Hasidic story in which a rebbe hears a gentile shepherd boy singing a tune. The rebbe likes the tune and asks the boy if he is willing to sell it to the rebbe. The boy thinks, "Foolish Jew! How is it possible to sell a tune?!" But he readily agrees to the transaction. After the rebbe pays the boy for the tune, he touches the boy's head and the boy forgets the tune forever. The rebbe then "frees the hidden sparks of holiness" in the tune and transforms it into a deeply spiritual expression.[58] The Hasid who told me this story likened the rebbe in the story to the Bostoner Rebbe and stressed, "When a *tsaddik* [a righteous person] takes even a normal melody and deals with it, it adds *kedushah* [holiness]!"

Idelsohn quotes Reb Nahman of Bratslav,[59] who asserts that the tsaddik, the righteous Hasidic leader, is able to gain access to "the heavenly spring of music." He can use it "as a tool to purify the fallen soul, heal the sick, and perform all sorts of miracles" (1929:414).[60] On one level, the Bostoner Rebbe wants only to work minor miracles in his choice of tunes for *Lekhah dodi*. Not unlike leaders and members of the other worship communities examined, he stresses the importance of participation in prayer. He chooses tunes that "move," that will hold the worshippers' interest, that will not be "boring." He wants to celebrate and recognize the rhythms of community life and mark the weeks in which those celebrations occur with meaningful and appropriate tunes. Through his choice of tune, he wants to convey the experience of Shabbat joy, teaching the proper manner in which to welcome and bring in this most special of days. On a higher level, his goals are considerably greater. Every week the text of the Kabbalat Shabbat service in general, and *Lekhah dodi* in microcosm, tell and retell the story of the Jewish people. The liturgy points the way toward the glorious Shabbat when Israel will finally be redeemed. The hymn admonishes the people: "Be stirred, rise up, throw off the dust. . . . Arouse yourself . . . awake, pour forth your song!" (Rosenberg translation). With the proper tune and kavanah, singing this hymn becomes an act of *yihud*, bringing unity to the world and hastening the coming of the Messiah. Through the power of the tune of *Lekhah dodi* coupled with the Kabbalat Shabbat nusach, the Rebbe projects his followers into the historical and spiritual drama of the Jewish people, moving from darkness to light, from exile to redemption.

Conclusions

In the late eighteenth century Ahron Beer composed many melodies for Shabbat and holiday prayers. As a cantor in Berlin, he would alternate among them so that his congregants could not learn the tunes. He wrote, "For if a person hears a tune but once a year, it will be impossible for him to sing with the cantor during the service, and therefore he will not be able to confuse the chazzan. It has become a plague to the chazzanim to have the members of the congregation join the song" (Idelsohn 1929:218). Influential cantors and composers assumed that congregants participated in worship by listening to prayer beautifully rendered and by quietly offering their heartfelt devotion. This study shows how these contemporary communities have reconfigured many aspects of worship in an effort to redefine and ensure meaningful participation in prayer.

For many congregants, the service's metric tunes are the primary vehicle for participation in worship. Enthusiastic group singing is a prerequisite for personal religious experience. For example, the leader at B'nai Or explained that God's presence could be felt when the group was singing in such a way that "everybody is one and everybody is connected." The group experience in turn affects the individual. A participant at Tufts Hillel noted that when "everybody's singing well together, it makes me feel unified." While some congregants sing more and some sing less, the tune is indispensable for worship. At the least, they see their favorite tunes as an opportunity to join with their community for relaxation and celebration. At best, the tune lifts the worshipper out of the ordinary world, transforming both the individual and the community.

This stress on the importance of participation in worship has caused these communities to redefine the role of the leader and reexamine the nature of professional leadership in services. At Tufts Hillel and Shaarei Tefillah the deprofessionalization of leadership allows congregants actively to control the style of the service. This approach is even evident in the worship communities that have strong, charismatic leadership. At B'nai Or the members spoke warmly and enthusiastically about "Lev's service." Yet he conducts prayers only one week of the month and works regularly with members of B'nai Or's ritual committee, who lead services on alternate weeks. At the Bostoner Rebbe's, as at many traditional shuls, the honor of leading the service is distributed to different members each week. While the Rebbe's presence is palpable at Beth Pinchas, he rarely leads the davening for Kabbalat Shabbat. At Temple Israel the cantor described a service in which he is "superfluous," at least some of the time, and "the congregation leads itself," a situation that simultaneously pleases and frustrates him. This emphasis on congregationally led worship has parallels in both the contemporary Protestant and Catholic church and is seen as a prerequisite for a quality worship experience.[61]

A leader's humility and ability to conduct services without distracting fellow members from their worship was seen as necessary for meaningful, transformative prayer. The right service can provide an important religious experience; uninspired prayer leaves congregants cold and stiff. The images used to describe an "unexciting" or "boring" service were often connected to death. The Rebbe stressed that the wrong tune "will kill the service" and characterized the Lewandowski melody for *Lekhah dodi* "as dead as could be." At Shaarei Tefillah one member described how a cantor in a former shul "sang everything, no matter how happy, as if it were a dirge." In chapter 3 the cantor at Temple Israel refers to congregational nonparticipation as "Death Valley Days." Members worked to create vibrant communities, an endeavor that often entailed considerable initiative, personal risks, and in some cases the willingness to endure communal tension and conflict.

Two of these worship communities were created as breakaway services, separating from an established group in order to create the worship environment that reflected the liturgical and musical style desired by a subgroup of the congregation. Shaarei Tefillah broke away from Congregation Beth El, a split that caused considerable communal disruption. While members of the atrium service at Temple Israel did not separate from that temple, the establishment of the early service underscored significant conflicts between the congregation's old and new guard.

To ensure that worship was meaningful, members and leadership of all of these groups were willing to invest considerable energy to develop standards of worship and, within accepted limits, to change local customs. The Rebbe explained that the choice of a good tune for *Lekhah dodi* was so important that he altered his community's custom and took the responsibility of choosing upon himself. At Shaarei Tefillah, community members put pressure on the gabbayim to ensure that skilled, competent leadership was chosen for Shabbat. Members of Tufts Hillel organized "teaching services" and produced cassette tapes to teach new music and increase knowledgeable participation in worship. Temple Israel created a special prayer book for Kabbalat Shabbat, including full English transliteration for all the Hebrew prayers.

Members in all of these worship communities express pride in their services, pointing to large attendance and enthusiastic, voluntary participation. None of these communities complained about low attendance at worship or wondered how to recruit new or younger members. In all of them music was a key element that drew people to services. Congregational singing was understood to be one of the most important ways to meld individuals into a community.

It was difficult to plot the practices of these five worship communities along a denominational spectrum. Those who write about American Judaism tend to classify congregations on a continuum of observance. The more observant are classified Orthodox, less observant are labeled Reform. As should be clear, a careful reading of this data shows how such a categorization is an oversimplification.

To facilitate comparison, the discussion here began with the havurah, B'nai Or, and moved through Reform, Conservative, and Orthodox congregations, ending with the Hasidic shul, Beth Pinchas. One might assume that B'nai Or and Beth Pinchas are on opposite ends of the religious spectrum, and indeed they are. Yet in some ways, these two worship communities have the most in common. They are the most open to transcendent experience and most comfortable with the role of a charismatic leader. They are the only communities in this study that use dance in a socioreligious context. Furthermore, while Reform Judaism occupies the "left" of the spectrum in religious observance, there are many ways in which the Reform Jews of Temple Israel are scrupulously "conservative" with a lower-case *c*. The fact that they do not feel bound to observe traditional Jewish law does not mean that they are laissez-faire in their approach to ritual. They pay careful attention to the performance of the service as it has developed in their community. Members notice and complain if any essential aspects of worship are changed. In this regard, they are very different from B'nai Or, their close neighbor on a standard spectrum of religious observance. Members of B'nai Or both embrace experiential exercises during the service and have been educated to expect changes from week to week in the Kabbalat Shabbat liturgy.

This is all by way of illustrating the importance of recognizing the complexity of these issues. Labels such as "traditional" or "nontraditional," "Orthodox" or "Reform," do not adequately explain these separate groups. It is more productive here to concentrate on certain themes that recur in an examination of these worship communities, such as a search for transcendent experience, the willingness to lose or exert control, the struggle to define authentic practice, a desire to place oneself on a historical continuum, and the use of music to uncover deeper meaning in liturgical text. These themes are explored in chapter 3, which examines the concept of nusach in these five worship communities.

3

The Meaning of Nusach

Worshippers' Perspectives on
Traditional Jewish Chant

The Concept of Nusach

This chapter examines the meaning and function of nusach, primarily from the perspective of the worshipper.[1] The subject of nusach elicits strong responses from Jews young and old. One Conservative cantor remarked, "Nusach is a real 'hot potato' in the Jewish community right now." In truth, it is hard to get a handle on the concept of nusach: it means many different things to Jews across denominational lines. It is seen by some to be the last holdout of traditional Jewish music. As such, it is viewed by some as a powerful talisman, a magic door to religious authenticity. While many Reform Jews were rediscovering Jewish chant, one Reform worshipper said nusach was unintelligible, calling it a "mumble-fest." A Bostoner Hasid insisted that nusach was "the first rap music." I asked members of an Orthodox congregation, "When you lead a service, how do you know if you are in nusach?" One man laughed and answered, "You know you're in nusach if they don't yell at you to sit down!"

The word *nusach* comes from the Hebrew root meaning "pulled out" or "removed." The term originally referred to a specific section of Jewish liturgy that a scribe had copied out of a particular prayer book or text. It was later applied in a broader way to indicate a particular community's tradition of prayer or, more generally, the way the prayers were publicly presented. Judit Frigyesi explains that "Nusach means something like 'the traditional way [of singing] according to the given liturgical function and local custom'" (1993:69).[2] Following this understanding, the nusach for a particular service would include all of the music that was customarily used in that service, both recitative chant and tunes (cf. Wohlberg [1954] 1972:159). Still, most of the congregants in the worship communities studied here understand nusach to refer to chant rather than the metric tunes used in worship.

In traditional Ashkenazi Jewish worship, the leader intones the ending and sometimes the beginning lines of individual prayers, marking the place and setting the pace of the service. These short sections of the liturgy are chanted "in nusach," a simple, recognizable melody that a community accepts as correct for particular prayers in specific services. In the Ashkenazi tradition these melodies were associated with musical modes (*shtaygers*, Yiddish), which Eli Schleifer defines as "a musical corpus of melodic patterns that are related to a scale and are associated with particular prayers, functions, and services" (1992:41).[3] There are three main prayer modes, named after well-known prayers sung to those melodic patterns: *Adonai malakh* (The Lord reigns), *Magen avot* (Protector of the patriarchs), and *Ahavah rabbah* ([With] great love) (CD #20).[4] Certain sections of a service are chanted to a specific mode. For example, one can say that the nusach for the psalms in the Kabbalat Shabbat service follows the *Adonoi malakh* mode. Still, the modes are not service-, or even prayer-specific. One can find examples of all three modes being used in different sections of one prayer, such as certain versions of the Shabbat *Kedushah* (Kligman 2000:912).

The worshippers with whom I spoke did not think about or understand nusach in this way. For the most part, they knew little about musical modes and had never heard of the Yiddish cantorial term *shtayger*. They thought of recitative chant in terms of melody and had learned it that way in practice. They were concerned primarily with differentiating among the melodies associated with certain services, such as the simple melody used for daily worship, the particular Shabbat melodies used on Friday night and Saturday morning, and the increasingly complex chants for the festivals and the High Holidays (CD #36).[5]

Worshippers were also conscious that nusach allows the leader considerable opportunity for improvisation. Once the leader knows the melody used for the opening phrase of a particular prayer, for the cadential ending, and for the reciting tones in between, it was assumed that there was a certain freedom to improvise. For the professional cantor, improvisation can take many complex forms such as repetition, coloratura, or melodic extension.[6] However, when these lay leaders improvised, they primarily used simple melodic variation and ornamentation, as well as changes in dynamics (loudness and softness). A defining feature of Jewish recitative chant is that it is not in regular metrical rhythm, and simple rhythmic variations were also a way these leaders would improvise when chanting.[7] These communities also use a form of nonstrophic group chant that is often based on the prayer modes but is sung in unison by the congregation, necessitating a more regular rhythm in these sections (CD #21). Most lay leaders do not think a lot about improvising when they lead services; they simply aspire to complete an accurate recitation of the service. More ambitious leaders use improvisation to interpret and emphasize sections of the liturgical text.[8] Some skilled lay leaders, and most professional cantors, are also concerned with adding a dimension of esthetic beauty to the davening.

The performance of liturgical text does have aspects of a musical performance; after all, the leader is often singing solo in front of the congregation. Yet a number of additional considerations shape and complicate this "performance" of sacred text. Chanting the service in proper nusach implies that the leader is paying attention to a range of liturgical details. The leader must concentrate on the correct pronunciation of the Hebrew text. The leader is also responsible for knowing, remembering, and cueing certain rules, such as when to stand up and sit down, when special prayers are inserted or omitted. Furthermore, even if the job of the shaliach tsibbur appears to be a performance, the leader is obligated to be praying together with the rest of the congregation. I regularly hear leaders struggle with the tension between trying to be conscious of all the musical, textual, and interpersonal dynamics inherent in leading a group in prayer while at the same time trying actually to daven for themselves. While objectively it is not possible for congregants to judge the quality of the leader's kavanah, their perceptions of the leader's sincerity, knowledge of the prayers, intensity, and focus have a profound effect upon the experience of worshippers engaged in prayer. As one congregant expressed, "If the shaliach tsibbur is the captain of the ship, I want to make sure he is facing in the right direction. If he doesn't know where he's going, we *all* might crash!" Congregants rely on subtle signals and perceptions, many of them connected with the leader's musical realization of the liturgy, in order to assess if the ship is on course. Much of this dialogue between the leader and the congregation takes place in the realm of nusach.[9]

Nusach in Five Worship Communities

B'nai Or: Extending the Definition of Nusach

Across denominational lines, worshippers spoke about the importance of nusach as "authentic" or "traditional" Jewish liturgical music. B'nai Or, the most musically eclectic congregation, was no exception. Hasidic and contemporary niggunim, Israeli folk songs, Hindu chant with Hebrew lyrics, modern musical compositions, movement and dance all find their way into this service. Yet participants strongly affirmed the importance of nusach as a historical connection to Jewish tradition. One member said, "[Without nusach], there would be no continuity with our tradition." His wife added, "I think there's got to be *some* connection with tradition—as creative as we get—because part of the thing about Judaism is how this chain has gone on."

Both the leader and the ritual committee at B'nai Or exercise control over the atmosphere and decorum of the service.[10] Here nusach is seen as an anchor to authenticity, an example of normative religious practice that serves as a connection to mainstream Jewish worship. Another member expressed this idea clearly when she said, "I love [nusach]. It makes me feel like I'm really doing Jewish and that I'm not just being a New Age hippie."

She explained that many uneducated Jews did not affiliate and participate in traditional Jewish prayer because doing so required cultivating "hard" skills: Hebrew language expertise, reading ability, vocabulary, grammar, historical and literary familiarity with the tradition. She said, "I think that B'nai Or wants to be grounded and not just lifted off into trend or fad. Sometimes I think we've had the best of that and in other ways we need to keep grounding ourselves . . . maybe we're not grounded enough in tradition . . . and in a real working knowledge of *Yiddishkeit* [Jewishness, Yiddish] and Hebrew." She saw chanting the Hebrew liturgy as a difficult skill: "I don't feel like many people are dealing with the hard skills, I think it's mostly the 'soft entry.'" By soft entry, she explained, she meant the singing of niggunim, English davening, and other "nonskilled" approaches to prayer. Specific cultural knowledge and expertise were necessary, she explained, to keep their creative explorations authentically Jewish.

B'nai Or's leader also saw the congregation's use of nusach as a connection to the greater Jewish community, framing their liturgical experiments and creativity in traditional practice. He asserted, "I think it's fairly important we don't separate ourselves from the mainstream . . . there is some great stuff out there. Almost everything we do comes from someplace. It didn't get snatched out of the air. . . . It may seem new because this may be a different form . . . but it all has precedent."

For this congregation, nusach becomes a touchstone, a tether to the past. Many members of the congregation are not ritually observant: they do not follow the Jewish dietary laws or observe traditional restrictions that prohibit driving or using electricity on Shabbat. Men and married women do not cover their heads. Once these identity markers have vanished, nusach becomes invested with more importance and meaning as a connection to authentic Jewish practice. At the same time, this congregation's creative and nontraditional approach to Jewish liturgy also influences their approach to nusach. It is not unusual to chant the English translations of the Hebrew prayers in nusach, a practice pioneered by Rabbi Zalman Schachter-Shalomi in the late 1960s. In Example 3.1, even the page number is announced "in nusach" (CD #22).[11] Sometimes a leader switches from Hebrew to English, chanting in both languages alternately. At other times there are two leaders, one chanting the Hebrew and one the English. This practice is sometimes referred to by members as "stereo" English-Hebrew davening. It would be considered unacceptable to the Orthodox, where no English is used in the service, and silly to Conservative and Reform Jews, who simply do not pray that way. Yet it is common at B'nai Or as a way both to connect to traditional practice and to make the English translations of the prayers more "Jewish." The community defines itself simultaneously as traditional and innovative and affirms this self-definition with such musical choices.

However, in a community where most participants do not have a traditional Jewish background, there are few gatekeepers to judge whether a tradition or melody really does have a connection to Jewish tradition. In fact, the leader's nusach did not sound like Ashkenazi chanting of the Shab-

Example 3.1. Opening of *Ahavot olam* ([With] everlasting love), B'nai Or. This example is transcribed from an actual service. A slightly different version is presented on CD #22.

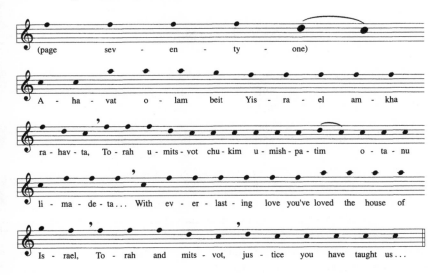

(page seventy-one)

A - ha - vat o - lam beit Yis - ra - el am - kha

ra - hav - ta, To - rah u - mits - vot chu - kim u - mish - pa - tim o - ta - nu

li - ma - de - ta... With ev - er - last - ing love you've loved the house of

Is - rael, To - rah and mits - vot, jus - tice you have taught us...

bat Maariv service, a fact that bothered his congregation very little. When I questioned him on the source of his Maariv nusach, he said, "I think that just came out of me. I'm into this major kind of mode." This leader understood that nusach was connected to time of day and time of the week, declaring "They're like ragas to me. They each evoke something." In fact, the Maariv nusach for Shabbat in the Ashkenazi tradition is commonly in the minor mode (cf. *Ahavat olam* as sung at Shaarei Tefillah, CD #23).

One of the few members of B'nai Or who knows traditional nusach and has worked as a part-time cantor in a variety of settings noted the leader's use of the "wrong" nusach in the Friday evening service. He commented, "It's not high nusach. [But] it's fine. If I were leading on a Friday night service, I might not use that one. . . . [He] does it major and I actually use the minor." He said that hearing that nusach on Friday night "sets up a dissonance" for him because he associates it with Shabbat morning. However, he was hesitant to be too critical, recognizing that this community was simply not interested in what constitutes "correct" nusach. He continued, "[But we're] splitting hairs here. [This is a community that] never *heard* the word 'nusach' before. . . . If [the leader] and I were to have a public debate about [that] . . . people would say, 'What's the point? What's the difference?' . . . [People would say,] 'What does it matter which nusach you use? You open your heart to God. That's the important thing.'"

What constitutes "authentic" nusach for this congregation? In this case it was not the traditional modal structure of the chant that established its authenticity. Among members of this community, melodic distinctions between specific *nuschaot* (pl.) were lost; the canvas was painted in broader strokes. Certain characteristics of Jewish chant, such as flowing rhythm, reciting tones, a cadential formula, bolstered by the prestige of a respected community leader, were enough to establish this nusach as authentic and comfortably linked to the chain of Jewish tradition.

Temple Israel: "I Don't Feel Good Just Sitting There Reading the Prayers"

In this Reform congregation, members spoke enthusiastically about the role of nusach in worship. Both the cantor and rabbis were committed to "proper nusach." Traditional Jews have criticized the Reform movement for bringing instrumental music into Shabbat worship, first the organ and more recently the guitar. The use of more English in the service, together with the shortening and altering of the liturgy, was seen as evidence of the Reform movement's increasing assimilation to the dominant Protestant culture, a move away from traditional Jewish practice. Yet since the 1970s, as many Reform Jews search for community and rootedness, they have increasingly explored and embraced certain traditional ritual practices, albeit selectively and on their own terms. Traditional chant has been introduced increasingly at Temple Israel since the inception of the atrium service, and congregants were excited about the new possibilities that it presented in prayer.

Several congregants spoke hyperbolically of nusach as ancient tradition, powerfully connecting them to thousands of years of Jewish history and experience. Before the atrium service was established, much classical Reform liturgy at Temple Israel was read in English by the rabbi. Other prayers were read responsively or in unison by the congregation. Yet as one member commented, "I don't feel good just sitting there reading the prayers." She explained that the very act of chanting the Hebrew opened up greater possibilities for spiritual experience. She explained, "[Chanting] comes from here [she puts her hand on her chest] . . . in your soul. The more senses you use, the more connection you feel . . . to read it and sing it and then to move with it. . . . [Chanting] just raises your level of participation and your sense of belonging. . . . I love using more senses."

The "multisensory" nature of davening and nusach (singing, chanting, breathing, moving, swaying) is seen to enhance prayer. To this worshipper, nusach facilitates a more integrated involvement in worship as well as a deeper understanding of the Jewish tradition. Nusach, more than any other musical choice, brings the worshipper into direct contact with traditional Hebrew liturgy. In fact, this member said that the introduction of traditional chant, and her enthusiasm for this Kabbalat Shabbat service, was a major factor in furthering her own Jewish education. She explained, "I find [chanting in nusach] just much more involving [and] it brought me to study Hebrew."

As she attended the Temple's adult education classes and as her Hebrew facility and comprehension increased, she wanted to engage the prayers on a deeper level. She explained, "Before I never needed to know the language. It wasn't really relevant. . . . But I realized that there was this really powerful language piece that I was missing out on. . . . All of a sudden I wanted to see the letters and connect them to the words, and then start understanding the liturgy in its rootedness." Her enthusiasm increased as she continued: "[This process of education] is like being on an archeological dig. It's allowed me to *do* the dig. What I think has been powerful about it . . . for those of us who are receptive to it [is that] it has encouraged us to study."

Other worshippers also stressed that the introduction of chant in the service was "wonderful" and created a feeling that pervaded Shabbat worship. Still, not every member at Temple Israel was comfortable with these changes. Some older members of this once classically Reform temple do not read or speak Hebrew and do not appreciate this move toward more traditional practice. Rabbi Mehlman said that "for some people there is the sense that there's too much Hebrew, which is a way of saying, 'I feel left out.'" One way the temple addresses this concern is by providing a full English transliteration of the Hebrew prayers and songs in their prayer book to facilitate participation for the multigenerational crowd that regularly attends services.

Even though members of this Reform congregation are enthusiastic about nusach and incorporate traditional chant increasingly in worship, one could not mistake Kabbalat Shabbat at Temple Israel for a traditional service. For one thing, the shortening of the liturgy precludes certain opportunities for chant that are found in a traditional Friday evening service. The Temple's prayer book has substituted a series of musical selections for the six psalms that precede *Lekhah dodi*, so there is no option to chant the openings and closings of those psalms (CD #5, #6). Furthermore, the two prayers before the *Shema* in the Maariv service, *Maariv aravim* ([God who] brings on evening) and *Ahavat olam*, are read out loud in unison in Hebrew rather than chanted by the worshippers and concluded by the leader. The guitar is heard throughout the service. The congregation joins in chanting other prayers without musical accompaniment, such as the *Hatsi kaddish* (CD #9), *Barekhu* (CD #10), *Ve'ahavta* (And you shall love [the Lord]) (CD #24), the *Amidah*, which in their service includes *Avot* (Patriarchs), *Gevurot* (God's power), and *Kedushah* (CD #25). The description of this service as "more traditional" Reform worship is subjective, as Rabbi Mehlman explained: "Traditional Jews don't feel that this is a traditional service . . . [but] for some people [in the congregation] it may be too traditional." As the atrium service has developed, the feeling and style of worship have changed dramatically: the congregation sings longer segments of Hebrew than it ever has, the sounds of traditional chant pervade the service. These musical traditions have become an integral part of this Reform community's worship, their historical authenticity accepted. The community has looked back selectively in order to move forward, and the integration of traditional chant is part of a cultural and spiritual awakening for a new generation of Reform Jews.

PARTICIPATION VERSUS CORRECT PERFORMANCE The cantor at Temple Israel spoke passionately of his commitment to teach the congregation to use and appreciate nusach. He believed it was important to sing "the proper music at the proper time" and wished to introduce the seasonal melodies "when [a specific holiday] comes around."

The cantor recognized that his community was special in this regard, commenting that in many Reform temples the congregation and cantor do not chant at all. He had arrived at Temple Israel during a time of transition. The cantor who preceded him had already introduced some chanting in the service, such as the *Avot* and *Gevurot* prayers in the *Amidah* and the *Ve'ahavta* in Torah trop. Encouraged by this history, the cantor wanted to teach more nusach and the rabbis and congregation gave him the "green light."

He began an informal educational program to teach his congregants to recognize and sing the traditional nusach. After a while, members learned Shabbat morning chant. He said, "I have stopped explaining it, because the crowd for the morning services is pretty constant." As a further way to educate the congregation, the cantor explained, "I have done some musical sermonettes or sermons in song where the rabbi and I have [taught together and have discussed] melodies that are peculiar to the holidays, so that you can identify holidays by melodies."

While there were weekly opportunities to introduce Shabbat nusach, it was harder to teach the special nuschaot for the High Holidays and the festivals of Passover, Shavuot, and Sukkot. The cantor confronted a dilemma in regard to his congregation's lack of knowledge of the unique musical traditions for the holidays. He considered the problem in this way: Using the proper holiday nusach is "right." However, because more people are familiar with Shabbat nusach, that works better and engenders more participation in services. He said:

> I think it's good for people to be singing the right thing at the proper moment, the correct melody, [but] I have fudged my philosophy on this with the High Holidays because everyone knows the [prayers] with Shabbat nusach, and the first year I sang High Holiday nusach, and it was "Death Valley Days!" I looked out: it was quiet. I may have done it for two years and then I decided I'm going to compromise my belief here because I think it's more important for them to be singing rather than hearing me sing the proper melody and just watching me.

He added that with his wife's encouragement, he decided to continue his educational program for the congregation. Eventually, he believed, they would come to learn, appreciate, and participate in these special, occasion-specific musical traditions. Still, in this liberal community, "correct practice" is a slippery concept, worked through with an eye toward Jewish law, local congregational custom, esthetic norms, a commitment to contemporary relevance, and creative expression. The tradition gets a vote but not a veto. Musical decisions are negotiated within a broad field of options, as leaders and members create worship that feels simultaneously authentic, participatory, and workable for this community.

Tufts Hillel: "When I Can Focus on the Words, It Feels Like I'm Really with a Prayer"

In the Conservative service at Tufts Hillel, students struggle to find the right balance between nusach, which they associate with davening the prayers on their own, and the spirited group singing that gives this service its particular character and appeal. While members stressed that they love the participatory singing, many said that it left them unsatisfied and unsure if they had really been engaged in prayer. Nusach allowed them to focus on the text of the liturgy and was seen to provide corrective balance to some of the problems caused by the group singing they embraced so enthusiastically.

Students recognize that they have built an unusual worship community, and they are proud of the reactions they regularly receive from visitors and guests. As one student said, "It's really remarkable, people . . . will come to a Tufts Hillel service for the first time . . . and they're speechless about the kind of community our singing and our service create."

Still, they expressed their concern that often they get so involved in singing that it is difficult to concentrate on the prayers and their meaning. As one student related, "I feel like sometimes I get so caught up in the fact that I'm singing it that I really fail to even know what I'm singing about." Students clearly saw this as a problem: concentrating on the text and themes of the prayers was seen as a prerequisite for meaningful worship. As another student explained, "I think that when I pray the *Amidah* alone, I honestly do read the words more [than when I'm singing]." She added, "[Nusach] feels more traditional and it feels more like praying." Another student said that while he liked the group participation pieces, "I get a very different inner feeling [when I am davening to myself]. When I can focus on the words for a little while before we get to singing again, it feels like I'm really *with* a prayer."

Another student struggled to delineate the difference between "religious experience," which she associated with private prayer, and a "community experience," which she associated with communal singing. She explained that she didn't "find it that much a religious experience to go to [Hillel for] Friday night services." With some discomfort, she related, "Sometimes I feel like I'm coming to services to sing." She continued, "I like the community aspect that's involved, but that makes it a *singing experience*." She felt that a tune, even a particularly beautiful tune, often becomes a distraction, diminishing rather than enhancing the experience of prayer.

When these students discussed "davening with nusach," they did not focus on a particular musical mode or the leader's vocal style. Rather, they concentrated on the process of approaching a prayer as privately chanted rather than communally sung text. While the leader marks the opening and closing of the prayer, as one member noted, the individual goes "one on one" with the text. These students assumed that "praying" is more than simply intoning the words of a prayer to oneself. In fact, these conversations about the role of nusach in the service prompted students to reflect on what they were actually thinking and doing when they were engaged in prayer. What did it actually mean to daven with kavanah?

One student explained that he understood prayer to be a highly personal confrontation and interaction with the text of the liturgy. Praying with proper kavanah entailed assessing where he was in his life, meditating on a prayer's meaning, and considering how the text raised questions and answers relevant to his own situation. As an example, he spoke about the prayer *Mi khamokhah* (Who is like you [God]), historically sung to celebrate the Israelites' deliverance from Egypt after they passed through the Red Sea (CD #26). He explained that when he came to that prayer, he thought about freedom and deliverance, the meaning of those concepts in his own life, and how he was historically connected to those ancient events. He felt that it was simply easier to go deeper into the siddur when chanting a prayer than when singing a rousing tune.

Still, while students desired the opportunity to daven and interact with the prayers, they so valued the community experience of group singing that they wished to preserve it even while chanting. This feeling shaped how nusach was used in this community in two ways. First, the students, influenced by the traditions of Camp Ramah, chant Kabbalat Shabbat nusach in a way that emphasizes group participation. The leader and congregation join together in chanting a prayer's opening and sections of its closing verses. Second, they sing in unison many nonstrophic sections of the liturgy to melodies that are based on traditional chant.

Although the melody many of them use for Kabbalat Shabbat nusach is very similar to that used by the Orthodox and even Hasidic worship community in this study, the interaction between the leader and the group is different. In the Orthodox Shaarei Tefillah, daveners finish the prayer by themselves, and then the leader intones the concluding verses, thereby giving the cue to proceed to the next prayer. At Tufts Hillel, however, students sing the opening phrases along with the leader, then daven through the psalm by themselves until the leader begins chanting the hatimah. At this point, the congregation joins the leader and chants the last words or phrases of the hatimah together. This can be heard on CD #28 for the conclusion of Maariv aravim.

The students' understanding that traditional chant functions in this way can also be seen in the way they speak about nusach. They assume that at some point everyone sings together. As one student remarked, "I always thought of it as the way to make sure the congregation stayed involved. It gave them something to look forward to at the end of each prayer. Even if they weren't understanding what the prayer was, they were still able to join in with the leader and see they're in the right place." Another student explained her conception of nusach: "I find the nusach almost hypnotic . . . , it brings everybody together and all the voices can combine." Upon further questioning, this student indicated she was referring to two aspects of davening: the way individual daveners create an undertone of many different voices and rhythms in the middle of a prayer, and the power of the community singing together at the prayer's conclusion. The fact that the voices "combine" in unison and everyone can "join in" at the prayer's conclusion is unique to this service among the communities in this study. In an Orthodox service the operative dynamic is between the shaliach tsibbur and the individual davener. In the Tufts Conservative service, the dynamic is between the shaliach tsibbur, the individual worshipper, and the full group, which is constantly joining the leader to sing short phrases of nusach in unison. In this way, the group experience continues to be stressed throughout the service.

The second way that the stress on participation has influenced nusach in this service is in the extensive singing of longer, nonstrophic sections of the liturgy to tunes that are often based on prayer modes and frequently interspersed or concluded by the leader's recitative (CD #21, #29).[12] I would place these nonstrophic tunes on a continuum between nusach, on one end, and strophic tunes on the other. These nonstrophic tunes are used much more frequently in this Conservative service than in either Reform or Orthodox worship. In general, Reform congregants do not have enough facility in Hebrew to sing these large blocks of Hebrew text, and many of these prayers are not in Reform Kabbalat Shabbat services.[13] To most Orthodox congregants, such singing would seem superfluous to the religious obligation of chanting the Hebrew text. Yet in this Conservative community, these tunes are well loved and have become important aspects of this service's musical tradition.

Why has this stress on group singing been so influential in the service that it has even shaped the approach to nusach? One student expressed this ideologically, emphasizing the value of community created through music: "I feel like the point of Shabbat is for the Jewish people *as a whole* to welcome Shabbos and accept the Sabbath and that when it's not sung together and it's just separate, it's not the Jewish people accepting the Shabbat or welcoming the Shabbat, it's each person and that's not the point. Shabbos should not be to separate us, it should be to bring us together." Another student simply noted, "In services that I've been to where there's less singing and more praying individually, you're less a community." Individual chant was important, yet too much personal davening felt isolating. In this regard, students drew a distinction between Conservative and Orthodox services, as expressed by a student who occasionally attends an Orthodox service when he goes home: "I go to morning minyan and . . . [they're] all trying to go through the services as fast as they can possibly daven and for me it's almost meaningless, it's a race to get through the service and get to work. Coming to Hillel is a more relaxing break and I'm actually feeling something and davening and praying, instead of mostly trying to plow through the Hebrew words."[14] Another student explained that for her the Conservative service brought together the best parts of Reform and Orthodox worship. She said, "In the Conservative service there's much more of a balance [between group singing and nusach], between songs and prayers. You sing the song and that has one level of meaning . . . and then you can go to another level of meaning and do a prayer. In the Reform service it feels like it's all songs and there . . . isn't as much time for you on your own to reflect. In an Orthodox service there's *too much* time on your own."

The students in this service represent the elite of young Conservative Jews. Shaped by their camp experiences, they are developing a service with musical traditions that balance their feeling of obligation to interact with the liturgy and their desire to create a group experience that is exciting, fun, and participatory. They are proud of their facility with Hebrew and their knowledge of sections of the liturgy, skills that they have polished at camp and in youth group. The nusach that they have carried with them from camp, and continued to develop in college, has a strong connection to place and shared community. In fact, students have developed particular ways in which they sing these prayers, marking them with various musical games, such as the use of syncopation in the prayer *Veshamru* (And they shall observe [the Sabbath]). Some students hold back while others continue singing, creating a syncopated rhythm (CD #30). Another example of rhythmic marking is found in *Al ken* (Therefore [we hope]), the second paragraph of *Alenu*: students stomp their feet in rhythm at certain points in this prayer (CD #31). Students enjoy these games, with their in-jokes and memories of a shared religious and cultural experience. There are a series of similar markings in the Conservative camp version of the *Birkat Hamazon* (Grace after meals), with rhythmic games, the insertion of English phrases that mimic the Hebrew, false endings, and puns. These markings are more than nostalgic re-creations of a camp or youth group experience. For many of these students, the act of altering musical and liturgical traditions fosters a sense of empowerment, ownership, and connection (cf. Summit 1993). In this way, Jewish practice is no longer the sole province of their parents or their grandparents. They have created their own worship community that, in certain purposeful ways, closes off participation to their uninitiated elders. As much as members of the older generation might object, these young Jews have created a musical tradition truly their own.[15]

When I asked a group of these students how much the service at Tufts was like their congregations at home, they laughed. As a group, they responded, "It's *nothing* like at home!" In the first place, students led the service at Hillel. As one student declared, "[At Tufts] the cantor is coming from one of us. It's not a set thing. It's sometimes Marshal and sometimes I do it and sometimes Aleza, and everyone participates." But there was more to this than the fact that the leader was one of them. These students did not want to listen to liturgical music: they wanted to sing. They explained that in general, their home congregations sang much less than they did at Tufts. While some said that their cantors at home encouraged participation, many did not.

Students claim to be "spoiled" by the level of participation and active ownership of the service at Hillel. Some are conscious that they are not alone in their desire to be more involved in prayer, and they are aware that deprofessionalized havurot or, in larger cities, unique congregations have developed. One woman said, "It's not that I don't think I'll ever find anything after this. I hate going to services at home and here I love it. . . . One time I went into the city [New York City] to B'nai Jeshurun and it was great. There were so many people and it was a lot of fun. So there have to be places that I'll like."

Many of these students looked to create change in the Conservative movement after they left college. One student stressed, "There . . . needs to be a change . . . to get people involved in their synagogues. . . . People are getting lost out there because the service is geared for the older people. . . . The [younger] people . . . aren't staying . . . because the synagogue doesn't do stuff for them. . . . [We need to] go to a shul and bring it with us and try to make a difference." Several students spoke of wanting to carry their experience in college on to the congregations they join after they graduate. The approach of these student leaders could have a profound effect on the Conservative movement. Even if they prefer to worship in a style that differs from that of their parents and grandparents, these students have grown into serious Jews who have embraced a style of Jewish prayer that they find meaningful and accessible. A balance of traditional chant and participatory singing has allowed them to construct a service in which they experience both the power of community and the relevance of the traditional liturgy.

Shaarei Tefillah: Nusach as Normative Practice

Among the liberal congregations considered in this study, nusach was just one of many possible musical choices for the performance of sacred text. However, for the modern Orthodox, correct nusach defined proper musical practice in the synagogue. When asked why nusach was so important to this community, one member answered, "Identification with tradition. . . . If you asked [Orthodox Jews], 'What's traditional about you? Do you study Talmud?' Some do, a lot don't. 'Do you know the *Shulchan Arukh*?' 'Never look in it.' 'So what's traditional about you?' 'Well, I do things right. I go to a synagogue where it's done right. . . . We do the tunes in the correct way.'"

When the members of this Orthodox congregation insist that they "do things right," they leave little room open for other musical choices in the service. Nusach becomes normative liturgical practice, and they have chosen to have no choice in this matter. In many aspects of their lives—their social circles, the food they eat, their leisure activities, how they spend their Friday evenings and Saturdays—they establish careful boundaries, limiting and narrowing their choices. Another member of this congregation spoke about how he grew up in the Conservative movement and has become more observant since having children. He felt this constriction and expressed how it was reflected in the congregation's music: "What's inter-

Example 3.2. *Arba'im shanah* (Forty years), Psalm 95. Father's nusach, Shaarei Tefillah, CD #32.

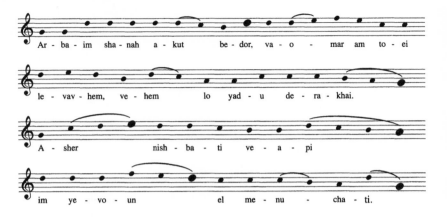

esting, at least for me, is that the nusach that I learned at Camp Ramah and USY was pretty fixed [but] is different than what my children are learning. There are similarities, but I think it's [different]. . . . It's not quite as melodic as we learned."

He proceeded to sing his nusach and his rendition of the nusach his son has learned (CD #32, #33; Examples 3.2 and 3.3). He commented on his son's nusach: "It's kind of more straightforward, . . . limited." He added, punctuating his comments with laughter, "I think that that's probably where we're going religiously, too." He pointed out that the nusach he grew up with had greater intervallic range and was more expansive, with more "flourishes." He perceived his son's nusach as simpler and more austere. While there is not a dramatic difference between the two examples, these observations are borne out in the transcriptions.

This member expanded on this musical observation. He described the ways that becoming more Orthodox had restricted his life, impacting on his job and determining the neighborhood in which he lives. He viewed all these developments as positive. He sent his children to Orthodox day school, and in many ways they lived a life more regulated and segregated than he had while growing up as a committed Conservative Jew. He explained that his family used to eat some foods in nonkosher restaurants, but as their standards of keeping kosher became stricter, they stopped doing this too. He spoke about their decision to separate themselves from many aspects of American society and said, "By choice I think we've ghettoized ourselves, and I don't think that we're any worse for it." He spoke of the legal restrictions on the Sabbath as "totally freeing," allowing him to spend time with his family. He explained how these choices enriched both his personal life and his professional life as a physician: "I think that . . . if you're strong in who you are, I think you can go out and face other people and appreciate them for who they are, and respect them for who they are better. . . . It doesn't get in the way of being a doctor. The only way

Example 3.3. *Arba'im shanah* Father's rendition of son's nusach, CD #33.

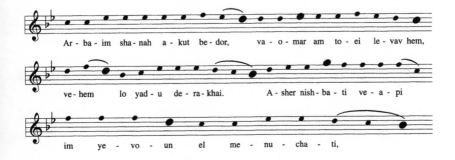

Ar - ba - im sha - nah a - kut be - dor, va - o - mar am to - ei le - vav hem,

ve - hem lo yad - u de - ra - khai. A - sher nish - ba - ti ve - a - pi

im ye - vo - un el me - nu - cha - ti,

to be a doctor these days, more than ever, is to have some kind of faith in something bigger than medicine."

In the Orthodox community, musical traditions are often passed from father to son, yet this member was not bothered that his son's nusach was different and that their family's social circle had become more constricted. He saw this tighter focus on family and community as a way to enrich their lives, strengthen his marriage, and give him more time with his children.[16]

"ACADEMIC TRADITIONALISTS" Many members characterized Shaarei Tefillah as a community that paid attention to the fine details of nusach and Hebrew pronunciation. They were proud that their High Holiday hazzan, one of the congregation's members, was "a stickler" for liturgical detail. Public affirmation for the importance of proper davening was very important. As this member remarked, "The concept of nusach with a capital 'N' is important." He elaborated, "As a principle, it's out there that we're supposed to care about nusach because that's the kind of people we are. . . . That's how we're different. We're academic traditionalists." This "academic approach," a studied attention to religious detail, was a defining value in their community.

However, in further conversation with this member, it became clear that while the basis of a "modern Orthodox musical tradition" was "sticking to nusach," in truth it was sticking to "people's best guess as to what nusach is." Actually, he thought that most members could not differentiate between fine points of liturgical chant. He gave the example of a special prayer for dew that is added to the service on the first day of Passover:

There are a lot of levels of gradation [in nusach]. The morning nusach is one you think people would hear every day and therefore know, and in fact there were only two or three people in the whole shul who know it. The point is, though, that when somebody gets up and does it flat without nusach, nobody calls him on it. So even the people who claim that nusach is very important to them don't know enough about this . . . whereas if somebody says, 'Oh, did you hear his *Tal* (Prayer for Dew)? He didn't know anything! Oh, yeah, his *Tal*, he really screwed that up.' Whether they really *know* what the *Tal* nusach is supposed to be or not is another question.

The Prayer for Dew is a *sui generis* liturgical performance. Members paid attention, or felt that they should pay attention, to endangered traditions, preserved correctly by relatively few congregations. They also felt that careful attention to nusach was particularly important during the High Holidays, a propitious time for personal and communal atonement. This member stressed that on the High Holidays "everybody has a strong sense of wanting to do it in the . . . hallowed and traditional way." He said that if someone did anything else, it would be "perceived as an overt attack, throwing away . . . what's supposed to be."[17]

Several worshippers felt that it was ironic that the congregation paid the most attention to High Holiday nusach, which was used only three days out of the year, while daily nusach received very little attention. This member observed, "There are hierarchies of what nusach is important. . . . Particularly on Rosh Hashanah and Yom Kippur—people get very uptight about that. . . . [We] pay more attention to [High Holidays] than nusach for holidays [the festivals: Sukkot, Passover, and Shavuot], . . . more attention is paid to them [than] for Shabbos. . . . The least attention . . . is paid to the weekdays, even though that's the most common."

This sentiment was also expressed by another member, who was especially concerned with the quality of daily nusach. He said, "[At Shaarei Tefillah,] Friday night nusach is pretty good. . . . Shabbat nusach is pretty good, although we have several people who [daven on] Shabbat using the wrong nusach. I don't understand how they do it! We have a policy that if people don't know nusach, we don't invite them to daven. . . . On weekday mornings you can hear anything. . . . I only recently found out that there is a standard nusach for weekday mornings, which I have learned—that there are three different melodies that you use. I've never heard anybody in our shul do it."[18]

As a matter of ideology, people care about nusach and profess its importance. However, it is too difficult to set an unrealistically high standard of liturgical performance from a congregation that depends on broad-based participation in leading daily and Shabbat services. Practically speaking, the gabbayim must find volunteers to daven every weekday and for the several services on Shabbat. If the community tried to enforce meticulous liturgical performance in the daily service, it would do more than alienate and anger members with average liturgical skills who enjoy the honor of leading services. It would severely limit the pool of qualified leaders. Insistence on a high level of performance would also conflict with another essential community value which has an even higher priority, the custom of giving mourners the honor of leading services, even if their liturgical skills are minimal. To demand professional standards of leadership would preclude the fulfillment of this important mitzvah, and that situation would be absolutely unsustainable for this community.

There are times, however, when the community is able to institutionalize its commitment to high liturgical standards. For the High Holidays the synagogue hires one of its own members to serve as hazzan for key services. This member is a noted authority on Jewish liturgical music. Because he is an insider, the congregation does not feel it is abandoning its self-image as a shul committed to communal participation. Throughout these negotiations, we see the congregation's struggle to balance its commitment to the proper performance of nusach with other values, such as its desire to encourage and allow broad-based liturgical leadership.

"DOWN-HOME ELITISTS": AN AVERSION TO PERFORMANCE There were some styles of davening that were seen as simply unacceptable to the members of Shaarei Tefillah. Even while asserting that people "did not know nusach," members said that in order to bring down community censure, "for people to exchange looks or something," a leader would have to be quite bad. One would not only chant the wrong melodies but would not be able to pronounce the Hebrew properly. However, if while leading the congregation, someone did a *"dreylikh, hazzonishe shtik"* (overly ornamented cantorial performance, Yiddish), that would be even "worse." One member commented, "I think we have no tolerance for that stuff. Who does he think he is? . . . Look who thinks he's a hazzan! . . . We don't do hazzanut here [laughs]. We do davening with nusach!" He went on to explain:

A lot of people have made a conscious decision against that kind of shul. If you wanted a hazzan, you would have stayed in a shul with a hazzan, or hired one, even though we don't have the money to do that. . . . There's a very interesting dichotomy here because, on the one hand, I think—not totally wrongly—there's a perception of a certain elitism that we pride ourselves in being more *frum* [observant, Yiddish] than the shul we came from. . . . But at the same time, if someone wants to come in and start with big time *hazonus* [hazzanut, Ashkenazi pronunciation] . . . we won't allow that! [laughs]. So, it's kind of—"don't be too grandiose." . . . We're down-home elitist.

This member further explained this antipathy toward "fancy" cantorial davening: "One of the reasons our shul was founded was because people didn't like to have a hazzan, and so, to the extent . . . if you're talking about . . . formal cantorial singing, I think my reaction and the reaction of my contemporaries has been a strongly negative one. . . . Our generation has been reacting against formal institutionalization, and cantorial singing with its distant and performative aspects . . . is almost a symbol of the kind of large, empty edifice which we are to varying degrees rejecting."

These "down-home elitists" have fairly simple goals when leading davening: pronounce the Hebrew properly, know what prayers are required at a specific service, know the tune for the appropriate nusach, don't stand out or call attention to the leader, and don't get too fancy (CD #34).[19] One member described his goals in this way: "I think what I try to do is not embarrass myself. . . . So, my own personal goal, and I think this holds true for many, although obviously not all, is just to get it in a way that's perceived as right, not to jar people, so that they don't wake up from their mental torpor, which is the usual state of mental alertness in a synagogue. In other words, if they don't say, 'What the hell was that?' then I've succeeded."

Whereas the emotional davening of the cantor was once considered pious and heartfelt, here it is seen as performance centered, showy, removed from true religious expression. These congregants have chosen to be more involved in all aspects of their Jewish lives, and this involvement extends to leading services, a skill shared by many in the congregation. They approach nusach with an understated simplicity, technical precision, and attention to detail that are in keeping with their general approach to modern Orthodox life.

ENFORCING NORMATIVE PRACTICE Members of Shaarei Tefillah distinguish between correct and incorrect nusach and are committed to its proper recitation. Yet it is difficult to control public performance without alienating members and hurting their feelings. Several people related how one member, an influential professor of Judaica, would rebuke a shaliach tsibbur if he used too many "frivolous tunes." At least one member left the community after such a confrontation.

I asked if there were other ways to control the performance of liturgical traditions. What would happen if someone came forward to lead Kabbalat Shabbat and started to sing the nusach for Shabbat morning? One member replied that it was the role of the congregation's gabbai to regulate such practice. He said, "I think what would happen would be that the gabbai wouldn't ask him again. The gabbayim . . . tend to be a conservative lot . . . who don't like innovation, who conceive of their job as defenders of the tradition, and who don't want to be criticized by the rabbinical types. . . . They can see their own role as doing the right thing, as maintaining the . . . correctness and appropriateness of institutional behavior." This worshipper told the following story:

I can think of one striking example—[someone's relative was visiting, and the family said he was a] "very good davener." He knew Kabbalat Shabbat like I know field hockey! It was really embarrassing. He couldn't get the words out. His tunes were not even tunes—you would think that somebody who knew as little as that would be embarrassed to go up and make a fool of himself, but obviously he didn't think he was making a fool of himself. So, two things happened. They would never ask him again, but that was no problem because he was from out of town, and, two, as the gabbai said to me, "Can you imagine these people say they know how to daven—how can I trust somebody that says he knows how to daven?" What he was saying was, this was reflecting on his job as a gabbai. It made him look like a fool because he's supposed to pick somebody who knows what he's doing. Now, conceivably that could lead to considerable tension, if that person really wanted to be asked again and had powerful friends. In fact, it doesn't happen very often, or hardly at all, because most people are not sufficiently obnoxious, or socially obtuse, to want to make an issue out of something like that—realizing full well that the implications go beyond whether you do Kabbalat Shabbat.[20]

I asked another knowledgeable member what would happen if a member led Friday night services and used the wrong nusach. He replied, "The person would be allowed to continue. Some people would prompt by responding in the right nusach, and that person then may switch or may continue. You would hear a lot of buzzing, and chances are that person would either be spoken to by one of the gabbayim or somebody self-appointed, and/or not asked to do it again."

While some worshippers took pride in the high musical and liturgical standard set by certain members of the congregation, others felt that this created unnecessary pressure and placed too much stress on proper performance of nusach. They did not think that leading prayer should be the territory solely of experts, and they wanted a broader range of people to feel comfortable leading the davening. One person said, "There are two or three people who . . . are extraordinarily knowledgeable . . . and they've made it their business to know. There's a certain intolerance for those who aren't quite up to that level, and that's . . . a real negative. I think that really damps down a sense of 'I can do that too —it's OK for me to do and to make a few mistakes.'"

This member spoke emotionally about the elitist stress on "proper" nusach creating a feeling of pressure and exclusion. He said, "They use it as a weapon . . . they use nusach as a club. . . ." He thought that this approach kept competent people from leading prayer, an issue that he felt was not discussed openly enough in the congregation. As an alternative, he thought that a leader's davening should fall within an acceptable range: "Like laboratory tests—there's a maximum normal and there's a minimum normal. So if it's within that acceptable range of normal [that should be acceptable]." He continued emphatically: "I have the strongest feelings against [policing proper practice.] I respect that knowledge, but it's like with anything . . . it has to be put in its place. . . . It's only davening." This member believed that there were other values, such as community solidarity, encouraging the use of new skills, communal participation, *derekh erets* (good manners), and mutual sensitivity between members of the congregation that were more important than enforcing the use of proper nusach.

PRESERVING ENDANGERED TRADITION Certain members gave other reasons for a commitment to "correct practice" in addition to the community's self-image as traditional and precise. The music professor spoke of the richness and diversity of Jewish musical and liturgical traditions. He feared that distinctions among nuschaot were being lost and spoke passionately about the importance of preserving these traditions in their unique and specific forms. He declared, "Now from the point of view of the ethnomusicologist in the twenty-first century, I'm sure they wouldn't care . . . if the tradition was maintained. They would say, 'Isn't it interesting, [a] new tradition, an American tradition is evolving and these old strains have gone by the wayside, and now there's this one musical tradition that's applied for all these services.' But for me, . . . I'm desperate to keep trying to see if we can keep these various strands going, and not just have them become homogenized into some strange *nusach America*." While he understood that musical traditions undergo development and transformation, he was emotionally and intellectually committed to their preservation. In fact, he devoted considerable energy to writing, lecturing, teaching, and directing an important Jewish choral group to ensure that these traditions were preserved, studied, and performed.

"NO ONE HERE REALLY KNOWS NUSACH" Still, even with this stress on the importance of nusach, I repeatedly heard members of this Orthodox synagogue insist that they "did not know nusach." One member speculated on what percentage of the congregation is committed to and actually knows these musical and liturgical traditions. He observed, "I would say [only] . . . about 10 percent really know. I may be exaggerating, but not by much. A lot of people pay lip service—'Oh, nusach is very important'—but if you sang them the nusach . . . they wouldn't know."

It was notable that even knowledgeable members of this congregation played down and derided their own liturgical skills and knowledge of "correct" nusach. A member of the synagogue who is admired for his liturgical skills, in both davening and chanting the Torah, claimed that he was "rather shaky about nusach." He said, "There are some parts of the nusach I know, because my father did make a point of teaching me this, but I'm not that conversant with the rest of it." Another worshipper, who has a reputation as a skilled leader, noted, "I'm probably at the lower range—and for some davening I really have not done it as often enough or known long enough to even consider myself to be competent." Listening to members of Shaarei Tefillah discuss this as they stood around outside their synagogue was rather like sitting in a locker room hearing semiprofessional players insist that they "didn't really know basketball."[21]

What does it mean when these members maintain that "no one really knows nusach"? Objectively, the level of Jewish knowledge at Shaarei Tefillah is as high as that of any Orthodox congregation in town. The majority of the members are liturgically skilled enough to lead daily services. Members of this shul know nusach as well as any "nonprofessional" cantor can be expected to know these musical traditions. I believe that when they insist that they do not know nusach, they are asserting that their musical and liturgical traditions are precise, detailed, historically specific, and not easily known. They are saying that the tradition they have chosen is subtle, varied, and complicated. Thus they affirm that there is a correct musical and liturgical tradition, rich in nuance and complexity. These modern Orthodox Jews are conscious that they live in a unique historical time: anti-Semitism is minimal, their access to American society is broad. However, they choose not to enter fully the "Goldene Medina," the golden country that lies spread out before them. The tradition they have chosen in its place is venerable and valuable. Their commitment to proper nusach is one further way to affirm their unique separateness in the face of the challenge and appeal of the seductive superculture.

Beth Pinchas: "Through The Music, You Reach The Feeling of The Moment"

When I spoke to the Bostoner Rebbe's son, Rav Naftali Horowitz, about nusach, he said, "Nusach is also a type of melody but it's not a melody where it's song. If you want to get more to the secular world, it's more like rap music. Rap music's not like song. [It's] like Jesse Jackson speaks. . . . We basically created the first rap music and that's called nusach."

It was notable that the only one who used contemporary metaphors in his explanations of Jewish liturgical music was a Bostoner Hasid who looked as though he had stepped out of nineteenth-century Poland. While working hard to isolate himself from the American superculture, Rav Naftali showed that he was hip. His proprietary claim of historical authenticity ("*We* created the first rap music . . .") underscores the primacy and validity of the Torah, its teachings and traditions.

Rav Naftali explained that as the nusach is applied to specific text, it might deal with feelings of joy or awe, mourning or longing for the Moshiach (Messiah). He stressed that in every case, "The music gets the words across and your kavanah in tefillah [your intentions in prayer] [is] much stronger. . . . Through the music and the melody, you can reach much more the feeling of the moment. That's what music does, brings over and clearer across to the soul, the *neshamah*, the feeling of the moment."

In this way, nusach functions to bring out the essential spiritual meaning in the prayers and helps the worshipper forge a direct connection between the soul and the text. Here we see that nusach is more than a way to interpret the meaning of the text: it functions as a shortcut, a direct path to the historical moments described in each prayer, the truth and experience of the liturgy.

When Rav Naftali's father, the Bostoner Rebbe, explained the function of nusach, he focused on the transformative role of music. He explained that nusach facilitated the transition from the weekday to the Sabbath, from the ordinary to the holy, from the everyday to the nearly messianic state of Shabbat:

The Friday night service, Kabbalat Shabbat, represents a mood change, represents leaving the world of exile, the world of *golus* [galut,

Ashkenazi pronunciation] and entering into the world of geulah, redemption, of almost *olam haba* [the world to come]. Shabbos is *me'eyn olam haba* [a foretaste of the world to come]. It gives us some sort of an impression of what olam haba is like. When you switch gears and you enter into that type of a world, there is ecstasy, there is excitement, there's fervor that accompanies what we do, and it expresses itself in the way we proclaim the event. It's an event that needs proclamation. The opening words of the service tell us how we do it. Because the first words of the Friday night service are *Lekhu nerananah* [Come, let us rejoice (in song)]. It doesn't say, *lekhu lehitpalel* [Come, let us pray]. It says *lekhu nerananah*, let us sing![22]

Through the nusach, the worshipper makes an experiential leap, a transition from the world of the profane to the world of the sacred. This heightened intensity and rejoicing are all conveyed in the nusach. Even the pitch of one's singing is raised through the excitement. The leader is able to move and elevate the worshipper with these sentiments. The Rebbe stressed that the leader's sincerity was paramount. The shaliach tsibbur must feel and understand the meaning of the prayers or else the nusach doesn't work. As the Rebbe emphasized, "You just can't convey the message if you're not the messenger." He continued, "The idea is, this is an occasion of song, an occasion of festivity, and therefore . . . we must not overlook it. And of course, when we say *lekhu nerananah*, we *feel* . . . we *experience* what's happening. The prayers come with more excitement, with more fervor, with more kavanah. It's louder than normal tefillah that you might just glance over. Usually . . . the sign of the change of mood would be in the tone of the prayer. You would be doing it in a higher pitch."

The Rebbe continued, "If you feel the words are precious, are important, you're going to emphasize them. You're not going to try to get to the next word before you give this word all it has. And therefore you would be concentrating on that rather than passing by the subject. . . . That's where the extra *dreydl* [ornamental turn, Yiddish] would come in, that's where the extra note would come in . . . to give it more feeling."

This heightened musical and spiritual intensity does more than convey the meaning of the words; it conveys the experience of the events. The Rebbe went on to say, "It is the nusach that tends to guide you to what's happening. It's via the tune of the nusach that you get the meaning of the words. Maybe even more than the words, you get the meaning of the events, which is the ultimate of what we would like to have. . . . There are the six chapters before *Lekhah dodi* which represent the six days of the week and getting closer every day, every *kapitel* [each Kabbalat Shabbat psalm, literally, 'chapter,' Yiddish], to the ultimate of your goal, the Shabbos" (CD #35).

The Rebbe believed that the actual tune of the Friday night nusach itself might be arbitrary. Still, history and tradition have imbued it with power and meaning and this nusach has become the tune that "gets us off." He said:

I don't know whether we can say that we know . . . exactly what the meaning of the tune [of Kabbalat Shabbat nusach] is as applied to the words. . . . Now, it's basically the nusach of the world, but of course everyone has their little *kvetch* [twist, Yiddish], their little *drey* [ornamental turn, Yiddish] . . . you hear the *Arba'im shanah* . . . you know we're taking off. So . . . there is no explanation why we are taking off with *this* tune. Maybe we could have taken off with another tune but we've taken off with this tune for millennia, forever, . . . so that's the tune that gets us into the new position.

The Rebbe teaches that as Friday night approaches, it is through the nusach that the worshipper is positioned to begin a journey that is potentially transformative, both for the individual Jew and for the Jewish people. The prayers of Kabbalat Shabbat celebrate the ever present possibility of personal and national redemption. Each worshipper becomes God's messenger, bearing witness that through the experience of Shabbos, we taste the possibility of ultimate salvation. In welcoming the Shabbos Queen and observing Shabbos with joy and attention, each Hasid prepares the way for the Moshiach and the World to Come. Nusach is the means to tell that story with an emotional intensity deeper than intellect, strengthened and bolstered by generations of musical meaning.

Conclusions

The *Mahzor Vitry*, a ninth-century religious manual, quotes a tradition that the melodies of the synagogue were taught to Moses by God on Mount Sinai: Jews have strong feelings about music (Samuel 1893:91). As these quotes show, contemporary conceptions of nusach are bound up in these Jews' struggles with modernity and efforts to clarify and assert their religious and cultural identity. For some, as external markers of identity fall away, nusach serves as an ever more powerful connection to Jewish history and tradition. Others see nusach as the key to a more participatory prayer experience, reconnecting them to traditional texts, with the rhythm of the body and their breathing. For some, a commitment to performing correct nusach underscores their belief in the importance and value of traditional religious practice. They reject other possible musical—and communal—choices as they separate themselves both from other Jews and from American culture. For yet others, nusach conveys the experience of Jewish history—past, present, and moving toward a messianic future. Nusach is performed and interpreted strategically as these American Jews define and present their identity.

4

Meaning and Melody Choice
in Jewish Worship

Identity, Choice, and Internal Bilingualism

In one of the talmudic stories explaining how the Jews became the chosen people, God asks those assembled at Mount Sinai, "Will you accept my Torah and live by its teachings?" Just as the question is posed, God holds the entire mountain over the heads of the Jews and adds, "It's your choice whether to accept the Torah or not, but if you don't, I will drop this mountain on you and it will mark your graves!" (text after a passage in the Babylonian Talmud, *Shabbat* 88a). Many Jews have felt ambivalent about choice ever since.

For the Jew at the beginning of the twenty-first century, Jewish observance and identification is bound up in the desire and ability to make choices within constraints. Most of these constraints are self-imposed. Melody choice in Jewish worship should be placed in a larger range of choices that American Jews make as they construct their identity in a society where ethnic and religious affiliation is increasingly voluntary.[1]

Musical choices are best viewed as one point on a continuum that includes how we speak, pray, chant, and sing (Titon 1988:xv). Jews have constantly dealt with issues of linguistic choice, as is shown by Max Weinreich's examination of how Jews historically functioned within at least two languages, a condition that he calls "internal Jewish bilingualism" (1980:247–314). Weinreich observes that "Ashkenazic Jews (just like other Jewish communities since the Diaspora) have always been a minority in a non-Jewish milieu; hence they always had to be bilingual" (ibid.:247). In addition to the language of Judaism's sacred texts, the Jewish community had to know the language of the "coterritorial majority." Weinreich calls this situation "external bilingualism." However, throughout the entire history of Ashkenazi Jewry, the community's *Weltanschauung* was formed by a "bilingualism within the Jewish community . . . the symbiosis of Yiddish and Loshn-koydesh [scriptural Hebrew]" (ibid.:247). The Jew always had, at the very least, two languages in which to express reality. In this way, language shaped Jewish reality as a "cofashioner of life, a cocreator of values "(ibid.:5). So deeply was this bilingualism ingrained in the Jewish folk psyche that people read it back into Jewish history, believing that the Yiddish translation of the Torah had been given to Moses on Mount Sinai (ibid.:249).

This internal bilingualism has affected Jewish culture in many ways. Speakers and writers were conscious that certain words had strong historical association, their multivalence rooted in ancient scriptural and liturgical traditions. Weinreich maintains that this grounding in two languages gave the members of the Yiddish community a "much wider spiritual horizon." Almost by default, Yiddish speakers assimilated and experienced the religious heritage of Hebrew. Through this "secular" vernacular, "spirituality pervaded the community" (Weinreich 1980:314). Internal bilingualism created a culture in which the ability to distinguish among shades of nuance in textual interpretation was raised to an art form and seen as the pinnacle of educational achievement. The *talmid hakham*, a wise disciple, was a wordsmith who, as it was said of the sage Rabbi Akiba, could even find interpretations for the ornaments adorning the letters of the Torah (Babylonian Talmud, *Menahot* 29b).

This bilingualism created a culture in which Jews continually played with the meaning of words. In his analysis of word play in Jewish *lernen* (Talmud study, Yiddish), the social anthropologist Samuel Heilman describes some of the symbolic associations that became connected to these Jewish languages as modern Hebrew entered the linguistic picture in the last century. Heilman writes that Hebrew can be divided into two types, "*Ivrit* or modern Hebrew and *Loshn Koydesh*, the holy language steeped in and associated with sacred literature." Modern Hebrew, with its Sephardic accents and cadences, is "capable of semantically handling even the most secular and modern matters." As such, it has become associated with contemporaneity and modernity. Heilman continues, "*Loshn Koydesh*, on the other hand, is filled with *gemore-loshn*, the unchanging language of talmudic idiom, and freighted with scriptural quotation. Along with Yiddish *taytsh* [the form of Yiddish used to translate and discuss Hebrew scripture], whose accents and inflections it shares, it has become generally associated with tradition and semantic stability" (1983:166–67). He goes on to say: "The Ashkenazic sound has come to be associated with Loshn Koydesh and its traditionalism. . . . speakers who wish to signal their association with tradition and holiness will often revert to an Ashkenazic pronunciation—even if they commonly speak Sephardic Hebrew." (ibid.).[2] For example, when praying, it is common to hear certain modern Orthodox Jews pronounce the phrase *melekh haolam* ([God,] King of the universe) as *melekh haoylam*. The sounds of Ashkenazi Hebrew, such as "oy," are understood to hearken back to the Eastern European yeshiva, a world imbued by these worshippers with more Jewish authenticity than either America or contemporary Israel. Heilman considers the symbolic meaning of this word play in his examination of a talmudic study circle (ibid.:160–200). His close analysis shows the extent to which the "people of the book" understand and manipulate the polysemic nature of words.[3] Jews do the same with the music used in worship, as I explore in the following sections.

Language, Code, and Music

I have found it productive to apply the concepts of code and code-switching from sociolinguistics to melody choice in Jewish worship (Summit 1993:54–56; also cf. Slobin 1992:61).[4] Monica Heller defines code-switching as "the use of more than one language in the course of a single communicative episode." She postulates that this phenomenon has received attention because it "violates a strong expectation that only one language will be used at any given time." Yet in the course of our everyday encounters, we constantly manipulate aspects of our language (accent, vocabulary, pronunciation) for strategic reasons. We use language as a code to forge connections with people, or to keep them at a distance, that is, to level or maintain boundaries between ourselves and others (Heller 1988:1).

Even when we are not explicitly thinking about what word to use or how we speak it, we pick our language strategically. Through linguistic switching, a speaker chooses the particular community with which he or she is identifying at a given moment. Samuel Heilman notes that in a situation where switching is possible, such as multilingual settings, each choice can be seen as an "implicit victory for the community in which that language is dominant" (1983:175). Insofar as music is also chosen strategically in Jewish worship, this methodology can also be applied to melody choice. As American Jews select melodies for public worship, they draw from a variety of musical and linguistic repertoires, such as nusach, "traditional" tunes from Sulzer and Lewandowski, Hasidic, Israeli, Sephardic, and contemporary American Jewish music. The use of the term *code* in this study, as opposed to repertoire or style, is meant to imply that melodies are infused with particular associations, coded meaning, and symbolic significance. I should stress that linguistic code-switching works only in bilingual settings, that is, where participants have facility in both the *unmarked* (familiar) and *marked* (unexpected) language (Scotton 1988:168). For this model to be productively applied to melody choice, participants must be familiar with both melodic codes used in the shift.

What is a melodic code? We can think of them functioning much the same way as brand names in advertising. They are recognized easily and quickly. Melodic codes are composed of redundant components with a high level of predictability. A code has an identifiable, stylistic profile, a bundle of recurring, packaged details, such as rhythm, melodic contour, the number of melodic repetitions, vocal quality, ornamentation, harmony, instrumental accompaniment, the relation between solo performance and congregational participation, and length of songs. While they are identified easily, their symbolic meaning and situational associations are different from community to community. I will present a number of examples of melodic code-switching and code-layering in Jewish worship, drawing from additional Jewish worship communities and religious services beyond those already detailed in this book.

It should first be said that nusach in Jewish worship functions as a complex system of melodic code in its own right. In worship communities where the nuances of this system are fully realized, nusach anchors the worshipper in the daily and seasonal liturgical cycle. Nusach is particular to the time of day as well as to weekday, Shabbat, and holidays. As one congregant declared, "Blindfold me, spin me around, and put me in any traditional synagogue and I'll tell you what time it is and what day it is!" In fact, this claim is hyperbolic. Within a given congregation, daily nusach is the same throughout the year. Festival nusach is the same for the three major festivals. Furthermore, many congregations are not so discriminating in their choice of nuschaot. Still, we see the power that this worshipper attributes to nusach; the music underscores occasions throughout the year and orients the worshipper to the liturgical cycle.

For other worshippers, nusach has emotional force growing out of its—sometimes imagined—historical significance. A graduate student who participated in the Conservative service at Tufts Hillel reflected, "I sit in synagogue and I listen to the melodies that our people sang for five thousand years and [the nusach] calms and centers me." No scholars have attempted to trace the music of the synagogue back to Adam and Eve. Still, by the reference to the Hebrew year, traditionally calculated as more than five millennia since the creation of the world, this worshipper honors the antiquity and the contemporary power of these musical traditions. In a world marked by constant and disruptive change, this worshipper finds it "calming and centering" to participate in "authentic" traditions that have existed, in her statement, since the birth of time. The fact that these statements are technically incorrect does not negate the importance and power of nusach. Worshippers sometimes hold symbolic associations to nusach that have more to do with their own search for authenticity than can be supported by the music itself.

Still, these prayer modes *are* rooted deeply in Jewish history. Venerable traditions have developed determining how and when this music is used in worship. CD #36 presents five recorded examples of the Barekhu (Bless [the Lord, who is blessed!]), the call to worship, beginning with daily nusach and proceeding through Kabbalat Shabbat, Shabbat morning, festival, and High Holiday. These examples reflect the tradition of nusach as sung by a knowledgeable baal tefillah at the Orthodox congregation Shaarei Tefillah (also cf. Levine 1989:28, example 2.12).

Melodic code-switching has long been established in synagogue tradition. An example from the public cantellation of the Book of Esther on the holiday of Purim illustrates how code-switching functions as an interpretive strategy to carry the meaning and emotive context from one ritual experience into another. Blom and Gumperz call this device *metaphorical* code-switching, "because the unexpected variety is a metaphor for the social meanings the variety has come to symbolize" (Heller 1988:5).

Sacred text is always chanted, never read, in the traditional synagogue. Although the same *taamei hamikra* (cantillation marks) are used throughout the Bible, they are sung differently according to the biblical book or special section in which they appear. While the accents serve as punctuation and have the same conjunctive/disjunctive function in every book, the melody of each accent is unique to each book or grouping of books. Specific books of the Hebrew Bible are read on particular holidays, and certain cantillation melodies and modes become associated with that holiday, its practices, and its observance. On Purim, in the midst of a carnival-like celebration, the Book of Esther is chanted in the synagogue. I would characterize Esther trop as major and narrative. Its cantillation motifs are simple, without as much ornamentation as is found in, say, the cantillation of the Prophets (see phrase #1 in Example 4.1). There is a switch common among Ashkenazi communities, where certain phrases of the Book of Esther (e.g., 1:7, 2:6) are customarily chanted to the melodic motifs normally used for the Book of Lamentations. This text is read publicly on Tisha B'Av, the ninth day of the Hebrew month of Av, commemorating the destruction of both the First (586 B.C.E.) and Second (70 C.E.) Temples in Jerusalem. Esther 2:6 describes the lineage of the story's hero,

Example 4.1. Cantillation for the Book of Esther.

Mordechai, and tells how the king of Babylonia, Nebuchadnezzar, took Mordechai's family in exile from Jerusalem (phrase #2). After using Lamentations trop for that verse, the reader then immediately resumes Megillah (Book of Esther) trop (phrase #3).

The switch to this trop functions in several ways as a metaphorical code-switch. For traditional Jews, the minor-mode Lamentations trop has many symbolic associations. Tisha B'Av is a fast day and is preceded by three weeks of communal mourning practices: many Jews do not eat meat in the period before the holiday, weddings are not performed, and instrumental music is not played in public celebrations. It is traditional to chant the Book of Lamentations by candlelight, sitting on the floor or on low stools, symbolic mourning practices. On one level, this melodic code-switch reminds the listener of the historic background of the Esther story—a history of persecution and exile—setting the stage for the book's atypical story of miraculous deliverance. On another level, the switch functions as time-travel within the Jewish liturgical cycle, briefly but powerfully shifting the knowledgeable listener out of the festive, raucous celebration of Purim into the dimly lit hall of Tisha B'Av, where worshippers sit on the floor, mourning Jerusalem's destruction.

Also chanted to the melody of Lamentations is Esther 1:7, *vekelim mekelim shonim* ("The vessels being diverse one from another"). This verse describes the vessels of gold used to serve wine at the lavish banquet given by King Ahasuerus. In rabbinic tradition these vessels were supposedly stolen from the Holy Temple after its first destruction. The code-switch from Esther to Lamentations trop in this verse serves several functions. For the learned, it recalls the rabbinic interpretation of the verse. For the ordinary Jew familiar with the traditional liturgy, the mournful, minor-key tune of Lamentations evokes the deep emotions associated with Tisha B'Av. The plaintive melody sets a tone for this otherwise innocent banquet, commenting on the character of Ahasuerus and his retinue and foreshadowing the danger that will confront the Jews of Shushan.

A subcategory of metaphorical code-switching in contemporary Jewish worship is melodic switching used to signal political or ideological identification, particularly in regard to Israel. In 1967 Israel's victory in the Six Day War stimulated a rise of Jewish identity and positive identification with Israel. At that time many Conservative and modern Orthodox congregations began to sing the prayer *Vahavi'enu leshalom* ("Bring us, in peace") in the morning Sabbath service to the tune of *Hatikvah*, the Israeli national anthem. One would expect to hear the text chanted as in Example 4.2; instead one would hear it sung as in Example 4.3.

Example 4.2. *Vahavi'enu leshalom*, nusach.

Va - ha - vi - e - nu   le - sha - lom   me - ar - ba   kan - fot   ha - a - rets...

Example 4.3. *Vahavi'enu leshalom* to the tune of *Hatikvah*.

Va - ha - vi - e - nu   le - sha - lom   me - ar - ba   kan- fot   ha - a - rets ...

The melody of *Hatikvah* is appropriate for the text of this prayer, which reads, "Bring us in peace from the four corners of the world and restore us to our homeland." Israel's national anthem celebrates the return to homeland from exile, "a free people in our [own] land." And yet it was only after the surge of Jewish identity following the Six Day War that the *Hatikvah* melody was introduced in the service. The use of this melody is also significant because of the position of this prayer in the service, immediately preceding the Shema, the central creed and statement of monotheistic faith in the Jewish tradition. In the 1960s many Jews were alienated from the synagogue and from the Jewish community in general. Israel's military victory, however, created a surge of community pride and an increase in communal and religious affiliation. For many, Zionism became their primary ideological creed, considerably more powerful and accessible than traditional Judaism. The switch to this coded, nationalistic melody—and its central placement in the service—enforces and reflects this identification with Israel. Currently the American Jewish community, at least in private, has a more problematic relationship with Israel, and today it is rare to hear the *Hatikvah* melody used for this prayer.[5]

Melody is also chosen strategically in the Shabbat morning service to foreshadow the approach of a coming holiday. The Sabbath service traditionally concludes with the fifteenth-century hymn *Adon olam*. Congregations usually have three or four melodies in their local repertoire for this popular, strophic hymn. The choice of melody each Sabbath is up to the prayer leader. The opening of one of the most popular tunes is transcribed in Example 4.4. Some ascribe this tune to Eliezar Gerovitsch; others refer to it as traditional (Nulman 1975:4, 5). In many congregations, on the Sabbath preceding specific joyous holidays such as Hanukah, Purim, or Passover, the leader will break away from the familiar repertoire and sing the hymn to the signature melody of the upcoming holiday. For example, on Hanukah it is customary to sing *Maoz tsur* at home every evening after kindling the Hanukah lights. Even though many compilations of Jewish liturgical song list the source of this melody as "traditional," it is important to note that this fifteenth-century German melody, adapted from a folk song, was used in church settings by Martin Luther and J. S. Bach.[6] Most worshippers are simply ignorant of the Christian associations to this tune. On the Shabbat before Hanukah it is common to sing *Adon olam* to this tune, a musical code symbolically associated with the upcoming holiday (Example 4.5). There is a playful element to this kind of switch. Wor-

Example 4.4. *Adon olam*, popular Shabbat tune.

A - don o - lam a - sher ma - lakh, be - te - rem kol ye - tsir niv - ra...

shippers greet the melody, the *leitmotif* of Hanukah, with nods and smiles. Melody becomes a bridge, foreshadowing and cueing the approach of the upcoming holiday.[7] This foreshadowing is not limited to joyous holidays. CD #37 is an example of *Lekhah dodi* sung to Sulzer's melody for the lament *Alei Tsion* (Rise up, Zion). This lament is traditionally sung on Tisha B'Av, and its tune is used for *Lekhah dodi* in many Conservative and Orthodox synagogues in the three-week mourning period preceding that holiday of remembrance.

Melody Choice and Conflict Management

Melodic choice is also used to manage conflict in communal worship. At the Hillel Foundation at Harvard University, participants avoided community conflict by mutually agreeing *not* to sing a tune for the Friday evening *Kiddush* (the Sabbath blessing over wine). The university is a place where, through choice and necessity, Jews from different movements must negotiate certain standards of religious practice such as the use of instrumental music on Shabbat, standards of keeping kosher, and the participation of women in religious ritual (cf. Summit 1993:55–57).

Harvard Hillel, like many university Jewish communities, draws Jews from Reform, Conservative, and Orthodox denominations. For the most part, these students worship and celebrate within their own denominational communities, but at certain occasions, such as Shabbat dinner, members of all the groups gather in religious celebration. In those contexts, participants continually negotiate religious practice that will satisfy the halakhic and ideological requirements of the pluralistic community.

The communal Shabbat dinner begins with the recitation of table prayers, including the Kiddush, the sanctification of the day, which is recited over a cup of wine. At Harvard Hillel, an intradenominational disagreement arose concerning whether a woman would be allowed to chant the Friday evening Kiddush for the full, assembled community. In a traditional context, it is customary for a man to chant this prayer. Many Hil-

Example 4.5. *Adon olam*, to the tune of *Maoz tsur*.

A - don o - lam a - sher ma - lakh, be - te - rem kol ye - tsir niv - ra...

lel students, including the majority of Orthodox students, wanted a woman to be able to make Kiddush for the entire community. The rabbi who works with the Orthodox community at Harvard studied the codes that govern Jewish legal behavior and found conflicting opinions on this issue. Joseph Caro's authoritative sixteenth-century code of Jewish law, the *Shulchan Arukh*, allows a woman to lead this prayer, especially in the context of her home and immediate family. However, the late nineteenth-century commentary on the *Shulchan Arukh*, the *Mishnah Berurah*, ruled that a woman should *not* make Kiddush. While a small group of students accepted this opinion, the majority of Orthodox students favored the position that Hillel functioned as home and family for the student community during the year, and that therefore a woman should be allowed to lead the Kiddush. It was therefore decided that the community would alternate: one week a man would lead Kiddush, the next week a woman. It appeared that the problem had been solved.

However, a second problem arose. A small number of the Orthodox students raised the issue of *kol ishah*, the prohibition against hearing the voice of a woman in song (Babylonian Talmud, *Berakhot* 24a). Historically, the rabbis feared that a woman's voice was sexually arousing and forbade men to listen to women sing lest they be distracted from study or work. While it is unusual for modern Orthodox university students to invoke this law, once it was brought up, the community was bound to find a compromise solution that answered the concerns of the entire group. To solve this problem, the community decided that a woman could lead Kiddush but she was not allowed to sing or chant the first part of the prayer, which is customarily chanted as a solo. In this egalitarian environment, it was then considered only fair to extend this prohibition to men. Neither men nor women would sing or chant Kiddush; the leader had to read the Kiddush until the section beginning *kivanu vaharta* (because you have chosen us), at which point the entire community would join together in the standard Kiddush melody that approximates Louis Lewandowski's setting.

This rather extraordinary example of strategic melody choice involves a switch from *melody* to *no melody* in a context where sacred text is always chanted. In a traditional setting, the *reading* rather than the *chanting* of liturgy is so unusual that the lack of melody encodes the liturgy powerfully. The community took the prohibition seriously. In several instances men broke into undertone recitative chant while leading the solo section of Kiddush and were later rebuked by the student community leaders. During the time that this compromise was being worked out, Harvard Hillel was interviewing for a new director. One rabbi, a serious candidate for the position, was spending Shabbat with the community. He was informed of this issue, but when given the honor of making Kiddush, still insisted on chanting the prayer, a factor that contributed to his not getting the job. He was accused of singing! To which he reportedly replied, "You call *that* singing?" Yet the community was very serious about their negotiated compromise; it was precisely the elimination of melody in the first section of the Kiddush that enabled this multidenominational community to gather, pray, sing, and eat together. Over time, this compromise solution did not remain workable; everyone simply missed singing Kiddush. The stricter group of students relented, allowing both men and women to chant the prayer.

At Tufts Hillel, melody choice to manage conflict was less successful. The students were planning a "teaching service," a program conceived both as an actual service and as an educational program to introduce new students to the meaning and structure of Shabbat worship. During the service, students and staff presented short explanations of the prayers and meditations on their meaning. Students from both Reform and Conservative groups planned and co-led the service, one of the few occasions during the year that the two communities attempted to pray together.

The planning committee struggled to construct a service that would be acceptable for both communities. They searched for common ground—especially common musical ground—that would be consistent with the halakhic orientation of the more traditional service and still express the worship style of the Reform students. Student leaders had high hopes that compromise solutions could be found; as one person said, "If we can sing together, we can pray together!" Ultimately, singing together proved harder than either group had imagined.

The planning committee did not have an easy job; these two services differ considerably. The Conservative service, often called "the traditional service," uses nusach and has almost no English. Most of the tunes were learned in the youth movement and summer camps of the Conservative movement. Davening is led by the shaliach tsibbur, who stands in front of the group. The majority of Conservative students hold the traditional position that instrumental music is halakhically forbidden on the Sabbath, and they would not think of using an instrument in Shabbat services. For the Reform students, the guitar and the role of the enthusiastic song leader have become emblematic of Reform worship in high school and college. Most view the guitar as essential to meaningful, participatory prayer. While there is a student leader and a song leader in the Reform service, the leadership role in this group moves person by person around the circle, as all worshippers take turns reading a section of the service. While many of the prayers and the structure of worship in both services are basically the same, it was clear to the planning committee that they were attempting to meld two services with essentially different styles.

Still, students believed that they could negotiate a joint service. In many ways, these Conservative and Reform students do not appear to be so different in their Jewish practice or approach to Jewish issues. They work together organizationally and are socially friendly. Students from both groups are deeply committed to building an active Jewish community on campus. Still, a certain tension marks relations between the two communities. Reform students sometimes feel that they are not treated as serious Jews by the more traditional Conservative students. It is in fact true that Conservative students sometimes criticize Reform students for not respecting traditional Jewish practice, such as the dietary laws or Sabbath observance. While both groups are part of Hillel, they work hard to maintain their separate active connections with their movements' national college groups, *Kesher* (Connection) for the Reform students and *KOACH* (Strength) for the Conservative students. As the discussion unfolded, it became clear that while Reform and Conservative students might not be so different in their private Jewish observance, they held tenaciously to their own styles of public worship. That public display was understood to be a major differentiating factor in their particular denominational identity.

The planning was difficult from the beginning. Reform Jews felt that the service was already skewed toward the traditional community. To accommodate the participants, the service needed to be held in the larger chapel, the room where traditional services were regularly held. Because Conservative students wanted access to the full text of the prayers, the traditional prayer book would be used. To bridge the gap between these two groups, a number of compromises were suggested, beginning with the easy issues. The planning committee decided to reconfigure the seating to a circle, reflecting the setup of the Reform service. A Reform student suggested that they use a guitar and tried to argue that the Conservative students' position forbidding an instrument was not consistent with their personal practice. He charged that Conservative students were not so strict in their personal observance concerning music on Shabbat, declaring, "But after Hillel, you'll go to a party where there's music. You'll listen to music in your room!" Still, leaders of the traditional service rejected the use of the guitar out of hand and insisted on differentiating between private and public observance. As private observance has diminished among American Jews, display of public Jewish observance such as worship traditions have become increasingly important in establishing boundaries between Jewish denominations.

To accommodate the Reform community, Conservative students had an easier time agreeing to change a number of the tunes, substituting Reform youth group tunes for prayers regularly used in the traditional service. The tunes chosen by the committee were rarely if ever sung in the traditional service. A traditional student suggested that they use a popular Reform youth group tune for *Mizmor shir leyom haShabbat* (a psalm, a song for the Sabbath day) and said, "It will make the Reform Jews feel welcome." This text is regularly sung to Kabbalat Shabbat nusach in the traditional service but there was no halakhic problem, nor any objection, to singing it to a tune instead. At the same time, other traditional students assumed that the rest of the psalms in the beginning of Kabbalat Shabbat would be chanted to the appropriate nusach, a style of music that is never used in the Reform service.

The Conservative students felt uncomfortable with the Reform students' proposal that they all sing Debbie Friedman's tune for the English text of the *Ve'ahavta*. They had never included a song in English in their service and one student said, "It feels *Protestant* or something!" Yet, in the spirit of compromise, the Conservative students agreed that if the prayer was first chanted in Hebrew, it could then be sung in English.

The Conservative students felt better about the next proposed change. At the conclusion of the silent *Amidah*, members of the traditional service often sang *Oseh shalom*. The Reform students are more familiar with a Reform youth group tune composed by J. Klepper and D. Freelander for the prayer *Shalom rav* (Great peace) (Davidson 1987:No. 58). The students chose to sing *Shalom rav*, whose text is found in the traditional liturgy but normally is prayed silently by the traditional congregation. While this was a departure from the minhag of the traditional service, there are no halakhic difficulties in singing this text to a different melody. Furthermore, many members of the traditional community knew and liked both tunes.

Throughout this meeting the modus operandi was to include enough of both communities' music to make both groups feel welcome. In this way, music, like language, could "signal shared culture or be used to create it" (Heller 1988:270). Members of both groups attempted to choose melodies to create, even briefly, a shared community in which all the members could belong and participate (cf. Blom and Gumperz 1972, McClure and McClure 1988).[8]

In fact, these attempts to create a shared experience had limited success. While many agreed that the service was an effective educational program, it did not work as worship. After the service, a number of Reform students grumbled that they had to follow the "*frum*-est common denominator." *Frum* is Yiddish for pious or ritually observant. These students were especially upset that they could not use a guitar in the service. Even with the addition of NFTY melodies and the change in the seating arrangement, the use of traditional nusach and absence of the guitar made Reform students feel that they were at a traditional service. Conversely, Conservative students commented on the "Reform nature" of this service: more English explanations, unfamiliar melodies, and *even an English song*! The inclusion of even *one* English song was enough to make the service feel foreign to the Conservative students. Labov describes this reaction as the phenomenon of categorical perception, in which "deviation from the norm is perceived as far more salient than its actual frequency would warrant" (1966, quoted in Woolard 1988:57). Both groups of students were unable to foresee that music from the "other" service had such strong coded significance that its very inclusion excluded the other group. Both communities' musical styles had been disrupted, creating an atmosphere in which neither the Reform nor the Conservative students felt especially at home.

Music and Code-Layering

Music provides the option to layer one code on top of another, combining many elements such as text, rhythm, melody, and instrumentation. In this way, multiple identities and associations can be presented simultaneously. An interesting example of melodic code-layering took place at the havurah B'nai Or. Many members spoke of growing up in large suburban Reform and Conservative synagogues whose materialism, lack of partici-patory worship, and "boring" musical traditions "turned them off" to the organized Jewish community. During or after college they were influenced by Eastern religious traditions, particularly Buddhism. These members stressed that Eastern chant, yoga, and meditation had been formative fac-tors in their approach to spirituality. While not Jewish, these practices had touched them deeply, allowing them to reconnect to religion in a more substantial and meaningful way. It was common to hear members speak of time spent in ashrams or neo-Buddhist retreat centers such as the Kri-palu Center in western Massachusetts. However, as important as these traditions were, they were not *their* traditions. As one woman said of her experience in a yoga center, "It felt very spiritually good there, but the chanting was not Jewish chanting, it was Hindu chanting." By joining B'nai Or, these Jews were returning and reconnecting with Jewish worship and prayer.

Both their journey and their connection to Eastern traditions can be seen through their strategic use and choice of melody. The first time I re-corded a service at B'nai Or, I was surprised to hear the congregation sing what appeared to be a *kirtan*, westernized Hindu chant, as a meditation before lighting the Shabbat candles (CD #38). The text of this chant was a mixture of Hebrew and English: "Barekhu, Dear One, Shekhinah, Holy Name; When I call on the light of my soul, I come home." The community sang the same chant over and over, for more than twelve minutes. While chanting, certain members closed their eyes and sat in the lotus position, touching thumb and forefinger, resting their hands palms up on their knees. Lev, the leader, accompanied the chant on guitar. When I later asked him about the origins of this melody, he said that indeed he had borrowed it from Eastern tradition and substituted Hebrew and English for the origi-nal Hindi words. He continued, "I learned it as 'Hari Om' and 'Krishna,' . . . and I thought this was a nice melody. The 'Hari Om' and 'Krishna' don't work for me but 'Barekhu' and 'Shekhinah' would . . . so I just put those two together."

The use of this chant, reinforced by participants' affect while chanting, levels the boundaries between Eastern and Jewish spiritual traditions. The addition of the familiar Hebrew word *barekhu* (Bless!) anchors the chant for them as a Jewish ritual. The use of the Hebrew mystical name for God, Shekhinah, is also inclusive because it portrays God as female. The name Shekhinah is bracketed by loose English translation and commentary ("Dear One," "Holy Name") that makes the chant more accessible to the majority of the participants, who either do not know or are just beginning to learn Hebrew. The final English phrase ("When I call on the light of my soul, I go home") thematically connects the chant with the physical ritual of lighting candles. It also reflects the spiritual journey experienced by many participants as they move from Eastern religious traditions back "home" toward their Jewish identity. The strategic inclusion and manipulation of this melodic code mediates the conflict many participants feel in this dual attraction to both Eastern and Jewish traditions. Neither has to disappear.

In the chant, a fictional world is modeled where two religious traditions have found a peaceful coexistence (cf. Woolard 1988).

In another example of code-layering at B'nai Or's Friday evening service, both the leader and members assert their self-image as a unique Jewish community in which playfulness, spontaneity, and irreverence are not in conflict with Jewish tradition. Near the conclusion of the service the leader strummed his guitar and said that he would like to sing "an old Jewish melody, possibly one of the oldest of *all* Jewish melodies!" He then proceeded to sing the vocables "yai lai lai" in the style of a Hasidic niggun. In a moment the congregation realized that he was singing the tune "Happy Birthday to You." Members laughed and smiled, joining him in the melody.

After finishing the niggun, the leader extended birthday wishes to a woman who was a very active member of the havurah. Later I questioned Lev on his decision to add this "niggun" to the service. He replied, "It wasn't much of a forethought. She had come up to me to say it was her fiftieth birthday and she'd like some acknowledgment of it, and I said okay. I thought we'd do something [after services] but the thought popped into my head that it would be an appropriate thing to do, and it was fun. I've always felt that I wanted to be funny and to have fun at a service."

The congregation's response to this atypical code-layering was overwhelmingly positive. When questioned further about the appropriateness of this tune in the Shabbat service, Lev continued: "For me, there are two things going on: one is that I personally believe that anything done with dignity and a sense of inclusiveness in the experience of being in synagogue together is appropriate and that celebrating somebody's birthday . . . [is] a mitzvah." The mildly irreverent incorporation and judaization of this melody emphasizes the fact that fun and spontaneity are valued in this worshipping community. Many members said that when they joined B'nai Or they were looking for a community that was not as "stiff" and "formal" as the synagogues in which they grew up. The leader and members of B'nai Or used this humorous melodic code-layering to underscore these core values of their community that they see as differentiating them from the larger and more impersonal organized Jewish community.

Melody Choice and Boundary Violation

In the preceding example, melody choice affirms a community's identity but a choice of a particular melody can also violate a community's boundaries, threatening and challenging a group's self-image. Such an example took place at a minyan in Newton, Massachusetts. This minyan is a knowledgeable, participatory community; congregants take turns leading prayers, reading Torah, and giving sermons. The service is comprised of the complete Hebrew liturgy.

On the late December Shabbat in question, the leader chose an unexpected melody for the Musaf *Kedushah*, a central prayer in the service declaring God's holiness. According to this minyan's minhag, the *Kedushah* can be either chanted or sung to one of several tunes that are known by the members of the congregation. On this Shabbat, which coincided with Christmas, this leader chose to sing the *Kedushah* to the tune of *Adeste, fideles*, "O Come, All Ye Faithful."

First several worshippers chuckled. Then a few members walked out of the room. Although a small number of worshippers joined him, the leader finished the piece by himself and proceeded to complete the service without any unusual melodic variations. After services he was, in his words, "accosted" by a group of worshippers who roundly criticized him for appropriating the tune of "O Come, All Ye Faithful" for the *Kedushah*.

I interviewed a number of people about this incident and collected the following comments. A principal of a synagogue religious school said, "I spent too much time in grammar school and high school arguing that I shouldn't have to sing Christmas carols. I don't have to do it in my shul!" A university professor said, "I was embarrassed for our guests." This minyan rents space from and meets in the basement of a church. Another person said, "It was an insult to the church: I was afraid that the minister would walk by and think we were making fun of them." A lawyer in the group said, "The leader is supposed to help the congregation's kavanah, not distract from it!" When I interviewed the leader, his response was defensive: "Well, the hell with them if they can't take a joke!" When he cooled down a bit, he added, "That's great music. I thought, why shouldn't we be able to use it?" It should be noted that not everyone in the congregation reacted negatively to this melody. An artist commented, "I thought it was great . . . and ecumenical, like, we're not the only ones who believe in God!" Still, the criticism far outweighed the approval. The congregation's cueing (nonparticipation) and confrontation had been effective. I saw this leader daven several times after that Christmas weekend and, in his words, he has been "on good behavior," choosing from an accepted range of melodies for Shabbat worship.

It made little difference that Jews, especially the Hasidim, have a history of appropriating melodies from host cultures for use in worship. The melodic code of this Christmas carol was too loaded to be judged acceptable by this congregation. In this switch, which was intended to be playful, the leader pushed beyond the limits and challenged the community's self-definition. The community took up the challenge and asserted its self-definition as a subculture opposed to assimilation and committed to separation from the Christian superculture.

I have found that it is difficult to predict, even within specific communities, which boundaries are inviolable and which remain open and permeable. In that same minyan, it is acceptable for the children to sing *Adon olam* to the tune of "Rock Around the Clock." Some adults grimace, but the majority of parents indulge this childish conceit. Many of the children learned the tune at the Conservative Jewish day school, Solomon Schechter, where it is an acceptable if somewhat humorous melody. I discussed the use of this tune with some of the children in the congregation, my son included, and although they know it is humorous, most of them are not familiar with the original song. Once I was listening to the radio with my son Zack when he was nine years old and we heard the original version of Bill Haley's "Rock Around the Clock." Zack laughed and said, "Hey dad! It's *Adon olam!*" As James Clifford notes, such shifting reference points are common in the study of contemporary ethnography (1988: 14, 15). In any case, rock and roll apparently presented less of a challenge to that community's self-definition than did Christianity.

Finally, I wish to discuss a parody of the *Kiddush*, the blessing over wine, that is recited on Purim. Rather than taking melodies from the American superculture, this parody relies on elaborate, internally referenced melodic code-switching for its humor. Purim is a minor holiday celebrating the miraculous deliverance of the Jews of Persia from their enemy, Haman. The Book of Esther is chanted in the synagogue. Drinking, humorous skits (*purimshpil*), raucous behavior, and the wearing of costumes mark the celebration of this holiday. Whereas both the Sabbath and the festivals begin with the chanting of a *Kiddush* particular to the holiday, Purim begins with no such formal blessing over wine.

Among Ashkenazi Jews, the custom arose of beginning the *seudah* (festive meal) on Purim with a special *Kiddush*. While the text of this "Kiddush" parodies the festival and Sabbath Kiddush, key words are used as "pivot points" or "switch points" to branch off into well-known phrases of liturgical and scriptural Hebrew text. Each of these textural phrases is encoded with its own particular melody. Following is the beginning of a Purim Kiddush sung by Moshe Waldoks, recorded at a seudah at a home in Newton in 1993 (CD #39). In the analysis, the base text is the text that the Purim Kiddush is parodying. Pivot points are marked in **bold.**

Analysis of Purim Kiddush

Purim Kiddush:	*Vayehi bayoym hashishi*
Translation:	And it was on the sixth day
Melody:	Shabbat Kiddush
Base Text:	This begins as a parody of the Shabbat evening Kiddush, based on the text: *Vayehi erev vayehi voker, yom hashishi*
	(And it was evening and it was morning, the sixth day)

Purim Kiddush:	*vayakhulu **hashamayim***
Translation:	And the Heavens were finished
Text Source:	Shabbat Kiddush, Genesis 2:1–3
Melody:	Shabbat Kiddush

Purim Kiddush:	*(**hashamayim**) mesaprim kevoydoy*
Translation:	The heavens tell of God's glory
Text source:	Psalm 19, Shabbat morning
Melody:	Shabbat morning davening
Comment:	The Ashkenazi pronunciation, *kevoydoy*, as opposed to *kevodo*, is humorous, making fun of the stereotypically pious Eastern European Jew.

Purim Kiddush: ... *oy male oylam*
Translation: where the world is full ...
Text Source: Kedushah, Musaf Amidah
Melody: Kedushah, Musaf Amidah

Purim Kiddush: *meshartav shoalim, shoalim ze leze,* **ayei** *mekom kevodoy*
Translation: and call this one to that, where is the place of (God's) glory?
Text Source: Kedushah, Musaf Amidah
Melody: Kedushah, Musaf Amidah

Purim Kiddush: **ayei** *ayei Sawrah ishtekhaw?*
Translation: where is Sarah, your wife?
Text Source: Genesis 18:9
Melody: Parody, Torah cantillation

The Purim Kiddush progresses through Shabbat morning melodies (*Shema, Alenu*), Torah cantillation, piyyutim for the High Holidays (*Melekh al kol ha'arets* [King over all the earth], *Hayom* [This day]), selections from the Passover seder (The Ten Plagues, *Ehad mi yodea* [Who knows one?]), as well as other popular liturgical selections spanning the Jewish calendar year. The *Kiddush* concludes with several false endings, also using pivot words as puns to alter the meaning of the text. These endings create a sense of tension; they give the impression that the leader is about to recite an actual *berakhah* (blessing). According to Jewish law, it is considered a transgression to say a formulaic blessing that does not fulfill a specific commandment or is not connected to a commanded action. This is termed a *berakhah levatalah* (a wasted blessing). However, at the last moment the reader switches to a different word, nullifying the religious meaning of the blessing. Part of the humor of the Purim *Kiddush* relies on the tension created as the reader nearly transgresses a commandment.[9] Throughout the *Kiddush*, pivot points create junctions for melodic switching. Here, the pivot words pull one back from the edge of a transgression just as it appears irrevocable.

For example, one false ending to this Purim Kiddush begins "*Barukh atah Adoshem,* **shehakol** ... [slight pause]. This gives the impression that the reader is about to say the general blessing over unspecified food, "Blessed are you God, for everything (is created by his word)." However, the leader actually concludes "**shehakol** *kol Yaakov, vehayadayim yedei Esav*" ("the voice is the voice of Jacob, but the hands are the hands of Esau," Gen. 27:22). This switch plays on the Hebrew homonym, *kol.* Depending how it is spelled, *kol* can mean either "everything" or "voice." On one level, this pun is funny because of the unexpected switch pivoting on the word *kol.* On a deeper level, this text is the Jewish tradition's classic description of a situation where things are not as they seem. In this story from Genesis, Isaac says these words when Jacob comes to him disguised as Esau in order to steal Esau's blessing. On Purim, the world is turned upside down, a liminal situation mirrored in the ever-shifting texts and melodies of the Purim *Kiddush.* Nothing is as it appears. Masks cover people's faces. Men and women dress in each other's clothes. The musical switching in this parody liturgy creates a surreal landscape where the orderly progression of the liturgical year is purposely disrupted, a reflection of the holiday itself in microcosm. Unpacking all this material requires significant familiarity with traditional text and the cycle of the Jewish liturgical year. The ability to do that is a large part of the delight experienced by the knowledgeable listener.

By examining melody choice and code-switching in the performance of liturgical text, we see various strategies employed by these American Jews as they construct, maintain, and present their cultural and religious identity. They create or diffuse boundaries between themselves and other segments of the Jewish community and define their relationship with the non-Jewish American superculture. Melodic switches in Jewish worship also play upon the expectation that melodies are associated with certain times of day and certain occasions in the holiday cycle. The act of uprooting these melodies from their calendric position and context underscores both the existence of this musical/liturgical cycle and its power in organizing and hallowing time throughout the liturgical year.

Conclusion

American Jews and American
Religious Experience

A Walk across the Street

During the time I was writing this book, I made it a practice to "walk across the street" and speak with Protestant and Catholic colleagues at my university and in greater Boston about music in their worship services. Often, when I started talking about an issue, my Christian colleagues would finish my sentence. When I would ask, "So when it comes to music, what are you arguing about in *your* church?" they responded eagerly. Here my research was informal and the information I received is anecdotal, yet I was struck by how much we seemed to be standing on common ground.

The Christians with whom I spoke addressed many of the same issues that these Jews did when choosing music in prayer. They discussed their struggle to establish traditions that felt both modern and at the same time in touch with the past. They described their search for music that seemed historically authentic and yet spoke to the contemporary soul. I listened to congregants who valued their active participation in worship, involvement that is realized primarily through communal song. I met both clergy and laity who felt that their worship experience was compromised by poor-quality performance. Clergy, music directors, and organists put serious thought and effort into their choice of music, yet I heard conflicting answers to the question, "What makes a good hymn?" Both Catholic and Protestant worshippers wanted to affirm the unity of their church by the simple act of singing together, yet congregants brought very different ideas of what they should sing, how it should be orchestrated, and who should sing it. In the words of an Episcopal priest, "People don't like to change or be challenged that much. These days, discussions about music and liturgy always seem to be contentious." These Christians were acutely aware that their religious and sometimes cultural identity is bound up in the music they sing—and occasionally refuse to sing—in church.

147

The minister at the First Baptist Church explained that his congregants came from many different backgrounds and as a result, preferred different styles of music in worship. Some simply did not feel that they were worshipping if they could not sing the music they remembered from their childhood. He described how their church focused on more formal "straight hymns directed toward God," hymns that used "we" as opposed to "I." Yet some members had grown up deeply moved by gospel hymns, in which the text focuses on the individual worshipper's relationship with Jesus. The minister spoke about how people expected to have a choice, and that expectation created a certain conflict in the church because, "we just might not sing what they remember." The minister added a theological dimension to the general consensus not to sing gospel hymns: the language of the hymns shaped the concept of community in the church. He declared, "I don't want it to be just me and God. I want it to be a real gathered worship. If it's just a bunch of individuals singing about their personal experience with God, then it's not a gathered community."

A deacon at this Baptist church reflected on music's power to create community through participation, with its advantages and its pitfalls. He chuckled and commented, "The Roman Catholics have recently discovered [the power of congregational participation] . . . and found it to be a bonanza, so they've adopted many of our hymns, many of the good ones and many of the bad ones, but they sing them very enthusiastically because they've found, like we've known for a long time, that having the congregational participation is important." Still, like the cantor at Temple Israel, he felt that participation should in some way be controlled and limited. At times it went too far and distracted from the worship experience. He gave the following example: "In a lot of churches they will have these sing-alongs. They will take parts of [Handel's] Messiah and get the whole congregation to sing the Hallelujah Chorus. I find that somewhat of a turn-off. I'm fussy enough that I like that stuff performed nicely, and to have a bunch of well meaning folks unrehearsed just singing along doesn't do much for me in a worship service."

While the majority of members liked their "high church" service, not everyone appreciated the stress on professional music with a leaning toward Bach. Both the minister and congregants recognized that while the church drew its music from local history and tradition, they "built their liturgy from scratch." As with B'nai Or and Temple Israel, authority was locally based and the national denomination could not tell an individual church what to do. Still, they were hesitant to invoke too much religious authority for their musical choices, which many members attributed simply to a well-developed sense of aesthetics. The minister felt strongly that one should not confuse community authority with theological authority: "Never assume that a majority vote is the same as the will of God."

At the Lutheran church one of the most difficult musical issues being addressed was that of participation versus performance, specifically in regard to the children's choir. The pastor explained, "One live issue in our community has been music for the children and the balancing of easy expression and accessibility with the challenge of performance and standards. This is especially challenging when you are dealing with a small congregation." He expressed his concern: "When the children do a children's song in church, we want it to be an authentic experience for them. But there are also aspects of performance to it, so the issue is to what extent do we keep some esthetic standards? If a child hasn't been able to rehearse, then should he be told not to sing with the children's choir?" If church leadership refused to let a child participate, they risked making the parents angry and the children disappointed. Yet if some children were totally unprepared to sing with the choir, their singing detracted from the worship experience.

In this Lutheran church, members and leadership struggled with how serious and formal the liturgy should be. For a church with a relatively fixed liturgy, it was difficult to balance these issues of formality versus informality, polished performance versus less demanding participation. The pastor explained, "Within the church we've been talking, should we offer a second, shorter, easier, more accessible liturgy? I've seen churches that have done that and there's a feeling that it's 'liturgy lite.' We're a congregation that holds together and I'm loath to split it. But would it serve more people? Would the blessing be greater? In fact, would it be somewhat liberating to be this way, or that way?" Should the church strive to remain one community or split to accommodate different musical and liturgical approaches? At both the atrium service at Temple Israel and Shaarei Tefillah, they decided that a split was the better solution.

This discussion of the nature of the worship experience led the pastor to speak about his approach to hymns. When the congregation sang together, a primary focus for him was the text of the hymn. He explained, "My own Swedish background was one in which the words had a significant value apart from the music. The words of hymns would function as prayers. They were often quoted at baptisms and funerals, where the minister would address the child, or the deceased, with words of this hymnic poetry." For him, those words carried the theology of the community in a way similar to that described by the Bostoner Rebbe as he focused on liturgical text.

The pastor often felt that members of his church paid more attention to the music than to the words of a hymn. He said, "A common dispute is 'Pastor, this is a nice hymn, but do we have to sing all the verses?' [Then I think] But the words are so wonderful and they tell a story! What could you cut out of this? Which of your children are you going to kill? For someone who is text oriented, the question seems strange, but in many churches people say we don't pay so much attention to the words." This comment reminded me of the conflict experienced by students at Tufts Hillel who wondered if enthusiastic participatory singing was actually prayer. The pastor went on to say that for many worshippers, it was possible to get so caught up in the music that one might unwittingly miss the meaning of the words. He related that this had happened to him when he was younger. It took him until his mid-20s to realize that he must have sung the hymn "Ye Watchers and Ye Holy Ones" at least a hundred times before he realized "that the words that I had sung over and over again in the second stanza were addressed to the Virgin Mary! Here we were, good Protestants, and we had been praying to the Virgin Mary and calling on her prayers! I'd been singing those words and I didn't know!"

When we spoke about how music functioned in Protestant and Catholic worship at Tufts, the university chaplain, a Unitarian Universalist, spoke about the conflict between "old and new music." He said that for many students the canon of the hymns of Martin Luther feels "old and tired—the church as it was." That music might be majestic and triumphal, but in college the Protestant service that has the greatest draw and power relies on folk music. He related, "We've tried to use the organ and the piano, but the guitar has the greatest impact. It's accessible, informal, unstructured, and anti-institutional."

The same situation exists with the Catholic Mass, a folk Mass that draws hundreds of students each Sunday evening at 10:00 P.M.. Enthusiastic group singing is led by a student ensemble composed of guitar, bass, piano, and drums. The university chaplain stressed that in a college congregation, the social experience of worship is very important for these students: "Students come looking for community. They want a relational experience and the informal, participatory music at worship supports that." This was a theme of all of the Jewish communities I studied.

The Episcopal priest at Tufts said, "It's very much piano or guitar with a rhythm and beat that inspires students to participate. If it's music that will get their feet moving, make them sway, make them want to clap, that becomes very, very important." She contrasted worship at Tufts with the parish she also serves: "The opposite is true in the parish. There we have a canon of acceptable church music and it's to be played in very traditional ways. It's not about moving anything but your mouth, if that!"

As with the Jewish students at Hillel, the move toward participatory music in worship has been influenced by students' experiences in youth groups and camps. The priest continued, "A lot of these students have belonged to church youth groups and have been taught to sing Christian camp songs, accompanied by guitar, that's very common even in Episcopal circles." She also explained, "Other groups, like Intervarsity, have made tremendous efforts to develop musical forms which are compelling and engaging to young people." She commented, "I have no problem with that kind of music but I'm glad that my personal repertoire is bigger than that." The priest added that even though the form of this music in the college community is different from traditional hymns, the message is more traditional than ever. She explained, "The students want a different sound but the theology is still a very traditional Christian theology: Jesus died for my sins, Jesus was sent by God to redeem humanity. Good Heavens, sometimes they even say, 'mankind'!"

This Episcopal priest went on to describe how some of these issues played out differently in her parish in Boston. She told of her experiences balancing tradition and innovation. "We use different hymns every week, but if you want to be safe with the congregation, to tell you the truth, you toss in one or two of those familiar tunes every week. . . . A new hymn might not sound so good, and people don't like to be uncomfortable in a service. They really do come there for that time out from daily life, to find that comforting word, in all aspects of the service, including the sung pieces."

She went on to describe a theological imperative for making musical changes in the Episcopal worship service: "In Christian theological terms, we are taught by the Gospel that part of what we need to do is go out, reach other people, tell them about Jesus, and bring them in. In all of its history, the Church has adapted itself to its environment, and therefore if our environments have changed and if we want to continue to be witnesses of the Gospel, we must change what we're doing and find ways to make what we are saying relevant to the people we want to reach. That's theological and practical: you want to stay open, you've got to change something. The dinosaur died and other species took its place."

I asked what she, as a worshipper, wanted when she was able to go to another church to worship. She replied, "Like every other Episcopalian, I have my favorite list of traditional hymns, and you're going to make me very, very happy, I will feel like I struck it rich, if at least three out of the four or five hymns they pick are hymns I know and love. And I'll like it if the one or two that I don't know are singable hymns." She stressed, "What I want is music that I can participate in. It's fine with me if they have a paid choir or a soloist and that person does a piece, but it is almost offensive to me if the whole thing is taken over by a musical show."

I spoke to a Roman Catholic priest I had known when he worked in campus ministry. Now he served a large suburban church. He also reflected on the importance of the group experience that was created by participatory music and how that experience of community formed the core of Catholic identity. He believed that worship should be "a deep spiritual experience, something that really lifts them and raises them up and brings the congregation together." Worship should "focus our attention on those things which are transcendent, those things beyond us." Like the rabbis at Temple Israel, he believed that it was "absolutely essential" that the musicians be skilled, "not as performers, but as people who can move the congregation to participate as one voice." He understood "coming together" as the essence of Catholic identity: "The Catholic Church is never more itself than when it is gathered around the alter and around the word in worship. That is the identity, that is the center. Everything has to begin from there." He saw music as the vehicle that creates this communal unity. He stressed, "For Roman Catholics, the Mass isn't something you *go to*, it's something you *are*. Active, informed, well-done participation is absolutely essential—with a priest who is a good leader and has a sense of ritual and presence, readers who are articulate and have good diction, and musicians who are excellent and professional." Here the priest understood that music in prayer did more than provide an experience for the worshippers; it determined the nature of their identity as Catholics, creating and sustaining their community.

The purpose of sharing these quotes from members and leaders of local churches is not to make a quick comparison and imply that Jews and Christians are the same. They are not. All of these men and women are bound by different historical, religious, and cultural constraints that determine how they choose and use music in worship. But after I spoke with these Christians, it struck me that the Jews in the worship communities I studied were describing larger issues than music; they were discussing concerns common to middle-class religion in America. The expectation that worshippers can find or create the kind of service they need, the role of the empowered individual in creating new structures and institutions, and the ready tendency to form communal associations are all themes common to American religious life. Additional issues, such as the therapeutic uses of ritual and the notion that religion should provide self-fulfillment and transcendent experience, grow out of the larger milieu of Protestant worship in America.

Conclusions

When the members of each of these Jewish worship communities discussed their spiritual lives, they did not devote a lot of time to speaking about God. Mark Slobin suggests that many people do not talk about God because contemporary religious expression is primarily about themselves. Throughout these interviews, there is a stress on the importance of the self, a common theme in American religious experience. Robert Bellah examines the tradition of "religious individualism" in America and explains that for both Catholics and Protestants, "There are thousands of local churches in the United States, representing an enormous range of variation in doctrine and worship." Yet most define themselves as communities of personal support, "focusing on the needs and concerns of the individual" (1985:232). He writes that in America, "It is the self . . . that must be the source of all religious meaning" (ibid.:229).

In fact, many members of the worship communities described in this book look to religion for personal support and self-fulfillment. Peace and quiet are in short supply. The synagogue becomes a place to gather strength after a hectic, stressful week. A busy professional woman at Temple Israel speaks of the Kabbalat Shabbat service as the one place where "nobody interrupts me." When another member describes how she "can just start to feel the tension draining out of [her] body as the music starts," she is describing how religious ritual contributes to her physical and psychological well-being. The Jewish tradition has long stressed the power of Shabbat to transform both the individual and community, but in America this journey for personal fulfillment and peace has its own background and context. America has always encouraged its citizens to focus on the needs and desires of the self. The result of this utilitarian individualism, rooted in the writings of Thomas Hobbes and John Locke, was assumed to bring both public and private prosperity (Bellah and Hammond 1980:170). At the same time, this focus on self-fulfillment is part of the therapeutic worldview that shaped American culture throughout the twentieth century. This view is described by Jackson Lears as "a constellation of concerns about self, energizing a continuous, anxious quest for well-being" (1981:304). The Jews discussed in this book are surrounded by Americans who concentrate on the self and search for personal well-being in many areas: relationships, therapy, and recreation. The members of these worship communities are participating in this American quest, yet by choosing to look for answers within their own religious tradition they bolster their personal search with historical validity, traditional structure, and authority. Religion, and the specific experience of worship, provide them with some precious commodities: time to be with family and friends, time to be by themselves, time to breathe and think and sing, time to be a part of something larger and more important than their own individuality. Religious services offer a safe haven, an idealized moment in the week when people can be free of social pressure and experience the warmth of a community.

They were not willing to join large impersonal religious institutions and suffer in silence with a style of worship that felt meaningless or alienating. This attitude too has its roots in the American experience. Bellah explains that by the mid-nineteenth century, religion in America "operated with a new emphasis on the individual and the voluntary association. . . . Religious membership was no longer unified. Even in the smaller communities, it had become highly segmented" (1985:222). Religion was seen as an issue of individual choice, and America legitimized a tremendous diversity of religious practice. Influenced by the approach of American Protestantism, which created scores of worship styles, together with American consumerism with its assumption of unlimited choice, these Jews believed that a community *should* exist that reflected their level of observance and style of worship. If it did not exist, it was certainly possible to create one. They left college and graduate school well prepared to organize new communities as the need arose.

Many members of these worship communities, including Beth Pinchas and Shaarei Tefillah, came of age in the late 1960s.[1] In the words of Robert Bellah and Phillip Hammond, they had been affected by the "massive erosion of the legitimacy of American institutions—business, government, education, the churches, the family" during that tumultuous period (1980: 168). They were involved in reforming and refashioning political, educational, and social institutions during the late 1960s and early 1970s. Among them were experienced community activists and organizers. Establishing a worship community was hardly a daunting task.

At the same time, their experience in the 1960s affected them in other ways. Many left college believing that it was difficult to have an effect upon the political system. Even the fleeting victory of the antiwar movement in the early 1970s did not transform America. Major problems facing American society—crime, hunger, and poverty—were still unsolved. They felt there were too many areas of life where they were standing on the sidelines. At least in their religious communities, they refused to be spectators. This move toward participation took many forms, including the creation of breakaway communities, a reconstruction of congregational leadership, and the adoption of new musical repertoires.

When they are seen against this historical backdrop, we can better understand the individualistic, anti-establishment tendencies in each of these worship communities. While the majority of these Jews are middle and upper-middle class, they shy away from formal, large worship settings, professionalized religious leadership, and conspicuous displays of wealth at services. In fact, "revolution" is a theme in the establishment of a number of these groups. The majority shun fixed pews, gravitating toward more intimate, flexible worship settings. Their search for meaningful spiritual experience is bound up with their struggle to establish control over their Jewish lives, wresting it from the older generation by manipulating style, space, and the structures of congregational authority.

The search for spiritual, cultural, and historic authenticity pervades the religious lives of the members of these five worship communities.[2] We see this in the way a member of Tufts Hillel (inaccurately) romanticizes nusach as a connection to "five thousand years of Jewish history" or as a member of B'nai Or describes how traditional chant connects her to an "unbroken chain" of her people's historical experience. When Jews in these worship communities speak of the "real" or "correct" version of Lekhah dodi, they construct a version of Jewish history in which uncontested answers and immutable truth can be found. We see this quest for authenticity in the meticulous approach of members of Shaarei Tefillah to the performance of sacred text, even as one member observes that such stress on an accurate Torah reading is a relatively recent innovation. We see this search for authenticity when members of B'nai Or are quick to characterize niggunim written in the last ten years as "folk" or "Hasidic" and, in doing so, invent a historical lineage for recent musical compositions. In a rootless age, historical connections, both real and imagined, provide validity and authenticity for these worshippers.

While many of the themes that frame their search are common in American religious life, their answers are uniquely Jewish. These men and women have created worship communities rich in ritual complexity. In some cases they accepted the structure and strictures of traditional rabbinic law to order their personal and communal life. In other cases they struggled with the meaning and interpretation of Jewish law, and at the least, accepted it as a contextual map for their ongoing spiritual journey.

All of these Jews thought a lot about who they were in relation to the American culture which they simultaneous embraced and, in the very act of making their particular communities so central in their lives, rejected. Through the use of music, they mark the passage of the seasons and celebrate the Jewish life cycle. They actively rejected styles of worship that to them seemed trivial or nonparticipatory. They chose music strategically in worship, to affirm their connection to Jewish history, to experience viscerally being part of the Jewish people, to carve out a separate space within the American superculture and negotiate their relationship with other Jews similar and different from themselves.

When the Jews were first exiled from Israel to Babylonia, they looked longingly toward home and sang, "How can we sing the Lord's song in a strange land?" (Psalm 137:4). These American Jews have puzzled out the answer to that question. They have done so by affirming the value of Jewish practice and tradition while at the same time yielding to the profound influence of the strange American environment on their identities and religious expression.

Notes

Introduction

1. Three terms will be used for the Jewish Sabbath, which begins at sunset on Friday evening and continues until after sunset on Saturday: the English "Sabbath"; the Hebrew "Shabbat," the Sephardic form of this word; and "Shabbos," used primarily in quoting Ashkenazi informants who use that pronunciation.

2. This issue has special resonance for Jews conducting ethnographic work within the Jewish community. See Kugelmass's "self-reflective" essays on American Jewish ethnography, in which he discusses the researcher's need to reconcile interests that are "purely scientific" with "the personal quest" for authenticity and community. He says that this approach to research speaks to "the ethnotherapeutic value, the search for wholeness, that ethnography can bring to bear in postmodern society" (1988:1, 2). Also see Belcove-Shalin 1988; Myerhoff 1988; Staub 1988; Prell 1988b; Heilman 1992:xi–xxi. For longer, fine examples of self-reflexive ethnography, see Shelemay 1991; Heilman 1984.

3. As I participated in prayer in each of these five communities, at times I would lose myself as I became fully engaged in the music and davening. In Jewish terminology, I was praying with *kavanah* (focused attention). Then a new tune or an interesting interaction would refocus my attention and I would again become a critical observer. In his essay "Knowing Fieldwork," Jeff Todd Titon discusses a similar dialectic in his "phenomenological account of music making." Describing why he believes this is a strong stance from which to do fieldwork, he writes, "Making music, I experience the disappearance of my separate self. . . . But I also experience the return of the knowing self. The experience of music making is, in some circumstances, in various cultures throughout the world, an experience of becoming a knowing self in the presence of other becoming, knowing selves. This is a profoundly communal experience and I am willing to trust it." Titon explains that in this kind of experience, the researcher becomes "emergent rather than autonomous." He continues, "Emergent selves . . .

are connected selves, enmeshed in reciprocity. Connectedness is a value that challenges the postmodern critique of contemporary society. I am willing to assert this ecological value and its intimate relation with music-making and fieldwork on the grounds that the survival of far more than ethnomusicology depends on it" (1997:99).

4. It is problematic to study liturgical music divorced from the context of its ritual performance. Kay Kaufman Shelemay observes that Zema (the sacred music of Beta Israel) is "virtually inseparable from the qalocc (words) with which it is associated." She notes that priests were "usually unable to speak texts during interview sessions" and quotes a priest who is asked to "speak" a prayer rather than sing it. He answered: "It is better to the zema [i.e., to sing the prayer]. . . . When I just speak the words it has no meaning, but when I do the zema, then it will benefit you" (1986:99–101). Also compare the comments of a Hasid interviewed by Chemjo Vinaver, who asked him to sing the melody for a particular section of the Shabbat liturgy. The Hasid replied that he was not able to "sing" melodies of prayer. He could "daven on Shabbos" but could not sing those melodies, out of context, during the week (Vinaver 1985:35, 36).

5. Compare Peter Manuel's study of the use of the cassette tape in North India and its influence on cultural and social identity (1993). Oral tradition is often seen to be threatened by technology, yet Manuel examines how such sociotechnical developments have strengthened subcultural musical traditions in North India, allowing people to broaden their musical choices and "create and enjoy . . . syncretic hybrid musics that are at once modern and affirmative of diverse community aesthetics and values" (ibid.: 153).

6. Of course these categories are valid and in many ways they define an essential dialectic in the development of American Judaism. For the relationship between German and Eastern European Jews in America, see Rischin [1986] 1997; Szajkowski 1973:13–44.

7. In this regard, consider Paul Berman's article "The Other and the Almost the Same" (1994), in which he offers some explanations for the current tension between blacks and Jews in America based on the suggestions of Vladimir Jankelevitch (d. 1985), a hero of the French Resistance and professor of music at the Sorbonne. Jankelevitch suggested that relations between people who are *almost* the same tend to be especially highly charged. He quotes Freud's *Moses and Monotheism*: "racial intolerance finds stronger expression, strange to say, in regard to small differences than to fundamental ones."

8. Mark Slobin identifies "interaction within subcultures" as "one of the last frontiers of ethnomusicology, [that poses] a set of crucial issues about the way people organize their social and aesthetic lives" (1992:57). Little attention has been paid in ethnomusicology and anthropology to comparisons among the various groups that compose a subculture. One exception is the collection of essays edited by Kugelmass that considers the ethnography of American Jewish subcultures and their relationship with the larger Jewish community. See the section entitled "Subcultures" in Kugelmass (1988:105–221).

9. See Joseph Greenblum's and Marshall Sklare's pioneering study of Jewish identity in suburban America, in which they examined five synagogues in a suburban community called "Lakeville" (1967). Four of their five communities were identified as Reform, yet behind that label they found "considerable diversity . . . in "religious outlook, . . . social and eco-

nomic stratification, . . . intergroup attitudes and behavior and some in the newer area of cultural taste and style of life" (ibid.:179).

10. For a full examination of the Jewish community in Boston, see Sarna and Smith 1995.

11. See "The 1998 Directory of the Synagogue Council of Massachusetts" (Newton, Mass: Synagogue Council of Massachusetts). Also see Rosenzweig 1995.

12. There are measures of community affiliation other than synagogue membership. Israel also examines membership and affiliation with non-synagogue fraternal organizations, Zionist and community relations organizations, Jewish community centers, and the Jewish federation itself (1997:42–45, 58–61,63).

13. For an examination of these issues, see Petuchowski 1968:31–43.

14. For a comprehensive treatment of American Jewish history, see Marcus 1989. For an important collection of essays on the American Jewish experience, see Sarna [1986] 1997. See Seltzer for a one-volume overview of Jewish history, with articles on Jewish religious movements (1989).

15. The founder of the Reconstructionist movement, Mordecai Kaplan, defined Judaism as an "evolving religious civilization," deemphasizing the supernatural and aspects of particularism such as the concept of the Jews as "chosen people" (1981 [1957]).

16. See Dinnerstein on anti-Semitism in America (1994).

17. Since 1977 all four major movements have published new prayer books. The Reform movement published *Gates of Prayer* (1977), the Conservative movement published *Sim Shalom* (1998), and the Reconstructionists published *Kol Haneshamah* (1989). The Orthodox Rabbinic Council of America recently edited its own version of the Artscroll siddur. Orthodox congregations use a variety of *siddurim* (prayer books, pl.). Shaarei Tefillah makes available copies of the Birnbaum siddur (1977). Beth Pinchas publishes its own siddur, which includes customs specific to the Bostoner Rebbe's community. In both the Reform and B'nai Or communities examined in this study, the siddur is seen more as a menu than as a blueprint for prayer. The Reform siddur is arranged to encourage many liturgical choices, providing leaders with a resource to create different Shabbat services each week.

18. The Reform rabbinic school is the Hebrew Union College–Jewish Institute of Religion, with branches in Cincinnati, New York, Los Angeles, and Jerusalem. Its cantorial school, the School of Sacred Music, is located on its New York campus. The Conservative movement trains rabbis at the Jewish Theological Seminary in New York and the Ziegler School of Rabbinic Studies of the University of Judaism in Los Angeles. The Conservative movement's cantorial school is the Cantors Institute. Orthodox rabbinic training is far less centralized. Valid rabbinic ordination is granted by a number of yeshivot throughout America and Israel. Still, the rabbinic-training program at New York's Yeshiva University and its cantorial school, the Cantorial Training Institute, exert important influence over modern Orthodoxy. Among the Hasidim, rabbinic leadership is a dynastic succession. Qualified men are ordained as rabbis after studying in a particular group's yeshiva. Among B'nai Or, and its national affiliate P'nai Or, rabbinic ordination has been conferred by the movement's founder, Rabbi Zalman Schachter-Shalomi. In affiliation with ALEPH: The Alliance for Jewish Renewal, P'nai Or is presently expanding a decentralized rabbinic ordination program. This study does not examine a Reconstructionist con-

gregation. Its rabbinic school is the Reconstructionist Rabbinical College in Philadelphia. For more information on Reconstructionism see Kaplan 1981 [1957]; Alpert and Staub 1985. Also see the new prayer book for Shabbat Eve published by the Reconstructionist movement, *Kol Haneshamah* (Teutsch 1989).

19. The youth group of the Reform movement is the National Federation of Temple Youth (NFTY). The Conservative movement's youth group is the United Synagogue Youth (USY). Orthodox youth groups include the National Conference of Synagogue Youth (NCSY) and B'nai Akiva. Youth group activity is directed toward students in high school. In addition to running after-school and weekend programs, all these youth groups sponsor summer camp programs.

20. Throughout this study I use the terms "ethnic group" and "ethnic identity." Anthropologist and dance ethnographer Anya Peterson Royce defines an ethnic group as "a reference group invoked by people who share a common historical style (which may be only assumed), based on overt features and values, and who, through the process of interaction with others, identify themselves as sharing that style. 'Ethnic identity' is the sum total of feelings on the part of group members about those values, symbols, and common histories that identify them as a distinct group" (1982:18). See Royce's first chapter, "Neither Christian nor Jewish . . . ," on the problems inherent in defining ethnic identity and ethnicity.

21. Mark Slobin refers to these choices as "methodologies of belonging" (personal communication). Also see Slobin on issues of choice, affinity, and belonging (1992:37).

22. Throughout, this study focuses on "emic" data. The terms *etic* and *emic*, from phonetic and phonemic, were coined by Kenneth Pike in his study of language and human behavior (1967:37–72). He explains, "The etic viewpoint studies behavior as from outside of a particular system, and as an essential initial approach to an alien system. The emic viewpoint results from studying behavior as from inside the system" (ibid.:37).

23. Perry London and Alissa Hirshfeld argue that all the ideas of identity or self in the literature of psychology can be reduced to two general themes. The first is "the notion of identity as a person's *entire sense of self or ego* . . . without reference to a social or other external source or object of expression" (1991:32). The second might best be called "social identity" or "group identity," which Barry Schlenker calls "the point of intersection between the individual and other people" (as quoted by London and Hirshfeld, ibid.:33). London and Hirshfeld assert that this definition of identity is "most pertinent to Jewish identity and the one that has chiefly interested social scientists because it pertains directly to the study of social groups and their relationships, to ethnicity and ethnocentrism, and to intergroup and cross-cultural conflict" (ibid.).

24. Ethnomusicologists have examined the power of music to express a person's core identity. In Jocelyne Guilbault's study of zouk, the popular dance music of the Caribbean, she writes that because zouk is sung in Creole and created by black Antilleans, it has been "endowed . . . with the very specific mandate to assert Antillean identity, locally and internationally" (1993:9). She quotes Eric Virgil, one of Martinique's leading zouk singers: "Why zouk? Because it's truly *me*. The feeling we have about zouk is that it reflects our way of walking, laughing, dreaming, and speaking. All of our Creoleness is in zouk, all of our everyday life" (ibid.: 20).

25. Christopher Waterman observes that "the irreducible object of eth-nomusicological interest in not the music itself, a somewhat animistic no-tion, but the historically situated human subjects who perceive, learn, in-terpret, evaluate, produce, and respond to music" (1991:66).

26. Phillips (1991) presents a helpful overview of the seminal sociolog-ical studies of Jewish identity, including Sklare 1967; Goldstein and Gold-scheider 1968; Cohen 1983, 1988; Goldscheider 1986; and Herman 1977.

27. The discipline of ethnomusicology does not rely on a neat categoriza-tion of identities but rather, as Philip Bohlman says, on "allowing [those constructed identities] to represent the complex and contested cultural practices of the modern world" (1993a:25; also cf. Guilbault 1993:203). Bohlman asserts that identity has been "one of the most important foci of ethnomusicological research throughout the course of its history" (1993b). He describes two ways in which this concept has been used: first as a focus of research in ethnic folk music, where music serves as an ex-pression of ethnic identity; second, as a "framework in melodic analysis, where the identity of a tune family or raga is essential to our understanding of entire repertoires and music cultures." This book is concerned with the first definition of this term. Early ethnomusicological research did not focus on the issue of identity. Bartok is sensitive to musical influence from other traditions, but in general music was assumed to represent national music traditions (1931; also see Bohlman 1988:54–57 on the German folk music theory, *Kulturkreislehre*, theory of culture area). As described by Nettl, music was seen as the "sole property of a group of people who also shared a culture" (1985:19). Other ethnomusicologists looked to the concept of mode to classify repertoires and to ascribe national identity through modes (Idelsohn 1929). In later scholarship, it was widely assumed that people belonged to a particular group and as such were culture carriers for that group, one of the most extreme theories being Lomax's canto-metrics (1968), a method to measure, code, and systematically describe the features of a particular culture's music. In the 1950s, 1960s and 1970s, issues of difference between groups and musical change were addressed through the study of syncretism, acculturation, and ethnic boundaries (see R. Waterman 1952; Merriam 1964, Nettl 1964, Slobin 1976). Current research on identity in ethnomusicology has focused on concepts such as "self" and "other" (Grenier and Guilbault 1990), style and subculture (Slobin 1992), and cultural boundaries (Bohlman 1988). It has also ex-plored the role of music in the construction of ethnic, cultural, and na-tional identities (Seeger 1987, C. Waterman 1990, Guilbault 1993). Concepts developed in social anthropology, popular music studies, and cultural studies such as culture and hegemony (Hebdige 1979), the "invention of tradition" (Hobsbawm and Ranger 1983), and the negotiation and con-scious manipulation of multiple identities (Royce 1982) have been influ-ential in ethnomusicology.

28. See Hoffman 1979:160–71; Petuchowski 1968.

29. Alan Mintz says, "As for prayerbooks . . . , there are as many versions as there are groupings of synagogue movements" (1984:428). Also see Petuchowski's listing of more than a hundred different editions of liberal and Reform prayer books in Europe between 1816 and 1967 (1968:1–21). Also see Hoffman's chapter, "American Jewish Liturgies: A Study of Iden-tity," in which he discusses how prayer books developed as "party mani-festos" for the developing Jewish denominations in America (1987:60–74).

30. There is a history of contention in rabbinic literature about the proper use of music in worship. See Shiloah 1992:65–86; Adler 1975.

31. The great success enjoyed by Congregation B'nai Jeshurun, known as B.J., in New York, which draws up to 1,500 people for Friday evening services, can be credited to its development and use of a particular musical style.

1. An Introduction to Jewish Worship

1. See Hosea (14:3) where he taught that prayer, "the offering of our lips" would substitute for animals offered at the Temple. Also see these statements "When they read [the order of the sacrifices] before me, I will account it as if they had brought them to me and I forgive their sins" (Babylonian Talmud, *Taanit* 27b). "Just as the worship at the Temple altar is called Avodah so is prayer called Avodah, that is, "the service of the heart" (Babylonian Talmud, *Taanit* 2a).

2. For a comprehensive treatment of prayer in the Jewish tradition, see Elbogen [1913, 1972] 1993; also Heinemann 1977. Recent scholars have challenged certain assumptions about the early development of Jewish worship. See Fleischer 1988. Also see Langer 1998, as well as Langer's perspectives on Fleischer (1999). For a solid introduction to Jewish prayer, see Hammer 1994. Jacobson presents a detailed analysis and translation of the Sabbath service (1981) and the weekday service (1973). Samuel Heilman, in the field of social anthropology, offers a comprehensive analysis of the life of an Orthodox synagogue and the interpersonal dynamics of worshippers in prayer and study (1976, 1983). His discussion of the physical setting of the synagogue is extremely helpful (1976:25–61). Readers may also consult a series of articles on Jewish prayer in *The Second Jewish Catalog* (Strassfeld and Strassfeld 1976:264–309). Their countercultural orientation provides important insight into the approach to prayer of many Jews from the generation of the 1960s and early 1970s. Also included in *The Second Jewish Catalog* is a helpful chart explaining the body movements (standing, sitting, swaying, bowing) that many Jews make when praying (Saltzman 1976:292–95). Although the works mentioned above collectively provide a comprehensive introduction to Jewish worship, I encourage the uninitiated reader to attend several synagogue services. Only through firsthand observation and participation can one begin to understand the nature of Jewish worship, the role of music in prayer, and the interaction between the leader and congregation.

3. This description refers to Ashkenazi prayer. In Sephardic prayer the entire congregation usually sings through the service together, although some prayers are done by individuals in the congregation.

4. The word *kavanah* comes from the Hebrew root *kvn*, to direct or to aim, and connotes prayer that is focused and spiritually intense. Both the Talmud and the Jewish legal codes stress the importance of kavanah in prayer. Indeed, prayer without kavanah does not fulfill one's obligations to pray (cf. Babylonian Talmud, *Berakhot* 5:1 and 31a; Shulchan Arukh, OH 98:2).

5. The etymology of "amen" is from the Hebrew root *amn*, to confirm or support, and means "truly" or "verily." See Donin 1980:227–30.

6. For a more in-depth consideration of the "cast of characters" in the house of prayer, see Elbogen [1913, 1972] 1993:368–74; Heilman 1976: 69–127.

7. For more background on the Kabbalat Shabbat service, see Arzt 1979; Elbogen [1913, 1972] 1993:91–95; Hammer 1994:212–20; Kimelman 1998 (Hebrew).

8. For an examination of spirituality in Safed, see Werblowsky 1987. Lawrence Fine presents a general introduction to Jewish mysticism in his essay "Kabbalistic Texts" (1984b).

9. This is implied in the rabbinic commentary on the importance of reciting the section of the Torah "the heaven and earth were finished," which precedes the blessing over wine on Sabbath Eve: "Rabbi Hamnuna said: He who offers the Sabbath Eve prayers and recites the verses beginning with 'and the heaven and the earth were finished' (Genesis 2:1–3), is considered in the Torah as though he had become a partner in Creation, for one can vocalize the word *vayekhullu* ["heaven and earth were finished"], as *vayekhallu*, 'they [man and God], finished the Creation'" (Babylonian Talmud, *Shabbat* 119b).

10. While the word *tikkun,* from the Hebrew root, *tkn,* means "repair," here Artz uses it in the sense of the ultimate cosmic repair, the redemption of Israel.

11. Solomon Schechter published sections of Cordovero's manuscripts in his essay on Safed (1908). See Fine's translations of Cordovero (1984a:34–38).

12. Fine translates these from Meir Benayahu's *Sefer Toldot ha-'Ari,* a collection of Luria's writings edited by his student, Hayyim Vital (1984a:65–77).

13. This expression refers to the Shekhinah, the feminine presence of God. See Fine's discussion of Scholem's explanation of this phrase (1984a:179, n. 32).

14. Sephardic and Oriental communities recite only Psalm 29 before *Lekhah dodi.*

15. The mystics looked deep into the hidden meaning of the rubrics of this service. According to the system of *gematria* (numerology), each Hebrew letter has a numerical value. The numerical value of words and phrases is seen as a key to understanding their deeper meaning. The mystics pointed out that when the first letters of these psalms are added together, they yield a numerical value of 430, equivalent to that of the word *nefesh* (soul), an allusion to the additional "Sabbath soul" that descends and fills us on the seventh day (Munk 1963:5).

16. In other congregations this section of Mishnah is chanted at the conclusion of the Maariv service.

17. See Shulchan Arukh, OH 267:2.

18. Originally the Kabbalists of Safed actually went out into a field and designated it "the field of holy apple trees," a name of the Shekhinah that is found in the Zohar, the central text of the Kabbalah (Fine 1984a:33).

19. See Elbogen [1913, 1972] 1993:91–95.

2. The Meaning of a Tune

1. Throughout this book various terms are used to describe music in Jewish worship. The worshippers I spoke with use *melody, tune, niggun,* and *nusach* in a general and often overlapping sense. Specific definitions for these terms will be given as they appear in the discussion. Mark DeVoto defines *melody* as "any group of tones meant to be heard as a succession, the succession being organized in some way." He states that a melody has "an identity, and an organization that is intended to be perceived" (Piston

1978:83). In defining *tune,* DeVoto states that song tunes are "usually conceived as matched syllabically to a text in rhymed verse. They are characterized by a relatively small range . . . , a quality of singability, and a lack of wide intervals or complex rhythms" (ibid.: 86). Other characteristics of tunes are "melodies with regular periods (such as four-bar groups), strong tonic and dominant cadences, and often an internal structuring within and between phrases, such as organization into rhythmic or intervallic motives" (ibid.). In this study I use the term *tune* for a fully developed melody to which the stanzas of a hymn, such as *Lekhah dodi,* are sung. Worshippers who were interviewed described and sang various tunes for hymns such as *Yedid nefesh* (Beloved of my soul), *Lekhah dodi,* and *Adon olam.* In some places a popular tune, such as the Israeli song *Erev shel shoshanim* (Night of Roses), is applied to a section of the liturgy that is not organized in stanzas, as in the singing of the Shabbat *Kedushah* (the Sanctification, the third section of the *Amidah*). A broad definition for the Hebrew word *niggun* is "tune" or "melody type," such as *gemore niggun,* the chant used by students when studying the Talmud. However in this study, the word *niggun* is used to refer to Hasidic devotional tunes, characterized by repetition and usually sung to vocables such as "rum, de, de, dum" or "yai, lai, lai." (cf. Koskoff 1978; Idelsohn 1929:414–32). The term *nusach* refers to a "specific musical mode to which a certain part of the liturgy is sung" (Avenary 1972b:1283). *Nusach* (see chapter 3) is a complex term and is used here to refer to traditional Ashkenazi recitative chant that is composed of a stock of characteristic motifs specific to a particular service. These definitions notwithstanding, it should be stated that there is certain overlap in these terminologies. It is possible to speak of "the melody of Lewandowski's tune of *Lekhah dodi*" or "recurring melodic motifs in a leader's Kabbalat Shabbat nusach." One could also say that a certain section of liturgical text is "sung to the tune of the Israeli song *Erev shel shoshanim.*" The strong identification of a melody, actually a melodic sequence, with an entire tune often led to a blurring of these terms by the worshippers interviewed. They often used the term *melody* in a much more general way, making it synonymous with *tune.* They would speak of "that melody of *Lekhah dodi*" in referring to a particular tune to which the hymn was sung. I use the term "melody choice," as opposed to "tune choice" for several reasons. Every tune has a melody, as does the nusach for Kabbalat Shabbat. In this way, the term "melody choice" encompasses a broader spectrum than "tune choice." Furthermore, when these worshippers are making musical choices in the service, they are dealing mostly with fragments of tunes that can accurately be described as melodies. When various sections of the liturgy are set to tunes or melodies, there is often not enough text to use an entire tune. More often, a melodic theme is chosen from a tune and then applied, more or less elegantly, to a particular text.

2. One theory is that piyyutim were developed during the Justinian religious persecution of Jews in the fifth century. The Justinians forbade biblical exegesis or talmudic interpretation in the synagogue, and this restriction led to the development of the new literature of poetry and prayer. Poets wrote hymns to interpret both the written and oral law as well as the meaning of Shabbat and holidays. These poems were written in obscure and difficult language in order to deceive the Byzantine oppressors. Heinemann raises many objections to this theory in his edition of Elbogen's text ([1913, 1972] 1993:219–37).

3. For the development of the piyyut, see Fleischer 1975 (Hebrew); Weinberger 1998.

4. "The injunction concerning the Sabbath found in Exodus 20:8 begins, '*Remember* the Sabbath day to keep it holy' while in Deuteronomy 5:12 it reads, '*Observe* the Sabbath day.' According to rabbinic tradition (*Shevu'ot* 20b) both forms were miraculously communicated by God simultaneously" (Fine 1984a:172).

5. "Beloved" refers, according to some commentators, to the *Sefirah Tif'eret*" (ibid.). Fine explains that according to the Kabbalah, *Tif'eret* is "male in character, 'husband' or 'lover' in relationship to *Shekhinah*" (1984a:165).

6. "According to Jewish tradition, the Messiah will be a descendant of King David, son of Jesse, of Bethlehem" (Fine 1984a).

7. "The imagery and wording in this and the following stanzas draw on the second part of Isaiah" (Fine 1984a). See Isaiah 49:19, 51:17, 52:2, 54:3, 60:1, 62:5.

8. "King David was descended from Perez through the biblical character Boaz (Ruth 4:18–22)" (Fine 1984a).

9. This is taken from the Reconstructionist Sabbath evening prayer book, *Kol Haneshamah* (Teutsch 1989). I observed this in practice at B'nai Or, where they use this prayer book. The leader encouraged the singing of *Lekhah dodi* in English, stressing that this translation worked extremely well. While most people sang the hymn in Hebrew, using either the original text or the accompanying transliteration, worshippers also sang the English version.

10. There were several different piyyutim based on the text "Come, my friend." An earlier version was composed by Moses ben Machir, a contemporary of Alkabetz, who lived in Safed as a youth. His version also used the same *Lekhah dodi* refrain and included one verse, *Bo-i beshalom* (Come in peace), that was exactly the same as Alkabetz's composition (Arzt 1979:19). On acrostics in piyyutim, see Elbogen [1913, 1972] 1993:228–29.

11. Idelsohn groups Alkabetz with Isaac Luria and Israel Najara, calling them the "last folk-singers, whose products were accepted throughout the Diaspora" (1929:361).

12. See Kimelman's paper given at the conference "Spirituality and Community: Religious and Communal Motifs in Transformation from the Bible to the Present," held at Brandeis University, Waltham, Mass., in April 1994. A videotape of the proceedings is available from the Tauber Institute, Brandeis University.

13. Munk notes that "'dodi,' (my friend) denotes God, himself" and references Isaiah 5:1 and the rabbinic interpretation of "dodi" in the Song of Songs (1963:6). In this view, the people Israel acts as a matchmaker, enjoining God to meet His Queen, the Sabbath.

14. For a broader treatment of the place of music in Jewish mysticism, see Shiloah 1992:131–56.

15. Savran is using the term *niggun* in a general sense to mean tune or melody.

16. The havurah movement should be contextualized in a wider discussion of the nature and meaning of social relationships in modern urban life and the search for community in modern society. See Neusner 1972:xiii; Gusfield 1975:83–105. For a comprehensive treatment, see Prell 1988a. In addition to presenting a historical overview of fellowship in the Jewish community, Neusner's anthology includes an early action plan by Zalman Schachter for the formation of the B'nai Or fellowship. Also see

Hecht 1993; Cohen 1979; Strassfeld 1989. A number of writers have examined the attempts of large synagogues to divide their membership into smaller, more personal "havurot." See Reisman 1977; Bubis, Wasserman, and Lert 1983; Elazar and Monson 1979.

17. Compare Buber's Hasidic tale "The Praying Rabbi" (1947:145–50).

18. *Shema* (Listen!) is the first word of the central creed of Jewish faith: "Listen, Israel! Adonai is God. Adonai is one."

19. It is interesting to note that this is the same leader who incurred community criticism (see chapter 4) when he chose to sing the Musaf *Kedushah* to the tune of *"Adeste, fideles"* (O Come, All Ye Faithful).

20. Charles Davidson credits the composition of this tune to M. Zeira (1987:No. 6). He presents his own arrangement, in which he divides the A and B sections into "Cantor" and "Cantor with Congregation." He repeats the chorus of *Lekhah dodi* in the B section rather than using the text "Shabbat shalom umevorakh," as is done by B'nai Or and Temple Israel.

21. The tapes and CDs of Debbie Friedman (no relation to Lev Friedman) are extremely popular in the Reform movement, especially among high school students in the National Federation of Temple Youth, the Reform movement's youth group, and increasingly with youth in the Conservative movement.

22. Lev Friedman plays this tune beginning with an A minor chord but capos up three frets so it is in C minor. When he says "It follows an A minor," he is referring to his beginning chord.

23. For a comprehensive history of the Reform movement, see Meyer 1988.

24. In Germany, until 1876 it was not possible to separate voluntarily from the traditionally controlled Jewish community without officially renouncing Judaism (Petuchowski 1968:32).

25. See Petuchowski 1968:105–27.

26. Mark Slobin discusses how Reform congregations have "slowly taken on the participatory mode as their basic service type," as is shown by these interviews (1989:196). For a reassessment of the dynamics of contemporary worship and issues of congregational participation, especially in the Reform movement, see the work of Lawrence Hoffman (1987, 1988; Hoffman and Walton 1992).

27. The editors of this service transliterate the Hebrew letter *kuf* as "Q."

28. Here I present a transcription of this tune as it was sung in an actual worship service. The recording session drew enthusiastic singers who sang with the cantor even more than the congregation did during worship.

29. Such melodies include Eric Mandell's composition for *Ahavat olam* based on traditional motifs (Nathanson 1974:59), the *Ve'ahavta* chanted to the melodies of Torah cantillation, *Magen avot* by Israel Goldfarb (ibid.:97) and Sigmund Sabel's *Alenu*, also credited to Salomon Sulzer (Davidson 1987:101).

30. For a fuller overview of the Conservative movement, see Nadell 1988; Sklare 1972.

31. Alexander III of Russia followed a simple plan to "solve the Jewish problem" proposed by his advisor Pobiedonostzev, the Procurator of the Holy Synod of the Greek Orthodox Church. One third of Russia's five million Jews should emigrate, one third should be baptized, and the remaining third should be starved. This program was initiated by savage pogroms

and followed by the formal enactment of the May Laws to forcibly relocate Jews in a smaller area of the Pale of Settlement and enact Jewish quotas in the Russian educational system.

32. Mark DeVoto observes that the B♮ can be regarded as an out-of-tune artifact.

33. I would also add that a measure of discord is often a normative state in some synagogues. I illustrate this with a story told to me by Richard Israel: Once a young rabbi accepted a position at a certain congregation. At the point in services when the congregation arrives at the Shema, the central creed of monotheistic faith, an argument breaks out over whether people should sit or stand during the recitation of that prayer. Some members yell that they should all sit down; others scream that they should all stand up. Disconcerted, the young rabbi visits an older sage in the community and poses this question: "During the Shema, some people yell at each other to sit down, other people yell at each other to stand up. What's the tradition?" The old sage ponders for a moment and answers, "In that synagogue, the tradition is for people to yell at each other."

34. This term was originally applied as a term of derision but was later adopted by this group. See Heilman 1992:367 n.21.

35. In the turbulent atmosphere of the Enlightenment, even Hirsch was at some points marked as a Reformer for making certain liturgical changes when he was a rabbi in Nikolsburg. It is of special interest to this study that some of those changes concerned music. Hirsch drew criticism for eliminating traditional chant both from his service and from Talmud study (Rudavsky 1967:222).

36. See Hirsch's *Nineteen Letters of Ben Uziel* (1899) and *Horeb* (trans. 1962).

37. For material on the history of Orthodox Judaism and its development in America, see Heilman and Cohen 1989; Bulka 1983; Liebman 1964–1965.

38. Mark Slobin describes this as a Hasidic tune, "with a lively, syncopated rhythm" (1989:200).

39. There is a rabbinic injunction against unduly lengthening a prayer and thus burdening a congregation. See Shulchan Arukh, OH 53:11.

40. On music in the Young Israel movement, see Nulman 1985:91–92; Slobin 1989:195–96.

41. Here the term is used to connote a non-Hasidic style of traditional worship. The *Mitnagdim* (adversaries), from the Hebrew *mitnaged* (to be opposed), were opponents of the Hasidim. They saw the reverence accorded to the *tsaddik*, the Hasidic rebbe, as bordering on cultic and understood much Hasidic philosophy as pantheistic. For a reassessment of the Mitnagdim, see Nadler 1997.

42. This issue of accuracy is connected to the larger issue of authenticity in current American Orthodoxy. Rabbi Daniel Landes writes: "What is the new ideological concern [of my *baalabatim* (congregants)]? . . . I can perhaps express [it] in one word: authenticity. It's a heavily laden word. Let me not define it so much as describe how it works itself out. They want to have *authentic* Jewish lives. And therefore, they often go back to models which they don't necessarily have in their own families, or if they do, they're often romanticized. This going back to models of authentic Jewish existence means complete halakhic compliance and also having a proper ideology which is in consonance with Torah values. . . . If for a moment any of my *baalabatim* felt that their experience in my minyan was somehow

not authentic Judaism, as taught in the past by Hirsch or Maimonides, or did not involve a proper understanding of Gemorrah, they would leave it instantly" (1991:176).

43. A current convention of some Hasidic Rebbes is to use an English honorific title such as "Grand Rabbi," suggesting a distinction between their roles and that of an ordinary rabbi.

44. For an etymology of the term traced through Jewish history, see Jacobs 1973:1–8.

45. For an introduction to Hasidism, see Dan 1989. For a treatment of Hasidic prayer, see Jacobs 1973.

46. For example, see George Savran's article on Jewish music in the *Jewish Catalog* (Siegel, Strassfeld, and Strassfeld 1973:211–15).

47. For an examination of the work of Buber and Heschel, see Silberstein's essay on the renewal of Jewish spirituality (1987). For examples of the influence of Zalman Schachter-Shalomi on contemporary Judaism, see the festschrift produced in his honor, edited by Wiener and Omer-Man (1993), especially the section on Jewish song, pp. 325–48.

48. See William Novak's comments on the religious dimension of Havurat Shalom: "The individuals who formed Havurat Shalom . . . used the term 'religious' unashamedly. This did not mean that they necessarily held in common a shared theology, or that they agreed about the nature and relative importance of Jewish observance. Likewise, the problem of a belief in God, while never easy, did not have to be resolved before one could speak meaningfully of religious acts, or attempt to create a religious society. 'Religious' was more attitudinal than theological; it described a tone rather than a content" (1972:247).

49. With the exception of Tufts Hillel, no other congregation examined in this study made such a direct link between the six days of the week and the psalms leading up to *Lekhah dodi*. When I lead services at Hillel, I occasionally expand on this kabbalistic interpretation. I encourage worshippers to think back through the week as they daven the six psalms, and suggest that they privately reflect on something that happened on each of the preceding days.

50. The seven uses of *kol* (voice) in psalm 29 are *kol Adonai al hamayim* (the voice of the Lord is over the water), *kol Adonai bakoach* (the voice of the Lord is mighty), *kol Adonai behadar* (the voice of the Lord is majestic), *kol Adonai shover arazim* (the voice of the Lord breaks cedars), *kol Adonai hotsev lahavot aish* (the voice of the Lord hews out flames), *kol Adonai yahil midbar* (the voice of the Lord makes the desert tremble), *kol Adonai yeholel ayalot* (the voice of the Lord makes the oak trees dance). These *middot*, or in Ashkenazi pronunciation, *middos*, corresponding to the seven lower *sefirot* (kabbalistic realms), are character traits that correspond to aspects of the divine in the kabbalistic system explaining the modes of divine manifestation. I wish to thank Nehemia Polen and Richard Israel for their helpful observations on the kabbalistic aspects of these middot.

51. Instead of pronouncing the text as it appears in the hymn, the Rebbe pronounces the phrase *lo tevoshi* in its plural imperative Ashkenazi form, *lo sevoshu*. At other times he uses the singular, *lo sevoshi*.

52. The Modzhitz Hasidic dynasty was founded in Poland by Israel of Modzhitz (d. 1921). He was a prolific composer of Hasidic tunes, a tradition carried on by his son, Saul Jedidiah Eleasar (d. 1947) (Rubinstein 1972:207–8).

53. The Ger Hasidim originated in the town of Gora Kalwaria, close to Warsaw, Poland. This celebrated Hasidic dynasty was founded by Isaac Meir Rothenberg Alter (1789–1866), a disciple of Levi Isaac of Berdichev. After the Holocaust, the Ger Hasidim relocated in Israel (Goldrat 1972:784–86).

54. The Rebbe and many other Jews are unaware that Lewandowski wrote different settings for the verses and chorus in this tune of *Lekkah dodi*. It is common to hear the entire hymn, verses and chorus, sung to the melody of the first chorus, creating a monotonous rendition. In practice, some congregations use variations of Lewandowski's settings for the verses but use his tune for the *Lekhah dodi* refrain throughout the hymn. Such is the version at Temple Israel. See Lewandowski, *Todah V'simrah* (Thanksgiving and Song) 1876, vol. I; 1882, vol. II. For a fine recording of Lewandowski's original arrangement, see "The Majesty of Holiness: Masterworks from the Great 19th-Century Synagogues of Berlin and Vienna," The Zamir Chorale of Boston.

55. Mark Slobin observes that the F naturals in verse eight suggest the normal modal shifts one encounters in Hasidic multipart tunes.

56. The Rebbe stressed that there were other examples of Hasidic music in which the music was determined by the text of the prayer. He explained that in the text of *Asadair* (I prepare [the Sabbath meal]), one of the zemirot composed by the *Ari Hakadosh* (the holy Rabbi Isaac Luria) and sung after Shabbas lunch, "there are a few words which say *velav milsa avsha*, 'Not a spoken word.' And it's at that point where [you stop singing] the words and you only hum the tune." The Rebbe's father taught that the tradition from the *Hozeh* of Lublin, the Seer of Lublin was that one specifically stopped singing the words at this point because such was indicated by the text, *velav milsa avsha*."

57. Vizhnits was a village in the Ukraine. The area was annexed to Russia at the end of the eighteenth century, and in the nineteenth century Hasidim gained a strong following in the community.

58. For a discussion of this type of tune borrowing, see Hajdu and Mazor 1972:1422. Also see their transcription of *Vald, Vald* (Forest, Forest) attributed to Rabbi Isaac of Kalov (ibid.:1427).

59. For a full treatment of the life of Reb Nahman of Bratslav, see Green 1978.

60. This quote is taken from Nahman of Bratslav's *Likkute Moharan* (Jerusalem, 1874:F. 79a).

61. The need to promote congregational participation and deemphasize the role of the professional leader is also found in contemporary critiques of Catholic worship. In his book *Why Catholics Can't Sing*, Thomas Day encourages priests to "Let the assembly hear its own voice, not the voice of an ego behind a microphone" (1991:169).

3. The Meaning of Nusach

1. Most explorations of nusach analyze the musical aspects of Jewish chant, examining such concepts as mode, scale, and the art of cantorial improvisation. Other studies have considered the historical development of Jewish prayer modes or their relation to the religious music of other cultures. For an overview of chant in Ashkenazi liturgical music, see Schleifer 1992:13–58. Also see the sections on liturgical chant and prayer modes in Avenary 1972a, Kligman (2000), Werner 1976:46–61, and Idelsohn

1929:72–91. For a detailed discussion of prayer modes, see Wohlberg 1972 [1954], Avenary 1972a, Glantz 1972 [1952], and Cohon 1950. For cantorial art music, see Avenary 1968. I see this work as a continuation of Mark Slobin's research in his final chapter of *Chosen Voices*, where he presents the first emic consideration of nusach (1989:256–79). Slobin describes the difficulty of establishing any single understanding and approach to nusach and observes that the "dividing up of a core insider term is bound to be artificial, as is any one gloss for a cultural concept" (1989:276, n. 4).

2. Judit Frigyesi presents the following historical overview: "The study of nusah goes back to the treatises of the eighteenth and nineteenth century cantors who first described the melodies and scales of Jewish music, either as part of the introduction to a collection of melodies or as a separate theoretical study. One of the most detailed treatises is Singer (1886) [for bibliography see chapter 16 in Idelsohn 1929]. In these studies, usually the word *Steiger* [Yiddish, shtayger] appears, literally meaning 'scale' but referring actually to the mode of the prayer. In cultural areas influenced by the Austrian-German cantorate, the word *nusah* often is replaced by or used alongside *Steiger* among cantors. Scholarly ethnomusicological study of the subject started with Idelsohn, who did not, however, use the word *nusah* but introduced the ethnomusicological term, 'mode' [Idelsohn 1914–32, 1929, 1933]" (Frigyesi 1993:82–83). While Frigyesi states that Idelsohn's classification and terminology of the modes are still used today, I would stress that these are familiar to professionals (cantors, musicologists, choir directors) rather than to laypeople.

3. Hanoch Avenary presents a more technical definition of prayer modes and asserts that their musical characteristics are defined by the following elements: "(1) Each is based upon a particular series of notes which may simply be a tetrachord, but more often a combination of several overlapping tetrachords, or another scale of less or more than eight notes; (2) each contains a stock of characteristic motives which undergo constant variation; (3) each combines these motives in a completely free order, forming an 'irrational' pattern; (4) the association of each nusah . . . is with a particular section of a specific holiday liturgy" (1972b:1283). In a later work he stresses that "Prayer-modes of the Eastern and Western synagogues cannot be described in the terms of scales and intervals alone. Their foremost characteristic is a stock of idiomatic motifs whose appearance indicates to the initiated listener the liturgical act he is attending in an Ashkenazi or Sefardi synagogue" (1987:106).

4. At the risk of oversimplification, one can grasp some of the flavor of these modes by comparing their structure to Western scales. *Adonai malakh* can be seen as a major scale with a lowered seventh, or as the Mixolydian mode. The structure of *Magen avot* corresponds to a Western natural minor scale, that is, with a lowered third, sixth, and seventh. *Ahavah rabbah* is characterized by the augmented second interval between the lowered second and natural third degrees.

5. The Jewish tradition is not the only religious tradition in which liturgical chant is connected to specific times of day and particular holy days. For this reason, scholars have compared nusach to the oriental *maqam*, the Indian raga, and early Christian liturgical music. See Avenary 1972b:1284, Idelsohn 1929:24–34, Werner 1959.

6. For a discussion of cantorial improvisation and recitative, see Wohlberg 1978. Eliyahu Schleifer draws the following distinction between professional cantors and lay service leaders, defining nusach as synagogue

chant that "serves today as the entire repertory for the lay precentor, but as the mere basis for the liturgical recitative of the professional cantor" (1992:29). A shaliach tsibbur aspires to daven in the basic nusach for a particular service while an accomplished cantor will often use this nusach as a springboard for a more sophisticated musical presentation of the service.

7. See Judit Frigyesi's article on "flowing rhythm" as a defining element in nusach (1993).

8. Most of the shaliach tsibbur's textual interpretation is fairly straightforward. Thus certain words in the liturgy become musical directions. *Kol demama* (a soft voice) or *raash gadol* (great noise) can guide the shaliach tsibbur. Other phrases, such as *hadesh yameinu kekedem* (renew our days as of old), call for emotional intensity. However, there also exists a more complex, culturally bound tradition of attributing various emotions and qualities to the modes and to their particular intervals. Idelsohn believed that synagogue chant used the minor third to express pain, longing, and hope but as soon as it wanted to express or confess truth, it turned to the emphatic sound of the major third (1929:78). Cantors and congregants have associated particular emotions with certain modes, connected to the textual theme of the prayer sung in that mode. In this way, grandeur and strength are associated with the *Adonai malakh* mode, love with *Ahavah rabbah*. For an analysis of melody choice that draws a complex relation between the culturally attributed meaning of the modes and the rabbinic interpretation of liturgical text, see Nulman 1985–1986. This approach has much to teach about the meaning of Jewish chant as understood by a particular community in a specific time. Yet just as textual interpretation changes in every generation, so does our perception of meaning in music. As I suggest throughout this study, the locus of musical meaning is not intrinsically found in the modes or their intervals, but in the individual as shaped by complex religious and cultural influences.

9. Compare Gerard Behague's comments on the importance of studying musical performance as both "an event and a process" (1984:4).

10. Members spoke of how the dancing during *Lekhah dodi* had gotten out of hand and children were making a game of throwing their stuffed animals in the air. This seemed inappropriate to the leadership, who conveyed to the congregation that this was not a *bekovedik* (showing proper respect) way of honoring Shabbat. Also, as has been mentioned, while the leader praised the children's enthusiasm, he asked parents of young children to control them and keep them from disturbing the service.

11. For an examination of Zalman Schachter-Shalomi's approach to davening, see Wiener and Omer-Man 1993:3–106.

12. Such examples include Mandell's *Ahavat olam, Ve'ahavta* chanted to the Pentateuchal mode, *Veshamru, Avot, Magen avot, Eloheinu velohei avoteinu* (Our God and God of our patriarchs), and the *Alenu*, including group chanting of the entire first, and sometimes the second, paragraph.

13. It should be noted that Temple Israel, with its move toward the inclusion of more Hebrew in services, sings a number of the same prayers in a similar style and provides English transliteration to help congregants who cannot easily read the Hebrew.

14. While this student is emphasizing stylistic differences between Conservative and Orthodox worship, it is an unequal comparison to equate a quick weekday service with more relaxed Shabbat prayer.

15. See Slobin's discussion of the larger context of the anti-Ramah and pro-Ramah division among Conservative cantors (1989:112–32).

16. One member of this community stressed that the dynamics of passing a musical tradition "from father to son" are often more complicated than they appear. While the following extended quote discusses that transmission of the *taamei hamikra*, the cantillation of the biblical text, the discussion has clear implication for understanding the complex transmission of musical traditions in general among modern Orthodox Jews: "I taught both my sons to read Torah, and they both became quite good and quite interested in it, particularly my youngest son. . . . He really is very good at layning. He's got a knack. . . . I must say that my son's enthusiasm for learning it—obviously I say this with a certain amount of paternal pride—means that he is interested in connecting with what I'm doing. Now, if I just left it at that, you'd say, 'Isn't that nice, passing on trop from generation to generation—it's a way of Jewish continuity,' but it wouldn't be accurate . . . because my father can't layn his way out of a paper bag. My father taught me how to layn, yet much of what he taught me was wrong. He never layned. It wasn't important for him to layn. His father didn't teach him. [My father] taught me that the *sof pasuk* (final cadence) was the same as *etnachta* (semicadence), which it isn't. When I used to read for my grandfather—[who was] a tyrannical and terrifying man—he used to make fun of me. He used to say, "That's wrong!" I used to look in perplexity at my father and say, 'What did I do wrong?' My father didn't know, because his father hadn't taught him. . . . And so [now], my precision is self-taught. I learned it from listening to other people, from paying attention to grammar lessons. So I didn't pick it up from my father. So when I'm passing it on to my children, is this a tradition, or this a self-conscious reinvention of tradition? Well, I think it's more accurate to call it the latter. I have no problem with it, but . . . it's always more complicated than it seems."

17. The stress on the importance of "correct" nusach on the High Holidays is not limited to this Orthodox synagogue. This was also evident at B'nai Or. One of the members, who helps lead services during the High Holidays, explained, "The strictest application of classical nusach . . . is on the High Holidays. [As] we plan the service every year, the discussion goes: 'Well, how much nusach and how much singing in English? How much reading in English?' Because there is a substantial portion of the community that comes to hear the classical nusach. To them *that* is the holidays."

18. This knowledgeable member described the resources that he consulted when looking for the proper weekday morning nusach: *The Musical Siddur* by Pinchas Spiro (1993), a Conservative cantor who published a number of resource books for the shaliach tsibbur; Macy Nulman's article on the weekday morning service (1985:167–78); and a cassette tape of the weekday service produced by Chadish Media (New York). This member added, "Most important, I called up a local respected hazzan, sang my nusach to him, and asked if I was doing it right." While this worshipper's studied approach to determine the authentic tradition for weekday nusach is atypical, it is in line with the highly educated modern Orthodox community's commitment to authentic tradition. It is interesting to note that this member is an authority on Jewish music and there are those in his community who might model their own nusach after his "authentic" tradition. In fact, he would be presenting a carefully constructed, amalgamated tradition, recently drawn from a variety of sources.

19. In recording examples of Kabbalat Shabbat nusach, worshippers from Shaarei Tefillah (CD #34), as well as from Tufts Hillel (CD #27) and

the Bostoner Hasidim (CD #35), all presented similar Eastern European traditions. The one exception was Gene Fax from Shaarei Tefillah. He ascribes his family's nusach to the Hasidic community of Demidovka in the Ukraine.

20. In reaction to this story, Joel Rosenberg observed, "There are instinctual limits to snobbery. In truth, this is a delicate and complicated issue because two religious imperatives are in conflict: ritual propriety versus the obligation not to shame someone publicly."

21. However, I found that occasionally when a person in the Orthodox community asserted that he "did not know nusach," he was simply telling the truth. At Beth Pinchas I observed an older Hasid approach a younger member in his mid-20s and ask him to daven. The young man said, " I've never davened. I don't really know nusach." The older man insisted, "Don't worry. Who knows nusach!? You'll be fine. Once I made your brother-in-law daven, and later he thanked me." As the young man made his way up to the reader's stand, he asked some people to help him if he forgot anything. In fact, he was not a very good davener. His Kabbalat Shabbat nusach was shaky: he hesitated in a number of sections and had trouble fitting the melody of the nusach to the text. Even when a community adheres to and affirms the importance of certain musical practice, that does not mean that all of its members have rhythm, can carry a tune, like to sing, or have mastered musical and liturgical traditions. Communities are made up of individuals, bringing their own talents, fears, and skills into the creation of the community's expressive culture.

22. Here and throughout their comments, both the Rebbe and his son switch between Sephardic and Ashkenazi pronunciation. Joel Rosenberg sees this as a mark of their sophistication and observes that they adjust their Hebrew usage to their listener's background. I agree and would add that the larger issue of linguistic code-switching between Sephardic and Ashkenazic pronunciation is a strategy employed to level or maintain boundaries in all of the worship communities examined in this study (see chapter 4; also cf. Heilman 1983:172–76).

4. Meaning and Melody Choice in Jewish Worship

1. This observation does not hold true in regard to visible differences such as race. It also does not apply to traditional Jews who publicly mark themselves as separate from the superculture by their dress, hairstyle, or language. Yet the majority of American Jews are able to "pass," easily appearing to be members of the dominant superculture. Barbara Kirshenblatt-Gimblett writes, "The folklore of ethnicity grows out of a heightened awareness of cultural diversity and ambiguity, out of mastery of multiple cultural repertoires and the ability to choose and switch among them" (1987:88, quoted in Kugelmass 1988:6).

2. Major differences between Sephardic and Ashkenazi pronunciation of Hebrew are as follows: Sephardic Hebrew is characterized by closed sibilants and accents placed on the ultimate syllable. Ashkenazi Hebrew is characterized by open sibilants and the accent on the penultimate syllable. Sephardic Hebrew pronounces the Hebrew letter *tav* as "t." The Ashkenazi pronunciation of *tav*, when it is not doubled or beginning a syllable after a closed syllable, is "s"; thus Shabbas (Ashkenazi) and Shabbat (Sephardic). The Sephardic pronunciation of the Hebrew vowel *kamats* is "ah," while the Ashkenazi pronunciation is "aw." Dialectic pronunciation varies from community to community.

3. As discussed by Heilman (1983) and analyzed in detail by Wolberger (1993:110–36), the language of Talmud study, *gemore-loshn*, is in fact a language of musical chant, *gemore niggun*. In the Jewish tradition, Talmud study and the recitation of both scripture and liturgy are all forms of ritual performance that require music.

4. William B. Gudykunst and Karen L. Schmidt say that language (and as I suggest in this study, music) and ethnic identity are related reciprocally; that is, language usage influences the formation of ethnic identity, but ethnic identity also influences language attitudes and usage (1988). The sociolinguist John J. Gumperz writes, "Codeswitching is perhaps most frequently found in the informal speech of those members of cohesive minority groups in modern urbanizing regions . . . in situation of rapid transition where traditional intergroup barriers are breaking down and norms of interaction are changing" (1982:64), a situation not unique to but especially relevant to the American Jewish community.

5. One can point to many similar examples. After the Yom Kippur War in 1973 it was common to hear many American Conservative and modern Orthodox congregations sing *Adon olam* to the tune of *Sharm El Sheik*, a popular Israeli song that celebrated the triumphant return of Israel's armies to the Sinai. We see an example of a similar metaphorical melodic switch in the liturgical use of "Jerusalem of Gold," the anthem of the Six Day War. Naomi Shemer's popular tune was sung both to the text of *Adon olam* in the Shabbat morning service and for the last *hakafah* (round or circuit of dancing with the scrolls) on Simhat Torah. The overlay of these melodies onto liturgical text reflects the American Jewish support and solidarity with Israel during those two wars (cf. Shiloah 1992:65–67).

6. Macy Nulman writes, "The opening bars of the melody were adapted by Martin Luther for the opening of his church chorale, "*Nun freut euch, lieben Christen g'mein*" [Now rejoice all you dear Christians together]. Johann Sebastian Bach also wrote a four-part setting of the same chorale" (1975:162,163). Nulman references Bach's 371 Four-Part Chorales, p. 82, no. 83 (New York: Associated Music Publishers) (ibid.).

7. The use of a holiday's signature melody to foreshadow its approach is not limited to *Adon olam*. Joseph Levine describes this custom in his discussion of prescribed seasonal motifs: "An excellent place to interpolate the motif is Kaddish for Friday night Maariv of the festival week. Its appearance is usually delayed until the second phrase, *be'olma di vera* [throughout the world, which (God) created]. This achieves maximum surprise since worshippers, anticipating the normal Sabbath chant, will instead 'round the corner' into Chanukah-awareness" (1989:163). Another example is the use of the High Holiday nusach for the Kaddish during Selichot, the penitential prayers chanted on the Saturday evening preceding Rosh Hashanah.

8. Kathryn Woolard discusses a similar attempt to bring two groups together in her analysis of the routine of a popular Spanish comedian who used both local languages, Castilian Spanish and Catalan, in his performance. In the comedian's jokes "a fictional world is modeled where the two languages have found a peaceful coexistence. Neither one has had to disappear; they are both in use, side by side, but there is no battle line between them like that encountered in the real world" (Woolard 1988:73). Yet in the case of the comedian, people were required only to *observe* him in action. The Hillel students had to participate and perform in both coded musical languages. Much more was required of them, and their level of discomfort was raised substantially.

9. This device is common in children's folk songs, such as "Miss Lucy Had a Steamboat" and "Hop-a-long Peter," where the rhyme structure and sense of a verse imply that the singer is about to use profanity, an expectation that is changed at the last minute.

Conclusion

1. During the late 1960s and early 1970s many students studied in a "rabbinical seminary" at the Rebbe's that provided deferments from the draft during the Vietnam War.

2. See Jackson Lears's discussion of antimodernism and its effect upon American culture at the beginning of the twentieth century. At that time, "liberal Protestantism lost much of its power as an independent source of moral authority" (1981:23). Ultimately these factors generated a crisis not only of moral but of cultural authority. Modern America did not turn out to be a "New Jerusalem," but rather "a wilderness of moral uncertainty" (ibid.:46). Lears asserts that antimodernism shaped our approach to cultural authority and authenticity in the late twentieth century (ibid.:300–12).

Glossary

Hebrew and Yiddish words are defined where they first appear in the text, with the exception of certain words that are common in English usage. The following words appear frequently.

Adon olam (Master of the world) A popular hymn in the morning service and closing hymn in Sabbath and holiday services.

Ahavat olam ([With] everlasting love) Blessing before the Shema in the Maariv service, proclaiming God's love for Israel evidenced by the giving of the Torah.

Alenu (It is our obligation [to praise God]) Prayer at the service's conclusion, proclaiming God's sovereignty and praying for the establishment of God's kingdom.

Amidah (standing prayer) A collection of benedictions said silently, while standing, that make up the core of the prayer service.

baal tefillah (master of prayer) The leader in prayer; one who knows the order and proper nusach and musical realization of the liturgy.

Barekhu (Bless! [imperative]) The formal call to prayer in morning and evening services.

bimah (raised platform) The stage from which the Torah scroll is read and on which the rabbi, cantor, or lay leader stands while leading prayer.

daven (*davenen*, noun) The Yiddish term meaning to pray, used by Ashkenazi Jews. Worshippers also use the word *davening*, a Judeo-English form in which an English suffix is added to a Yiddish or Hebrew word.

gabbai (sexton) The lay leader in charge of assigning ritual tasks in the synagogue.

halakhah (the way) The body of Jewish law.

hatimah (sealing) The concluding lines of a prayer, often chanted out loud by the prayer leader.

havurah (fellowship community) A worship community characterized by a high degree of participatory leadership.

hazzan (cantor) The leader who chants the prayers before the congregation.

hazzanut, hazzanus [Ashkenazi pronunciation] (cantorial performance) The corpus of musical, liturgical material sung by the hazzan, especially improvisation based on nusach.

Kabbalat Shabbat (welcoming or receiving the Sabbath) The first part of the Friday evening prayer service.

Kaddish [Aramaic] The doxology proclaiming God's holiness which marks the conclusion of certain sections of a service, also recited as a mourners' prayer.

kavanah Sincere devotion, concentration and intention in prayer.

Kedushah Literally "sanctification"; the third blessing in the repetition of the Amidah, which includes the response "holy, holy, holy."

Kiddush The blessing over wine recited on Sabbath and holidays.

kodesh Holy, separate, or unique.

layn (Yiddish) To chant the Torah.

Lekhah dodi (Come, my beloved) Central hymn in the Kabbalat Shabbat service, composed by Shelomo Alkabetz in the sixteenth century.

Lo tevoshi (Do not be ashamed) The sixth verse of *Lekhah dodi*.

Maariv The evening prayer service.

Minchah The afternoon prayer service.

minhag Local custom.

minyan The quorum of ten needed for public worship.

Moshiach [Ashkenazi pronunciation] (the anointed one), The Messiah.

Musaf Additional service following the morning service on Shabbat and holidays.

niggun, niggunim (pl.) A devotional tune, characterized by repetition and usually sung to vocables such as "rum, de, de, dum" or "yai, lai, lai."

nusach, nuschaot (pl.) Traditional Ashkenazi Jewish chant; the occasion-specific, traditionally accepted way in which a certain part of the liturgy is sung.

piyyut, piyyutim (pl.) Jewish liturgical hymn.

Rav Rabbi.

Rebbe Hasidic term for rabbi and spiritual leader.

Shabbat, Shabbos [Ashkenazi pronunciation] The Sabbath.

shaliach tsibbur (messenger or emissary of the congregation) The reader
who leads the congregation in prayer.

Shekhinah The feminine, indwelling presence of God.

Shema (Listen!) Central prayer in the morning and evening service
consisting of three biblical passages beginning with the creedal
statement, "Listen Israel! Adonai is our God, Adonai alone."

shul [Yiddish] Synagogue.

Shulchan Arukh (The Prepared Table) Joseph Caro's sixteenth-century
code of rabbinic law.

siddur Prayer book.

Tisha B'Av (the ninth day of the Hebrew month of Av) The solemn
holiday commemorating the destruction of both the First (586 B.C.E.)
and Second (70 C.E.) Temples in Jerusalem.

Yerushalayim Jerusalem.

zemirot Sabbath table songs.

Works Cited

Adler, Israel. 1975. *Hebrew Writings Concerning Music.* RISM Ser. BIX 2 Munich: Henle Verlag.

Alpert, Rebecca T., and Jacob J. Staub. 1985. *Exploring Judaism: A Reconstructionist Approach.* New York: Reconstructionist Press.

Arzt, Max. 1979. *Joy and Remembrance: Commentary on the Sabbath Eve Liturgy.* New York: Hartmore House.

Avenary, Hanoch. 1968. "The Cantorial Fantasia of the Eighteenth and Nineteenth Centuries—A Late Manifestation of Musical Trope." In *Yuval: Studies of the Jewish Music Research Center,* edited by Israel Adler. Jerusalem: Magnes Press, Hebrew University.

———. 1972a. "Music: The Evolution of East Ashkenazi Hazzanut." *Encyclopaedia Judaica.* Vol. 12:651–55. Jerusalem: Keter.

———. 1972b. "Nusah." *Encyclopaedia Judaica.* Vol. 12:1283–84. Jerusalem: Keter.

———. 1987. "The Aspects of Time and Environment in Jewish Traditional Music." In *Israel Studies in Musicology,* vol. 4, edited by Roger Kamien. Jerusalem: Israel Musicological Society.

Axelrod, Ira. n.d. *Seventy-Five Years of Chassidic Life in America: The Story of the Bostoner Rebbes, An Authorized History.* Brookline, Mass.: New England Chassidic Center.

Bartok, Bela. 1931. *Hungarian Folk Music.* Translated by M. C. Calvacoressi. London: Oxford University Press.

Bayer, Bathja. 1972. "*Lekkah Dodi*: Musical Rendition." *Encyclopaedia Judaica* Vol. 11:6, 7. Jerusalem: Keter.

Behague, Gerard, ed. 1984. *Performance Practice: Ethnomusicological Perspectives.* Westport, Conn.: Greenwood Press.

Belcove-Shalin, Janet. 1988. "Becoming More of an Eskimo: Fieldwork among the Hasidim of Boro Park." In *Between Two Worlds: Ethnographic Essays on American Jewry,* edited by Jack Kugelmass. Ithaca, N.Y.: Cornell University Press.

Bellah, Robert N. 1985. *Habits of the Heart: Individualism and Commitment in American Life.* Berkeley: University of California Press.

Bellah, Robert N., and Phillip E. Hammond. 1980. *Varieties of Civil Religion.* San Francisco: Harper and Row.

Berman, Paul. 1994. "The Other and the Almost the Same." *The New Yorker.* 28 February, 61–71.

Blom, Jan-Petter, and John J. Gumperz. 1972. "Social Meaning in Linguistic Structure: Code-Switching in Norway." In *Directions in Sociolinguistics,* edited by John J. Gumperz and Bell Hymes. New York: Holt, Rinehart and Winston.

Bohlman, Philip V. 1988. *The Study of Folk Music in the Modern World.* Bloomington: Indiana University Press.

———. 1993a. "Musical Life in the Central European Jewish Village." In *Modern Jews and Their Musical Agendas,* edited by Ezra Mendelsohn. *Studies in Contemporary Jewry* 9. New York: Oxford University Press.

———. 1993b. "Musical Identities." Paper delivered at Indiana University. April 1993.

Buber, Martin. 1947. *Tales of the Hasidim: The Early Masters.* Translated by Olga Marx. New York: Schocken Books.

Bubis, Gerald B., Harry Wasserman, and Alan Lert. 1983. *Synagogue Havurot: A Comparative Study.* Washington, D.C.: University Press of America.

Bulka, Reuven P. 1983. *Dimensions of Orthodox Judaism.* New York: Ktav.

Caro, Joseph. [16th century] 1874–75. *Shulchan Arukh.* 10 vols. Vilna.

Clifford, James. 1988. *The Predicament of Culture: Twentieth-Century Ethnography, Literature and Art.* Cambridge, Mass.: Harvard University Press.

Cohen, Steven M. 1979. "Conflict in Havurot: Veterans vs. Newcomers." *Response: A Contemporary Jewish Review* 12:34.

———. 1983. *American Modernity and Jewish Identity.* New York: Tavistock.

———. 1988. *American Assimilation or Jewish Revival?* Bloomington: Indiana University Press.

Cohon, Baruch. 1950. "Structure of the Synagogue Prayer Chant." *Journal of the American Musicological Society* 3/1:17–32.

Dan, Joseph. 1989. "Hasidism." In *Judaism: A People and Its History,* edited by Robert M. Seltzer. New York: Macmillan.

Davidson, Charles, musical editor. 1987. *Gates of Song: Music for Shabbat.* New York: Transcontinental Music.

Day, Thomas. 1991. *Why Catholics Can't Sing: The Culture of Catholicism and the Triumph of Bad Taste.* New York: Crossroad.

Dinnerstein, Leonard. 1994. *Antisemitism in America.* New York: Oxford University Press.

Donin, Hayim Halevy. 1980. *To Pray as a Jew: A Guide to the Prayer Book and Synagogue Service.* New York: Basic Books.

Elazar, Daniel. 1967. *Community and Polity, The Organizational Dynamic of American Jewry.* New York: Jewish Publication Society.

Elazar, Daniel J., and Rela Geffen Monson. 1979. "The Synagogue Havurah—An Experiment in Restoring Adult Fellowship to the Jewish Community." *The Jewish Journal of Sociology* 21/9:67–80.

Elbogen, Ismar. [1913, 1972] 1993. *Jewish Liturgy: A Comprehensive History.* Translated by Raymond P. Scheindlin. Based on the author's *Der judische Gottesdienst in seiner geschichtlichen Entwicklung* (1913) and the Hebrew version, *Hatefila beyisra'el behitpathutah hahistorit* (1972). Philadelphia: Jewish Publication Society.

Epstein, Isadore, ed. 1990. *Hebrew-English Edition of the Babylonian Talmud,* 30 vols. London: Soncino Press.

Erikson, Erik H. 1968. *Identity, Youth and Crisis.* New York: Norton.

Feldman, Steven, and the staff of *Genesis 2.*, eds. 1986. *Guide to Jewish Boston and New England.* Boston: Genesis 2.

Fine, Lawrence. 1984a. *Safed Spirituality: Rules of Mystical Piety, The Beginning of Wisdom.* New York: Paulist Press.

———. 1984b. "Kabbalistic Texts." In *Back to the Sources: Reading the Classic Jewish Texts*, edited by Barry W. Holtz. New York: Summit Books.

Fleischer, Ezra. 1975. *Hebrew Liturgical Poetry in the Middle Ages* [Hebrew]. Jerusalem: Keter.

———. 1988. *Eretz-Israel Prayer and Prayer Rituals* (Hebrew). Jerusalem: Magnes Press, Hebrew University.

Frigyesi, Judit. 1993. "Preliminary Thoughts Toward the Study of Music Without Clear Beat: The Example of "Flowing Rhythm" in Jewish *Nusah.*" *Asian Music* 24/2:59–87.

Glantz, Leib. [1952] 1972. "The Musical Basis of Nusach Hatefillah." In *Journal of Synagogue Music*, vol. 4/1, 2. New York: Cantors Assembly of America.

Glassie, Henry. 1982. *Passing the Time in Ballymenone: Culture and History of an Ulster Community.* Philadelphia: University of Pennsylvania Press.

Goldrat, Abram Juda. 1972. "Gora Kalwaria." *Encyclopaedia Judaica.* Vol. 7:284–786. Jerusalem: Keter.

Goldscheider, Calvin. 1986. *Jewish Continuity and Change.* Bloomington: Indiana University Press.

Goldstein, Sidney, and Calvin Goldscheider. 1968. *Jewish Americans: Three Generations in a Jewish Community.* Englewood Cliffs, N.J.: Prentice-Hall.

Green, Arthur. 1978. *Tormented Master: A Life of Rabbi Nahman of Bratslav.* University, Ala.: University of Alabama Press.

Greenblum, Joseph, and Marshall Sklare. 1967. *Jewish Identity on the American Frontier.* New York: Basic Books.

Grenier, Line, and Jocelyne Guilbault. 1990. "'Authority' Revisited: The 'Other' in Anthropology and Popular Music Studies." *Ethnomusicology* 34/3:381–97.

Gudykunst, William B., and Daren L. Schmidt. 1988. "Language and Ethnic Identity: An Overview and Prologue." In *Language and Ethnic Identity*, edited by William B. Gudykunst. Philadelphia: Multilingual Matters.

Guilbault, Jocelyne. 1993. *Zouk: World Music in the West Indies.* Chicago: University of Chicago Press.

Gumperz, John J. 1982. *Discourse Strategies*, ed. and *Language and Social Identity.* London: Cambridge University Press.

Gusfield, Joseph R. 1975. *Community: A Critical Response.* New York: Harper and Row.

Hajdu, Andre, and Ja'acov Mazor. 1972. "The Musical Tradition of Hasidism." *Encyclopaedia Judaica.* Vol. 7:1421–32. Jerusalem: Keter.

Hammer, Reuven. 1994. *Entering Jewish Prayer: A Guide to Personal Devotion and the Worship Service.* New York: Schocken Books.

Hebdige, Dick. 1979. *Subculture: The Meaning of Style.* New York: Methuen.

Hecht, Shirah Weinberg. 1993. "When Tradition Leads: Prayer and Participation in the Contemporary Jewish Equalitarian Minyan." Ph.D. Dissertation. University of Chicago.

Heilman, Samuel C. 1976. *Synagogue Life: A Study in Symbolic Interaction.* Chicago: University of Chicago Press.

──────. 1983. *The People of the Book: Drama, Fellowship, and Religion.* Chicago: University of Chicago Press.

──────. 1984. *The Gate Behind the Wall: A Pilgrimage to Jerusalem.* New York: Summit Books.

──────. 1992. *Defenders of the Faith: Inside Ultra-Orthodox Jewry.* New York: Schocken Books.

Heilman, Samuel, and Steven M. Cohen. 1989. *Cosmopolitans and Parochials: Modern Orthodox Jews in America.* Chicago: University of Chicago Press.

Heinemann, Joseph. 1977. *Prayer in the Talmud: Forms and Patterns.* Berlin: Walter de Gruyter.

Heller, Monica, ed. 1988. *Codeswitching: Anthropological and Sociolinguistic Perspectives.* Berlin: Mouton de Gruyter.

Herman, Simon N. 1977. *Jewish Identity: A Social Psychological Perspective.* Beverly Hills, Cal.: Sage.

Hirsch, Samson Raphael. 1899. *Nineteen Letters of Ben Uziel.* Translated by Bernard Brachman. New York: Funk and Wagnalls.

──────. 1962. *Horeb.* Translated by I. Grunfeld. 2 vols. London: Soncino Press.

Hobsbawm, Eric, and Terence Ranger, eds. 1983. *The Invention of Tradition.* Cambridge, UK: Cambridge University Press.

Hoffman, Lawrence A. 1979. *The Ganonization of the Synagogue Service.* Notre Dame, Ind.: University of Notre Dame.

──────. 1987. *Beyond the Text: A Holistic Approach to Liturgy.* Bloomington: Indiana University Press.

──────. 1988. *The Art of Public Prayer: Not for Clergy Only.* Washington, D.C.: Pastoral Press.

──────, ed. 1997. *My People's Prayer Book: Traditional Prayers, Modern Commentaries.* Vol. 1. *The Sh'ma and Its Blessings.* Woodstock, Ver.: Jewish Lights Publishing.

Hoffman, Lawrence A., and Janet R. Walton, eds. 1992. *Sacred Sound and Social Change: Liturgical Music in Jewish and Christian Experience.* Notre Dame, Ind.: University of Notre Dame Press.

Idelsohn, A. Z. 1929. *Jewish Music in Its Historical Development.* Holt, Rinehart and Winston. Reprint, New York: Schocken Books, 1967.

Israel, Sherry, ed. 1987. *Boston's Jewish Community: The 1985 CJP Demographic Study.* Boston: Combined Jewish Philanthropies of Greater Boston.

──────, ed. 1997. *Comprehensive Report on the 1995 CJP Demographic Study.* Boston: Combined Jewish Philanthropies of Greater Boston.

Jacobs, Louis. 1973. *Hassidic Prayer.* New York: Schocken Books.

Jacobson, B. S. 1973. *The Weekday Siddur: An Exposition and Analysis of Its Structure, Contents, Language and Ideas.* Tel Aviv: Sinai Publishing.

──────. 1981 *The Sabbath Service: An Exposition and Analysis of Its Structure, Contents, Lanuage and Ideas.* Tel Aviv: Sinai Publishing.

James, William. 1920. *The Letters of William James,* edited by Henry James, vol. 1. Boston: Atlantic Monthy Press.

Kaplan, Mordecai. [1957] 1981. *Judaism as a Civilization: Towards a Reconstruction of American Jewish Life.* Introduction by Arthur Hertzberg. Philadelphia: Jewish Publication Society; Reconstructionist Press.

Kimelman, Reuven. 1998. "A Prolegomena to Lekhah Dodi and Qabbalat Shabbat" [Hebrew, with English abstract]. In *Mehkerei Yerushalayim Bemahshevet Yisrael,* 14. Jerusalem: Hebrew University.

Kirshenblatt-Gimblett, Barbara. 1987. "The Folk Culture of Jewish Immigrant Communities." In *The Jews of North America*, edited by Moses Rischin. Detroit: Wayne State University Press.

Kligman, Mark. 1996. "On the Creators and Consumers of Orthodox Popular Music in Brooklyn." *YIVO Annual* 23:259–93.

———. 2000. "Music in Judaism." In *The Encyclopaedia of Judaism*, edited by Jacob Neusner, Alan J. Avery-Peck, and William Scott Green. Leiden: Museum of Jewish Heritage and Brill.

Kon, Abraham. 1971. *Prayer.* Translated by the author from his book *Si'ah Tefillah*. London: Soncino Press.

Koskoff, Ellen. 1978. "Contemporary Niggun Composition in an American Hasidic Community." *Selected Reports in Ethnomusicology.* Vol. 3/1.

Kugelmass, Jack, ed. 1988. *Between Two Worlds: Ethnographic Essays on American Jewry.* Ithaca, N.Y.: Cornell University Press.

Kushner, Lawrence. 1984. "Some Truths About Congregations." *New Traditions*, no. 1. Spring. New York: National Havurah Committee.

Landes, Daniel. 1991. "The Role of the Synagogue in Jewish Identity." In *Jewish Identity in America*, edited by David M. Gordis and Yoav Ben-Horin. Los Angeles: Wilstein Institute.

Landman, Leo. 1972. *The Cantor: An Historical Perspective.* New York: Yeshiva University.

Langer, Ruth. 1998. *To Worship God Properly: Tensions Between Liturgical Custom and Halakhah in Judaism.* Cincinnati: Hebrew Union College Press.

———. 1999. "Revisiting Early Rabbinic Liturgy: The Recent Contributions of Ezra Fleicher." *Prooftexts* 19/2:155–80.

Lears, T. J. Jackson. 1981. *No Place of Grace: Antimodernism and the Transformation of American Culture 1880–1920.* New York: Pantheon Books.

Levine, Joseph A. 1989. *Synagogue Song in America.* Crown Point, Ind.: White Cliffs Media Company.

Lewandowski, Louis. 1876, 1882. *Todah W'simrah.* 2 vols. Berlin.

Liebman, Charles S. 1964–1965. "Orthodoxy in American Jewish Life." *American Jewish Yearbook.* 66.

Lomax, Alan. 1968. *Folk Song Style and Culture.* New Brunswick, N.J.: Transaction Books.

London, Perry, and Alissa Hirshfeld. 1991. "The Psychology of Identity Formation." In *Jewish Identity in America*, edited by David M. Gordis and Yoav Ben-Horin. Los Angeles: Wilstein Institute.

Manuel, Peter. 1993. *Cassette Culture: Popular Music and Technology in North India.* Chicago: The University of Chicago Press.

Marcus, Jacob Rader. 1989. *United States Jewry 1776–1985.* 4 vols. Detroit: Wayne State University Press.

McClure, Erica, and Malcolm McClure. 1988. "Macro- and micro-sociolinguistic dimensions of code-switching in Vingard." In *Codeswitching: Anthropological and Sociolinguistic Perspectives*, edited by Monica Heller. Berlin: Mouton de Gruyter.

Merriam, Alan P. 1964. *The Anthropology of Music.* Evanston, Ill.: Northwestern University Press.

Meyer, Michael A. 1988. *Response to Modernity: A History of the Reform Movement in Judaism.* New York: Oxford University Press.

Mintz, Alan. 1984. "Prayer and the Prayerbook." In *Back to the Sources: Reading the Classic Jewish Texts*, edited by Barry W. Holtz. New York: Summit Books.

Munk, Elie. 1963. *The World of Prayer,* vol. 2. New York: Philip Feldheim Inc.

Myerhoff, Barbara. 1988. "Surviving Stories: Reflections on *Number Our Days.*" In *Between Two Worlds: Ethnographic Essays on American Jewry,* edited by Jack Kugelmass. Ithaca,: Cornell University Press.

Nadell, Pamela S., ed. 1988. *Conservative Judaism in America.* Westport, Conn.: Greenwood.

Nadler, Allan. 1997. *The Faith of the Mithnagdim: Rabbinic Responses to Hasidic Rapture.* Baltimore: Johns Hopkins University Press.

Nathanson, Moshe, ed. 1974. *Zamru Lo: Congregational Melodies and Z'mirot for the Friday Evening Service,* vol. 1. New York: Cantors Assembly.

Nettl, Bruno. 1964. *Theory and Method in Ethnomusicology.* New York: Free Press.

———. 1985. *The Western Impact on World Music : Change, Adaptation, and Survival.* New York: Schirmer Books.

Neusner, Jacob, ed. 1972. *Contemporary Judaic Fellowship in Theory and Practice.* New York: Ktav.

Novak, William. 1972. "Havurat Shalom: A Personal Account." In *Contemporary Judaic Fellowship in Theory and Practice,* edited by Jacob Neusner. New York: Ktav.

Nulman, Macy. 1975. *Concise Encyclopedia of Jewish Music.* New York: McGraw-Hill.

———. 1985. *Concepts of Jewish Music and Prayer.* New York: Cantorial Council of America at Yeshiva University.

———. 1985–1986. "A Perception of the Prayer Modes as Reflected in Musical and Rabbinic Sources." *Musica Judaica* 7/1:45–58. New York: American Society for Jewish Music.

Pasternak, Velvel, ed. 1968. *Songs of the Chassidim.* New York: Tara Publications.

———, ed. 1976. *Great Songs of Israel.* New York: Tara Publications—Board of Jewish Education, New York.

———, ed. 1986. *Siddur in Song: 100 Prayerbook Melodies.* New York: Tara Publications.

Petuchowski, Jakob J. 1968. *Prayer Book Reform in Europe: The Liturgy of European Liberal and Reform Judaism.* New York: World Union of Progressive Judaism.

Phillips, Bruce A. 1991. "Sociological Analysis of Jewish Identity." In *Jewish Identity in America,* edited by David M. Gordis and Yoav Ben-Horin. Los Angeles: Wilstein Institute.

Pike, Kenneth L. 1967. *Language in Relation to a Unified Theory of the Structure of Human Behavior.* The Hague: Mouton.

Piston, Walter. 1978. *Harmony.* Revised and expanded by Mark DeVoto. New York: Norton.

Prell, Riv-Ellen. 1988a. *Prayer and Community: The Havurah Movement and the Recreation of American Judaism.* Detroit: Wayne State University Press.

———. 1988b. "Laughter That Hurts: Ritual Humor and Ritual Change in an American Jewish Community." In *Between Two Worlds: Ethnographic Essays on American Jewry,* edited by Jack Kugelmass. Ithaca, N.Y.: Cornell University Press.

Qureshi, Regula. 1986. *Sufi Music of India and Pakistan: Sound, Context and Meaning in Qawwali.* Cambridge, UK: Cambridge University Press.

Reck, David B., Mark Slobin, and Jeff Todd Titon. 1996. "Discovering and

Documenting a World of Music." In *Worlds of Music: An Introduction to the Music of World's Peoples*, general editor, Jeff Todd Titon. New York: Schirmer Books.

Reisman, Bernard. 1977. *The Chavurah: A Contemporary Jewish Experience*. New York: Union of American Hebrew Congregations.

Rischin, Moses. [1986] 1997. "Germans versus Russians." In *The American Jewish Experience: A Reader*, edited by Jonathan D. Sarna. New York: Holmes and Meier.

Rosenzweig, Rosie, ed. 1995. *The Jewish Guide to Boston and New England*. Boston: The Jewish Advocate.

Royce, Anya Peterson. 1982. *Ethnic Identity: Strategies of Diversity*. Bloomington: Indiana University Press.

Rubinstein, Avraham. 1972. "Modzhitz." *Encyclopaedia Judaica*. Vol. 12:207–8. Jerusalem: Keter.

Rudavsky, David. 1967. *Modern Jewish Religious Movements: A History of Emancipation and Adjustment*. New York: Behrman House.

Saltzman, Shulamit. 1976. "Movement of Prayer." In *The Second Jewish Catalog: Sources and Resources*, edited by Sharon and Michael Strassfeld. Philadelphia: Jewish Publication Society.

Samuel, Simha ben. 1893. *Mahzor Vitry*, edited by S. Hurwitz. Berlin: H. Itzkowski.

Sarna, Jonathan D., ed. [1986] 1997. *The American Jewish Experience: A Reader*. New York: Holmes and Meier.

Sarna, Jonathan D., and Ellen Smith, eds. 1995. *The Jews of Boston: Essays on the Occasion of the Centenary (1895–1995) of the Combined Jewish Philanthropies of Greater Boston*. Boston: Combined Jewish Philanthropies of Greater Boston.

Savran, George. 1973. "Music." In *The Jewish Catalog: A Do-It-Yourself Kit*, edited by Richard Siegel, Sharon Strassfeld, and Michael Strassfeld. Philadelphia: Jewish Publication Society.

Schechter, Solomon. 1908. *Studies in Judaism*. Second series, 238–39. Philadelphia: Jewish Publication Society of America.

Schiller, Benjie-Ellen. 1992. "The Hymnal as an Index of Musical Change in Reform Synogogues." In *Sacred Sound and Social Change: Liturgical Music in Jewish and Christian Experience*, edited by Lawrence A. Hoffman and Janet R. Walton. Notre Dame, Ind.: University of Notre Dame Press.

Schleifer, Eliyahu. 1992. "Jewish Liturgical Music from the Bible to Hasidism." In *Sacred Sound and Social Change: Liturgical Music in Jewish and Christian Experience*, edited by Lawrence A. Hoffman and Janet R. Walton. Notre Dame, Ind.: University of Notre Dame Press.

Scholem, Gershom. 1941. *Major Trends in Jewish Mysticism*. New York: Schocken Books.

Scotton, Carol Myers. 1988. "Code switching as indexical of social negotiations." In *Codeswitching: Anthropological and Sociolinguistic Perspectives*, edited by Monica Heller. Berlin: Mouton de Gruyter.

Seeger, Anthony. 1987. *Why Suya Sing: A Musical Anthropology of an Amazonian People*. Cambridge, UK: Cambridge University Press.

Seltzer, Robert M., ed. 1989. *Judaism: A People and Its History*. New York: Macmillan.

Shelemay, Kay Kaufman. 1986. *Music, Ritual and Falasha History*. Ethiopian Series, Monograph No. 17. East Lansing, Mich.: African Study Center.

————. 1991. *A Song of Longing: An Ethiopian Journey.* Urbana: University of Illinois Press.

Shiloah, Amnon. 1992. *Jewish Musical Traditions.* Detroit: Wayne State University Press.

Siegel, Richard, Sharon Strassfeld, and Michael Strassfeld, eds. 1973. *The Jewish Catalog: A Do-It-Yourself Kit.* Philadelphia: Jewish Publication Society.

Silberstein, Laurence J. 1987. "The Renewal of Jewish Spirituality: Two Views." In *Jewish Spirituality: From the Sixteenth-Century Revival to the Present,* edited by Arthur Green. New York: Crossroad.

Sklare, Marshall. 1967. *Jewish Identity on the Suburban Frontier.* New York: Basic Books.

————. 1972. *Conservative Judaism: An American Religious Movement.* New York: Schocken Books.

Slobin, Mark. 1976. *Music in the Culture of Northern Afghanistan.* Tucson, Ariz.: University of Arizona Press.

————. 1989. *Chosen Voices: The Story of the American Cantorate.* Urbana: University of Ilinois Press.

————. 1992. "Micromusics of the West: A Comparative Approach." *Ethnomusicology* 36/1:1–88.

Smith, Ellen. 1995. "Strangers and Sojourners: The Jews of Colonial Boston." In *The Jews of Boston: Essays on the Occasion of the Centenary (1895–1995) of the Combined Jewish Philanthropies of Greater Boston,* edited by Johnathan D. Sarna and Ellen Smith. Boston: Combined Jewish Philanthropies of Greater Boston.

Sorin, Gerald. 1992. *A Time for Building: The Third Migration 1880–1920.* In *The Jewish People in America,* vol. 3, edited by Henry L. Feingold. Baltimore: Johns Hopkins University Press.

Spiro, Pinchas. 1993. *The Musical Siddur.* New York: Cantors Assembly.

Staub, Shalom. 1988. "Salim's Going to Be Muslim Someday: The Negotiated Identities of an American Jewish Ethnographer." In *Between Two Worlds: Ethnographic Essays on American Jewry,* edited by Jack Kugelmass. Ithaca, N.Y.: Cornell University Press.

Strassfeld, Michael. 1989. "Twenty Years of the Havurah Movement." *Sh'ma: A Journal of Jewish Responsibility* 20/382. 24 November.

Strassfeld, Sharon, and Michael Strassfeld, eds. 1976. *The Second Jewish Catalog: Sources and Resources.* Philadelphia: Jewish Publication Society.

Summit, Jeffrey A. 1979. *"The Song of Songs in the Biblical Tradition of the Yemenite Jews."* Rabbinic Thesis. Cincinnati: Hebrew Union College—Jewish Institute of Religion.

————. 1988. *"The Role and Function of the Part-Time Cantor: A Regional Study Based on Oral Histories of Part-time Cantors in the Boston Area."* M.A. Thesis. Medford, Mass.: Tufts University.

————. 1993. "I'm a Yankee Doodle Dandy? Identity and Melody at an American *Simhat Torah* Celebration." *Ethnomusicology* 37/1:41–62.

Szajkowski, Zosa. 1973. "The *Yahudi* and the Immigrant: A Reappraisal." *American Jewish Historical Quarterly.* September 63:13–44.

Teutsch, David A., ed. 1989. *Kol Haneshamah.* Shabbat Eve. Translated by Joel Rosenberg. Wyncote, Penn.: Reconstructionist Press.

Titon, Jeff Todd. 1988. *Powerhouse for God: Speech, Chant, and Song in an Appalachian Baptist Church.* Austin: University of Texas Press.

————. 1997. "Knowing Fieldwork." In *Shadows in the Field: New Per-*

spectives for Fieldwork in Ethnomusicology, edited by Gregory F. Barz and Timothy J. Cooley. New York: Oxford University Press.

Vinaver, Chemjo. 1985. *Anthology of Hassidic Music*. Edited with introductions and transcriptions by Eliyahu Schleifer. Jerusalem: Jewish Research Music Center, Hebrew University of Jerusalem.

Waterman, Christopher Alan. 1990. *Juju: A Social History and Ethnography of an African Popular Music*. Chicago: University of Chicago Press.

———. 1991. "Juju History: Towards a Theory of Sociomusical Practice." In *Ethnomusicology and Modern Music History*, edited by Steven Blum, Philip V. Bohlman, and Daniel M. Neuman. Urbana: University of Illinois Press.

Waterman, Richard A. 1952. "African Influence on the Music of the Americas." In *Acculturation in the Americas*, vol. 2. Proceedings of the 29th International Congress of Americanists, edited by S. Tax. Chicago: University of Chicago Press.

Weinberger, Leon J. 1998. *Jewish Hymnography: A Literary History*. Portland Ore.: Vallentine Mitchell.

Weinreich, Max. 1980. *History of the Yiddish Language*. Translated by Shlomo Noble with Joshua A. Fishman. Chicago: University of Chicago Press.

Werblowsky, R. J. Zwi. 1987. "The Safed Revival and Its Aftermath." In *Jewish Spirituality: From the Sixteenth-Century Revival to the Present*, edited by Arthur Green. New York: Crossroad.

Werner, Eric. 1959. *The Sacred Bridge: The Interdependence of Liturgy and Music in Synagogue and Church during the First Millennium*. London: Dennis Dobson.

———. 1976. *A Voice Still Heard . . . : The Sacred Songs of the Ashkenazic Jews*. London: Pennsylvania State University Press.

Wiener, Shohama Harris, and Jonathan Omer-Man, eds. 1993. *Worlds of Jewish Prayer: A Festschrift in Honor of Rabbi Zalman M. Schachter-Shalomi*. Northvale, N.J.: Jason Aronson.

Wohlberg, Max. [1954] 1972. "History of the Musical Modes of the Ashkenazic Synagogue and Their Usage." In *Journal of Synagogue Music*, vol. 4/1, 2. New York: Cantors Assembly of America.

———. 1978. "Aspects of Ashkenazic Hazzanic Recitative." In *Proceedings of World Congress on Jewish Music*, edited by Judith Cohen. Jerusalem: Institute for Translation of Hebrew Literature.

Wolberger, Lionel. 1993. "Music of Holy Argument: The Ethnomusicology of a Talmud Study Session." In *Modern Jews and Their Musical Agendas*, edited by Ezra Mendelsohn. *Studies in Contemporary Jewry* 9. New York: Oxford University Press.

Woolard, Kathryn. 1988. "Codeswitching and Comedy in Catalonia." In *Codeswitching: Anthropological and Sociolinguistic Perspectives*, edited by Monica Heller. Berlin: Mouton de Gruyter.

Ydit, Meir. 1972. "*Lekhah dodi.*" *Encyclopaedia Judaica*. Vol. 11:4–6. Jerusalem: Keter.

Contents of Companion Website
www.oup.com/us/lordssong

applied to the prayer *Magen avot*; the mode *Ahavah rabbah* ([With] great love) applied to *Tikanta Shabbat* (You [God] have established the Sabbath), Joshua Jacobson

#21 *Ahavat olam*, Tufts Hillel (Eric Mandell, based on traditional motifs)

#22 *Nusach* for *Ahavat olam*, Hebrew and English, B'nai Or, Lev Friedman

#23 *Nusach* for *Ahavat olam*, Shaarei Tefillah, Joshua Jacobson

#24 *Ve'ahavta* (And you shall love [the Lord]), Temple Israel (biblical trop, Jon Haddon, after Solomon Rosowsky)

#25 Friday Evening *Amidah* (standing prayer) selections, Temple Israel, *Adonai Sefatai* (God [open] my lips); *Avot*, (Patriarchs), *Gevurot* (God's power), (Adolph Katchko)

#26 *Mi khamokhah* (Who is like you [God]), Tufts Hillel, Marshall Einhorn

#27 *Hatimah*, Psalm 95, *Arba'im shanah*, (forty years), Tufts Hillel, Marshall Einhorn, Aliza Lipschitz, Neil Tow, Jennifer Madan

#28 *Hatimah, Maariv aravim*, ([God who] brings on evening), Tufts Hillel, Marshall Einhorn

#29 *Magen avot*, Tufts Hillel (Israel Goldfarb)

#30 *Veshamru* (And they shall observe [the Sabbath]), Tufts Hillel (Moshe J. Rothblum)

#31 *Al ken* (Therefore [we hope]), Tufts Hillel (based on a Hasidic niggun)

#32 *Arba'im shanah*, Shaarei Tefillah, father's nusach

#33 *Arba'im shanah*, Shaarei Tefillah, father's rendition of son's nusach

#34 *Arba'im shanah*, Shaarei Tefillah, Joshua Jacobson, Aaron Katchen, Jules Rosenberg, Avi Rockoff, Gene Fax. *Hatimah*, Psalm 29, *Adonoi lamabul yashav* (God sat enthroned at the flood), Aaron Katchen, Joshua Jacobson

#35 *Arba'im shanah*, Bostoner Hasidim, Rav Mayer Horowitz, Rav Naftali Horowitz

#36 *Barekhu*, examples of daily, Friday evening, Saturday morning, festival, and High Holiday nusach, Shaarei Tefillah, Joshua Jacobson

#37 *Lekhah dodi*, for the three weeks prior to Tisha B'Av, Shaarei Tefillah (after tune by Salomon Sulzer for *Alei Tsion* [Rise up, Zion])

#38 *Barekhu, Dear One,* B'nai Or (Lev Friedman)

#39 Purim *Kiddush*, Rabbi Moshe Waldoks

There is a traditional prohibition against pronouncing the name of God outside of the context of an actual prayer. When recording these liturgical selections, worshippers from Tufts Hillel, Shaarei Tefillah, and Beth Pinchas made certain changes in the liturgical text. For example *Adonai* is sung either as *Adomai*, which preserves the sound of the original, or more commonly as *Adoshem*. Worshippers make other changes, such as *kel* for *El*. Worshippers from B'nai Or and Temple Israel chose to record the prayers as they sing them on Friday evening. Where possible, musical transcriptions are taken from actual worship. Selections on the companion website were recorded outside of worship settings. As a result, recordings and transcriptions do not always correspond exactly.

One encounters problems when listing composers for Jewish liturgical pieces. While certain selections above have documentable composers, many melodies are part of a fluid oral tradition that is constantly reworked and applied to various liturgical texts. In some cases, someone inadvertently becomes known as a tune's "composer" by transcribing an unattributed melody. To compile the composers listed above, I referenced standard liturgical collections, such as Davidson (1987) and Nathanson (1974), as well as the work of Pasternak (1968, 1976, 1986). If the origin of a song was listed as "traditional" or "folk song," I leave the composer unattributed.

Index

Conservative movement
Camp Ramah and, 65–66, 67, 68, 69, 70, 71, 72–73, 75, 78, 114, 116
diversity in, 13, 16
Eastern European Jews and, 66–67
founding of, 66–67
Lekhah dodi and, 39
melody choice and conflict management and, 132–40
music in, 67, 68–69
nusach and, 105, 115
prayer book of, 159n. 17
prayer leader and, 27
rabbinic and cantorial schools of, 159n. 18
rise of, 15
roots of, 16
tunes of, 34
United Synagogue Youth and, 67, 68, 69, 70, 73, 78, 160n. 19
women and, 67
See also Tufts Hillel
conversion, 15
Cordovero, Moses, 29, 37

dancing, to *Lekhah dodi*, 49–51
davening, 26, 162n. 4
See also nusach
DeVoto, Mark, 163n. 1, 167n. 32
Dorf, Rabbi Shelly, 69

Eastern European Jews, 13
Conservative movement and, 66
Hasidism and, 94
See also Russia
Einhorn, Cantor Roy, 56–62, 112
Elbogen, 38
Eleasar, Saul Jedidiah, 168n. 52
Eliezer, Rabbi Israel ben, 93–94
Eloheinu velohei avoteinu, at Tufts Hillel, 171n. 12
Emancipation, 15
Enlightenment *(Haskalah)*, 15, 81, 167n. 35
Episcopalians, music in service of, 147, 150–51
Erev shel shoshanim, 85, 163n. 1

feminists, identity constructs and, 19

field recordings, 158n. 5
Sabbath music as unrecordable and, 9–11, 15–16, 158n. 4
fieldwork, music-making and, 6–7, 157n. 3
Fine, Lawrence, 35
Franco, Solomon, 14
Frank, Jacob, 94
Freed, 53
Freelander, D., 140
Friedman, Debbie, 21, 49, 70, 139, 166n. 21
Friedman, Lev, 7, 40–41, 43–45, 46–47, 48–49, 50, 141–42, 166n. 22
See also B'nai Or
Frigyesi, Judit, 33–34, 105, 170n. 2

gabbai, 27
gemore-loshn, 130, 174n. 3
Ger Hasidim, 98, 100, 169n. 53
Germany, Reform Judaism in, 53, 66, 166n. 24
Gerovitsch, Eliezar, 135
Gevurot, Temple Israel and, 111, 112
Glassie, Henry, 11
Goldfarb, Israel, 166n. 29
Green, Arthur, 95
Greenblum, Joseph, 158n. 9
Gudykunst, William B., 174n. 4
Guilbault, Jocelyne, 160n. 24
Gumperz, John J., 174n. 4

HaLevi, Shelomo Alkabetz, 37
Hameagel, Honi, 12
Hammond, Phillip, 153
Hanina, Rabbi, 37
Hanukah, code-switching and, 135, 136, 174nn. 6, 7
Haredim, 81
See also Hasidism
Harvard Hillel, melody choice managing conflict at, 136–38
Hasidic Song Festival, 54
Hasidism
Ger and, 98, 100, 169n. 53
history and background of, 93–96
Lekhah dodi and, 39, 77
Modzhitz and, 98, 99, 100, 168n. 52
music and, 88, 93, 95, 169n. 56

self-fulfillment, Jewish worship and, 152–53
self-reflexive ethnography, 6, 157n. 2
Selichot, 174n. 7
Sephardic prayer, 162n. 3
Sephardic pronunciation, Ashkenazi pronunciation *versus*, 130, 173n. 2
services. *See* Jewish worship
Shaarei Tefillah (modern Orthodox), 6–7, 8, 78–90
    accuracy and authenticity at, 89–90, 117–25, 154, 167n. 42
    Ahavat olam at, 109
    daily *nusach* at, 120, 172n. 18
    High Holiday *nusach* at, 120, 121
    history and background of, 79–81
    Lekhah dodi at, 74, 82–88, 167n. 39
    music at, 88–90
    music of Jewish community and, 21
    niggunim and, 88
    1960s and, 153–54
    nusach at, 114, 117–25, 132, 172nn. 16–19, 173n. 20
    prayer book of, 159n. 17
    prayer leader at, 79–80, 102–103
    women and, 78–79
    worship in, 82
shaliach tsibbur, 27
Shalom rav, at Tufts Hillel, 140
Sharm El Sheik, code-switching for *Adon olam* and, 174n. 5
Shelemay, Kay Kaufman, 158n. 4
Shema, 24, 166n. 18, 167n. 32
    at Temple Israel, 111
Shemer, Naomi, 174n. 5
Shir Hashirim, at Beth Pinchas, 91
Shleifer, Eliyahu, 106, 170n. 6
Shulchan Arukh, 81, 136
siddur, 25
silence, reasons for and significance of, 18
Six Day War, code-switching and, 134–35, 174n. 5
Sklare, Marshall, 158n. 9
Slobin, Mark, 7, 17, 34, 39, 152, 158n. 8, 166n. 26, 169n. 1
Spiro, Pinchas, 172n. 18

style, values and identity and, 19–20
subcultures, in Jewish community, 12–14, 158nn. 7–9
Sulzer, Salomon, 34, 39, 53, 131, 136, 166n. 29
Summer Havurah Institutes, 43
summer programs, 16
    See also Camp Ramah
Synagogue 2000, 62

Tal, at Shaarei Tefillah, 119–20
Temple Israel (Reform Judaism), 7, 51–63, 103, 104, 148
    atrium service in, 51–52, 54–56, 111
    cantor and participation *versus* correct performance at, 112–13
    history and background of, 52–54
    Lekhah dodi at, 21, 46, 58, 59–62, 166n. 20, 169n. 54
    Rabbi Bernard Mehlman and, 54–55, 57, 59, 111
    music at, 56–63, 104
    music of Jewish community and, 21
    nusach at, 110–13, 171n. 13
    personal support and self-fulfillment offered by, 152
    prayer leader at, 102–103
    Rabbi Elaine Zecher and, 57–58, 59, 62
Tisha B'Av, 39
    cantillation of Book of Lamentations on, 133–34
Titon, Jeff Todd, 7, 157n. 3
traditional chant. *See nusach*
traditional Orthodox, 81
    See also Hasidism
Tufts Hillel (Conservative movement), 8, 9, 63–78
    accuracy and authenticity at, 66, 154
    background and history of, 65–67
    Camp Ramah and, 78, 114, 116
    continuity in, 67
    Lekhah dodi at, 39, 45–46, 72, 74–78, 84, 166n. 20, 168n. 49
    melody choice and conflict management and, 132–40

music at, 66, 68, 69–71, 72, 102, 103, 114
music of Jewish community and, 21–22
nusach in, 113–17, 132, 171n. 12, 172n. 19
peer-led services at, 116–17
prayer leader at, 102, 103
recordings of music of, 10
service of, 65–66, 68–74
student-led services at, 71–74
United Synagogue Youth and, 78
tunes, 33–34, 163n. 1
borrowing and, 101
nusach versus, 33–34
sources of, 34
See also Lekhah dodi

Union of American Hebrew Congregations, 66
Union of Orthodox Jewish Congregations, 66
United Jewish Appeal, 12
United Synagogue, 66
United Synagogue Youth (USY), 67, 68, 69, 70, 73, 78

Vahavi'enu leshalom, tune of *Hatikvah* and, 134–35
Ve'ahavta, 166n. 29
at Temple Israel, 111, 112
at Tufts Hillel, 139, 171n. 12

Veshamru, at Tufts Hillel, 116, 171n. 12
Virgil, Eric, 160n. 24

Waldoks, Moshe, 144
Waskow, Arthur, 95
Waterman, Chrisopher, 161n. 25
Weiner, 53
Weinreich, Max, 129–30
women
Conservative movement and, 67
Kiddush and, 136–38
prayers and, 24
Reform Judaism and, 53
Shaarei Tefillah and, 78–79
Woolard, Kathryn, 174n. 8

Yedid nefesh, 163n. 1
at Shaarei Tefillah, 79, 88
at Tufts Hillel, 65
Yeshiva-rock, *Lekhah dodi* and, 48–49
Yeshiva University, 159n. 18
Yigdal, at Tufts Hillel, 72
Yom Kippur War, code-switching and, 174n. 5
Young Israel movement, 81, 86
youth groups, 16, 160n. 19
Debbie Friedman and, 166n. 21

Zecher, Rabbi Elaine, 57–58, 59, 62
Zeira, Mordechai, 40
Zevi, Shabbetai, 94

CPSIA information can be obtained
at www.ICGtesting.com
Printed in the USA
BVHW081346130119
537706BV00001B/35/P